LUNATICS, LOVERS AND POETS

LUNATICS, LOVERS AND POETS

The contemporary experimental theatre

MARGARET CROYDEN

McGraw-Hill Book Company
New York St. Louis San Francisco Toronto

Designed by Marcy J. Katz

LUNATICS, LOVERS AND POETS

123456789BPBP7987654

Library of Congress Cataloging in Publication Data

Croyden, Margaret.
Lunatics, lovers and poets.

1. Experimental theater. 2. Drama—20th century—History and criticism. I. Title.
PN2189.C7 792'.09'04 73-9904
ISBN 0-07-014780-9

Grateful acknowledgment is made to the following for permission to quote passages from copyrighted material: HARRY N. ABRAMS, INC., for Allan Kaprow, *Assemblage, Environment, and Happenings.* BEACON PRESS, for Herbert Marcuse, *An Essay on Liberation.* PETER BROOK, for Ted Hughes, "Orghast: Talking Without Words." CAMERA THREE, for an excerpt from the two-part Camera Three series "Jerzy Grotowski," broadcast on the CBS Television Network on January 4 and January 11, 1970. THE DRAMA REVIEW, for Antonin Artaud, "States of the Mind: 1921-1945," translated by Ruby Hohn, first published in *The Drama Review*, Volume 12, Number 3(T-39), Spring 1968, copyright © *The Drama Review*, all rights reserved; for Eugenio Barba, "The Kathkali Theatre," first published in *The Drama Review.* Volume 8 Number 2 (T-22), Winter 1963, copyright © *The Tulane Drama Review,* all rights reserved; and for Richard Schechner, "Extensions in Time and Space: An Interview with Allan Kaprow," first published in *The Drama Review*, Volume 9, Number 3 (T-27), Summer 1967, copyright © *The Drama Review*, all rights reserved. FARRAR STRAUS & GIROUX, for Richard Schechner, *Dionysus in '69*, text copyright © 1970 by the Wooster Group Inc., and for Edward Braun, ed., *Meyerhold on Theatre*, copyright © 1969 by Edward Braun. GROVE PRESS, for Antonin Artaud, *The Theatre and Its Double*, translated by Mary Caroline Richards, copyright © 1958 by Grove Press, Inc. JEAN-CLAUDE VAN ITALLIE, c/o International Famous Agency, for Jean-Claude van Itallie, *The Serpent*, 1969. MACMILLAN PUBLISHING CO., INC., for Maurice Nadeau, *The History of*

TO
PHYLLIS DAIN
AND
ALFRED H. RIFKIN

Preface

This book, a distillation of years of viewing, reading, discussing, thinking, is designed primarily for the layman, although I hope that it has something to offer to scholars and specialists, too. It is intended to give the perceptive theatregoer and student of the theatre a historical and social perspective as well as an aesthetic evaluation and description of a phenomenon of the 1960's—a theatre that did not depend on the playwright. I have tried to trace the historical sources of the movement, perhaps somewhat arbitrarily, but as every historian and social critic knows, setting dates for origins of movements always presents a problem and implies ambiguities. The important thing is that historical antecedents for the contemporary experimental theatre can be found, and it is interesting to see where and to discover that not too much is ever too new. But the book is not offered as a work of historical scholarship: I have attempted merely to delineate decisive influences from the past upon the modern avant-garde. Nor is it a definitive study of that movement. Rather it is an effort to analyze and depict the work of exciting and promising artists who were searching for new forms of theatrical expression in a rapidly changing world. I have concentrated only on those who developed a body of work. Certainly there were others not mentioned who were experimenting but who for one reason or another could not sustain their efforts. And certainly playwrights black and white were also struggling to break old forms—Café La Mama, for example, offered these writers a showcase—but this book does not deal with playwrights past or present even though they may have contributed to the experimental movement.

I am profoundly grateful to my dear friends Phyllis and Norman Dain for their hours of talk and tea and for their unstinting advice and love during the years of research and writing and for their critical reading of the completed manuscript. I also want to thank Cleo Dana for carefully reading the manuscript; Jack Dana for encouraging the writing of it; David Engler for his interest and efforts on its behalf; my sister, Sylvia Rosenberg, for typing and xeroxing parts of it and for coming to my assistance in dozens of ways whenever things got really rough.

I particularly want to thank my colleagues at Jersey City State College who, by their understanding and patience, eased my work on this book; the MacDowell Artists Colony where I spent two glorious months working on parts of this volume; Dan Pollack who lent me his extensive file on Peter Brook; George Ashley for his clips on Robert Wilson and the Bread and Puppet Theatre; Dr. Thaddeus V. Gromada of the History Department of Jersey City State College for his discussions about Poland and Polish history and for his generosity with his personal library; Ruth Arnold, librarian at Jersey City State College, for her gracious help in tracking down certain articles and books; and the Polish Institute of Arts and Science in New York for allowing me access to its extensive library.

My appreciation also to Seymour Peck, that splendid editor of the *New York Times* Sunday Arts and Leisure section who helped me secure some of the interviews in this volume and previewed some of this material; to Berenice Hoffman for her invaluable and intelligent editing of this manuscript, and to Sara Blackburn who painstakingly worked on its numerous details.

Perhaps my greatest debt is to the many theatre people who spent time with me in long interviews and informal conversations: Joe Chaikin, Roberta Sklar, Joyce Aaron, Kay Carney, Barbara Vann, Peter Feldman, Jean-Claude van Itallie, Allan Kaprow, Ida Kaminska, Slawomir Mrozek, Anthony Abeson, Patrick McDermott, John Vacarro, Andre Gregory, Richard Schechner, Joan MacIntosh, Peter Schumann, Carl Einhorn, Judith Malina, Julian Beck, Robert Wilson, David Hays, Ryszard Cieslak, Jerzy Grotowski, Alan Howard, Barry Stanton, Peter Hall, Trevor Nunn, Ted Hughes and Peter Brook.

And finally, I would like to express my appreciation to all the artists discussed in this volume for some enriching and memorable evenings of theatre.

MARGARET CROYDEN

New York
May 1973

contents

Introduction

" . . . there is only one question. What is living theatre? We have no answer today. Whatever we know, is not it. Whatever we have seen, is not it. Whatever is labeled theatre, isn't. Whatever is defined as theatre, misses the point. Whatever has been handed down to us, has been cheapened out of recognition. Whoever claims to know what theatre was or could be, doesn't. We are now before a long period of perpetual revolution, in which we must search, attempt to build, pull down and search again."

Peter Brook
Introduction to Tell Me Lies

When, in 1949, Bertolt Brecht returned to the rubble and ashes of Germany to create his Berliner Ensemble, it was clear that the contemporary theatre was in the process of redefinition. Five years later, Paris saw the triumph of Samuel Beckett's *Waiting for Godot* and the emergence of the Absurdists—further proof that a new theatre was in the making. But new theatres for old is an inevitable process; it is neither unique for our times, nor will it find its ultimate expression in the foreseeable future. Still, artists like Brecht and Beckett always had an eye for the future. Armed with a definitive aesthetic that evolved from a lifetime of struggle and work, Brecht consciously set out to revolutionize the theatre by successfully synthesizing art with Marx, and to found a company quite unlike any other in the West. Equally inspired, but striving in opposite directions, Beckett combined absurdist metaphysics with metaphor, and, in his unique way, developed an individualistic art.

By 1960, Brecht had been dead for four years, but his theatre was very much alive, even on the road to being institutionalized. Beckett and the Absurdists, having achieved international acclaim, were curiously on the road to quietude.

Meanwhile, Antonin Artaud's theories of cruelty (a complex concept that will be discussed in a separate chapter of this book) were surfacing. Attracting a new generation of experimentalists, Artaud damned the theatre of the playwright, and declared that visual images, gestures and "sounds beyond words" could be more theatrical than a standard text.

At the beginning of the sixties, however, neither Brecht, Beckett, nor Artaud had made any decisive dent on the work of American playwrights (with Edward Albee an exception) although plays by Brecht and Beckett were produced. Established, conventional playwrights still dominated the stage, and struggled with worn-out patterns and outmoded forms to tell tales of lost youth from the vantage point of middle age. Young audiences dwindled, many theatre houses were dark, and fewer serious plays were optioned. Elsewhere, another kind of theatre was in the making. Meeting in any convenient sort of place they could find, actors, directors, painters—aware of the aesthetics of both Brecht and Beckett, but followers of neither—were gathering to examine new concepts and new forms. These artists, the Happeners, the Living Theatre, the Open Theatre, the Environmentalists, Jerzy Grotowski, and Peter Brook, were determined to redefine the theatre once again—and, in the process, were to become the center of a new movement, later to be known as the non-literary experimental theatre. Some were radical only in form, others, in content, but each in his own way was searching to express his times and contributing to the Zeitgeist that was to comprise the experiments of the 1960's. It was no accident that their appearance coincided with a decade that ushered in confrontation politics, participatory democracy, black power, and sexual revolution, hippies, yippies, hell's angels, and women's liberation. Indeed, this new theatre, sensing the theatricality of real life, was ultimately to question the value of theatre itself. This book is about these groups and their leaders.

New movements are to some extent continuations of old ones. And all old ones were at one time new. So it was with romanticism and naturalism, with surrealism and absurdism; each has had its antecedents, prophets, and radical fringe, and each, after producing innovations, shocks, and sensations, reached its full tide before ebbing and reappearing in another form. The cycle, repeated with almost every avant-garde, has acted not only as an impetus for radical change but, given the recurrence of historical forces, has perhaps been necessary, even inevitable. Thus it was inevitable that in the 1960's the young should rechallenge two thousand years of verbal theatre dominated by the playwright and his medium: the word. To a generation bombarded with over-sell and over-kill jargon, the programmed rhetoric of synthetic technocrats and hypocritical politicians, small wonder that new theatre artists mistrusted talk and relied on the physical, rather than on the verbal response, on a felt, rather than an intellectual experience.

The young, in avowed rebellion against a political and economic system that encouraged racism, that betrayed its own commitments to ameliorate poverty, and that created a gap between the rhetoric of freedom and a free, emotionally "valid" life style, also looked upon the conventional theatre as an instrument of oppression, a business supported by the system and by the system's words that turned language into lies, dreams into nightmares, and youthful aspirations into early spiritual death. Words, equated with the mealy-mouthings of the power elite, were to be distrusted in the theatre as well as in mass media, and playwrights who adhered to words were to be disclaimed. The young who disdained the system, and saw it as unredeemable, developed their own mores, culture and language—not of words, but based on visceral responses that could be easily and quickly communicated to those on the same "vibes." They repudiated theatre as literature and substituted in its place a non-verbal theatre, one of "cruelty" and ritual, celebration and religion, and one of communal participation which might induce a more total or organic experience than the past had made possible. Inevitably, too, they abandoned not only the proscenium arch (which had already been forsaken by some of their predecessors), but the actual theatre site itself, as being too restricting and artificial; they replaced it by theatre in churches, garages, studios, cellars, cafés, streets, stadiums, gymnasiums, schools—or simply in any open space. It was clear, too, that the relationship between actor and audience had become static and passive, so that when "participatory democracy" became a popular concept throughout much of the world, the radical theatre artists responded in kind. Was it then essential for the audience to be only spectators, or could audiences participate in aspects of the production as well? Could one take a clue from primitive rituals, in that ritual encompasses the *whole* of man in a liturgy of mind, body, intellect, and senses? Could audiences be involved in a *total* experience? Some directors, reacting to the fragmentation of contemporary life, took participation seriously. Under the influence of Artaud's "cruelty" theories and of confrontation politics, they attacked the audiences verbally. Others, influenced by ritual theatre, designed settings called Environmentals, which included the spectators in the action of the play. For them, the time had passed when "clean-cut" bourgeois audiences would be expected to sit passively in rows of chairs and watch a "show."

The new practitioners, believing that their efforts should be collaborative and egalitarian, organized themselves into communes; others worked in cooperative groups. The spirit of the times had produced a compelling need for connection and collectivism among the youth, who felt intensely alienated from the adult world. Actors and directors, like college radicals who were "tuned in" to Timothy Leary's admonition to "drop out" and "turn on," became part of the counterculture groups springing up all over the country, not because of political revolutionary convictions alone (for some were non-political), but to find through group activity some measure of human contact that was apparently missing in their lives. Indeed, groups in the early and late sixties became a mass phenomenon. Imbued with Timothy Leary's slogan on the one hand, and Herbert Marcuse, Fidel, and Ché on the other, the "group," the hippies, and the activist revolutionaries merged, so that when mass demonstrations, the killing of students, and political repression supplanted love-ins and be-ins, the "Woodstock Nation" was already a counterculture movement which represented an alternative force with its own language and style and its own claim to philosophical and psychological thought. The "group" had become an emblem and focal point for revolt, dissent, and revolution. Various new theatre artists envisioned a unity between the group, theatre, and revolution. And for them, this trinity became a means to detach themselves from the establishment. For others, who were neither politically or socially oriented, the group was not only a commitment to art, but an act of faith—a commitment to life.

The group attempted to be the antidote to corruption and alienation, to the System itself, but it also served an important aesthetic function. It enabled the actors, who had always been exploited artistically as well as economically, to demand a creative role equal to that of the director, the scenic designer, and the playwright. In fact, the actors—unseating the playwright—claimed that they could collaborate in writing their own plays, or could at least bring their own sensibilities to bear on old masterpieces, and with their own bodies and voices create the *mise-en-scène.* Acting in the new theatre came to mean something other than portraying a "realistic" character that conveyed the "illusion." Acting, went far beyond anything sought after by Lee Strasberg's Actor's Studio; acting became not the grafting on of a new persona, but the unmasking or the developing of the actor's hidden self. Eventually this led to a new freedom, to the depiction of sex and nudity, to the portrayal of heretofore repressed and forbidden themes. Since actors were no longer shielded by words nor confined to a playwright's text, it was their vision and that of the director which supplanted the dramatist's vision. Thus the "new" theatre, deliberately submerging the playwright, depended more than ever upon the art of the actor and to a greater degree upon that of the director.

Further, the established American playwright of the sixties no longer expressed the younger generation's social and political attitudes. By and large, Broadway had become dominated by the musical comedy, which had degenerated into faded carbon copies of its original self—its form stereotyped, its content predictable. (*Hair* was an exception.) But as Broadway deteriorated, other branches of the arts advanced: innovators in dance and film had long ago abandoned naturalistic explicitness and concentrated on allusion and ambiguity, on image and metaphor. Only the theatre lingered in the past. The "slice-of-life" play, proscenium staging, traditional seating, "realistic" acting, colloquial rather than poetic language—all helped support a rotting, dying theatre, corroded by catering to expense accounts, profits, and the soft sell of press agentry.

Admittedly, the American theatre's concept of itself was never very sophisticated. The theatre had always encouraged "show biz" rather than art. Traditionally it could never develop or sustain repertory companies, or actively support experimentation. On the other hand, it could not support stars either, who frequently abandoned the stage for Hollywood: a Broadway actor's choosing "bigger things," in preference to his artistic development, was accepted as normal in American life. In view of the fact that these attitudes and conditions had prevailed over four decades, the younger generation of the fifties and the sixties, radical or not, regarded the traditional theatre as decadent, despite the development of regional and off-Broadway theatre, which too soon had come to ape the commercial establishment.

In addition, the onslaught of film and television had brought into question the need for the theatre and the relevancy of the live experience. The electronic age, a formidable challenge to all sensibilities, posed problems that eventually were to affect form, perception, and consciousness. Marshall McLuhan, hailing the arrival of the global village, predicted that television would enlarge our horizons, change our life styles, and usher in a need for a cool, visual, non-literary, multi-dimensional experience. He predicted that TV sound and image would change our "body perceptions," advance non-verbal communication, create a revolution in education, discourage literature, change our dress, popularize new music, promulgate mass action and mass participation. In other words, advanced technology was to color all our reactions and future relationships. Conditions in the sixties had opened up an age for questioning, evaluating, and redefining. Why should the theatre remain outside this upheaval? It didn't.

The revolution in theatre was on full force. The basic art of illusion and the precepts of the mimetic theatre, formulated by Aristotle and adhered to for centuries, were being uprooted. True to McLuhan's concept that the medium is the message, the revolution in theatre began through form; ultimately it was to affect content, but, for the moment, it was form that defined the extent of a group's radicalism. A company no longer playing in a Broadway or off-Broadway house, but in a downtown New York garage, in a Fourteenth Street loft, in a Greenwich Village church, or in a Brooklyn environmental, was to a great measure considered radical. The new theatre's unifying characteristic was its departure from the System's *concept* of theatre; its departure from the establishment's techniques and production structures: its producers, playwrights, and stars, its box office and press agentry, its reliance on elaborate costumes, sets, and lights—and especially its bourgeois audiences, whose bourgeois taste supported pallid, unpoetic language and predictable plots and characters. In short, everything the establishment theatre supported, glorified, and merchandised was despised.

The new theatre groups turned to nudity and sex, LSD, and rock; sensitivity training, group encounter, and consciousness raising; anarchy, primitivism, and Oriental philosophy; pastoral and commune life; bisexuality, homosexuality, and group fornication; acting out and being one's self; patterned responses and spontaneous feeling; and the merging of art and reality. These themes—considered radical—became incorporated not only in the groups' life style, but dominated the subject matter of their art. And it was precisely this subject matter that was able to attract youthful audiences. Nevertheless experimentalists were faulted for boorish amateurism and purist objectives. In fact, during the sixties admonishments and adorations characterized a running debate in the arts. Friend and foe, critic and layman, vied to discover the innovators and the imitators, to separate the fads and the fashions from the authentic and the genuine. (That each spokesman had a personal and often ill-founded conception of authenticity did not diminish the flow of criticism.) As a result, whatever genuine aesthetic concepts germinated during this period were continually undermined by instant evaluation—in a society that demands instant success. At the same time, various experimentalists gingerly accommodated themselves to the system and at the first opportunity merchandised their originality, forfeited long-range experimentation, and sacrificed their potential. Looking backward, it is painful to recognize how easily movements can be co-opted, codified, and stereotyped. Yet one realizes that certain aspects of new movements have always made their way into the mainstream (and are calmly accepted by those who once rejected them), and it is almost axiomatic that each avant-garde leads to another—though, paradoxically, each finds its antecedents in tradition. It is not astonishing to discover then that the contemporary experimental movement with which this book deals is also a continuation and extension of the past, and is part of the constantly changing historical spiral of the forever old and the forever new.

Thus some scholars believe that the beginning of the avant-garde spiral dates back to 1896, when a French actor walked out on a Parisian stage in Alfred Jarry's *Ubu Roi* and uttered the fatal five-letter word "*merde.*" Or to the work of Mallarmé and the symbolist theatre, to Stanislavsky's First Studio, Meyerhold's "biomechanics"; for some, surrealism and Antonin Artaud's "cruelty" theories are the most important theatrical developments in the twentieth century. To be sure, all these influences did contribute (and their importance is discussed in subsequent chapters). But the philosophical and aesthetic origins of the non-literary experimentalists discussed in this book do not stem from any single phenomenon, but arise from a world view that finds its roots in romanticism. For the spirit of the Romantic movement—its literary and artistic style, its tempestuous mood and search for inner vision, its glorification of the individual, and its belief in intuition and imagination, rather than logic and reason—perhaps more than that of any other period, comes closest to defining our own times and our own theatrical innovators. True, our contemporaries probably gave little thought to the past when they began their work (although some consciously looked backward), but there are, nevertheless, remarkable similarities—as well as differences—between them and the Romantic movement. The similarities are neither direct, exact, definitive, nor pure; all the same, they exist. The Romantics had produced a remarkable shift of values, and virtually no movement was immune to their influence. As a starting point and frame of reference for its offshoots and opposites—symbolism, naturalism, surrealism, absurdism—the Romantic movement is helpful in placing our contemporary non-literary theatre into historical perspective.

The Romantics of the early nineteenth century came to the forefront during a period of economic, social, and political upheaval and revolutionary ferment. Rousseau's "man is born free and is everywhere in chains" spoke directly to the conditions that prevailed. Along with Rousseau's "Social Contract," Paine's *The Rights of Man* (1791) and Godwin's *Political Justice* (1793) gave specific focus to dissent against aristocratic tyranny and the status quo. Rousseau fused his political radicalism with a radical vision of man—his belief in the superiority of the "noble savage," his personalization of love, his identification with nature, and his criticism of the education of children—which captured the imaginations of subsequent generations. And his *Confessions* regenerated the genre of self-revelatory literature, in which sensory and subjective responses to life became aesthetic values in themselves.

The Romantic movement was stamped not only by dissent and revolution, but by the apotheosis of the Self, by a distrust of logic, by a love of nature, by heightened consciousness achieved through drugs and the occult, and by an attempt to break down the barriers between art and life. Dreams, intuitions, and the purity of the child, as well as a belief in the perfectibility of man were the hallmarks of various Romantic poets, who sought to find new means of self-discovery and creativity that would displace the empty virtues as well as the hypocritical vices and social strangulation of accepted society. While God's divinity was called into question, these artists worshipped the divine in themselves. Self-confrontation took various forms—the celebration of the child in oneself, a probing into the self through opium and induced hallucination, the development of political consciousness, the forging of a romantic persona as exemplified by the Byronic hero, and the challenging of established poetic forms and diction. Above all, romanticism was conscious protest against the stifling superstructure of the institution of civilization and despite its variety, this protest was unified by a faith in the imagination and in its unbridled ability to create new art and new life styles.

But writers no longer separated their art from their life style. Their awareness of history and their sense of drama were keen. Glorifying the French Revolution, they attacked classicism, associated it with reaction, and ridiculed those who adhered to eighteenth-century aesthetics. Some became drug cultists;. others, sexual adventurers, mystics, and political activists. Politically they ranged from the liberal to the revolutionary, but aesthetically they were in agreement in aim: they believed in the felt experience expressed through image, myth, and symbol. The function of the artist was to reflect subjective perceptions, and they adopted "Intuition, Instinct, Imagination, and Vision" as their chief weapons to fight the accepted standards of taste. A century later, counterculture artists were to do the same.

Though the Romantic writers of the first half of the nineteenth century did not revolutionize the theatre of their day, their importance lies in their linking of romance and revolution, and in their concentration on the occult and the primitive as sources of inspiration. Moreover, they elevated individualism to the center of the stage; an eccentric, unorthodox life style and cultish dress and manners became the badge of the romantic revolutionary artist. Thus, the elevation of felt experience over a rationalistic approach to life resulted in an idiosyncratic aesthetic through which the Romantic artist sought first to expand his consciousness, and then to transform the world.

To transform the world was, for example, Shelley's moral, artistic, and radical mission. He was a forerunner of the flower children; everything in his life and art centered around the love of his fellows and his devotion to man's liberation. A born radical, he was expelled from Oxford for preaching atheism, arrested in Ireland for distributing leaflets, and ridiculed in the press for writing on free love and divorce. All the same, Shelley continued to preach the Godwinian doctrine that man's natural goodness would lead him to revolution. But most of all, Shelley believed that man could liberate himself through universal love; that hatred, oppression and deception resulted only from a lack of love, not merely between two individuals, but between those who could not free themselves from love based on possession. Love, for Shelley, was the embodiment of perfection, beauty, and moral worth, the force that would transform mankind. Though he supported political revolutionary movements everywhere, he believed that man's irrepressible need to love would produce an egalitarian society, and that this love, once achieved, would inevitably transform man's nature. Hence, Shelley's image became associated with a new moral beauty. His vision became a moral quest; and his personal life, an exemplar for the indestructible and deeply human need to love. Ideal love, the Revolution, and the perfect state were inexorably linked in Shelley's mind. It is not so mystifying, therefore, that subsequent young anarchist revolutionaries (perhaps unconsciously) should echo what seems to be Shelley's doctrine of Love and Revolution.

If Shelley stood for purity of youth and the innocence of love and revolution, Byron, who took an active part in revolutionary politics, nevertheless stands for another strain within romanticism—jaded, rebellious youth attracted to revolution by way of excessive sensuality. Perhaps this aspect of Byron corresponds more than any other to the phenomenon of contemporary middle- and upper-class intellectuals and artists who may be more attracted by revolutionary "chic" than by revolutionary action. The Byronic hero—a perpetuation of the Self as a literary character—became a pattern for subsequent decades, one that was later to find expression in the theatre and life of Alfred Jarry. But the Byronic hero was not the only romantic type perpetuated in the future. The link between drugs, the language of dreams, and poetic inspiration, so wonderfully asserted by Coleridge, as well as the mysticism of Blake's visions, were also to live on in subsequent romantic heroes.

Taken together, Rousseau, Blake, Wordsworth, Coleridge, Shelley, Byron, the German Idealists, and the entire intellectual and aesthetic Romantic movement of which they were a part, set the tone for a revolution in artistic form and content and for radical protest in poetry, fiction—and eventually, in theatre. Their rejection of scientific rationalism as a foundation for art put into motion a new aesthetic doctrine and raised fundamental social and political questions that later were to be fought out repeatedly on many battlefields.

It is in the progression of these battles, discussed in Part I of this book, that the reader will recognize the antecedents of our contemporaries discussed in detail in Part II. The Romantics initiated changes that were to reappear in new guises, new imaginative associations, and new experiments. How lasting an effect artistic rebels have is determined, to some extent, by what ensuing eras see reflected in them, and perhaps to a greater extent by the durability of their talent—whatever aesthetic they are seeking. It is too soon this early in the 1970's to make an ultimate judgment on the non-literary theatre of the 1960's, but that the scene has been lively and teeming with possibilities cannot be doubted. This book seeks to describe the people and groups—the lunatics, lovers, and poets—involved in this experimental movement, not uncritically, but with acknowledgment that they are remaking theatre, and that they reflect the fragmentation as well as the vitality of our times.

Lovers and madmen have such seething brains,
Such shaping of fantasies, that apprehend
More than cool reason ever comprehends.
The lunatic, the lover, and the poet
Are of imagination all compact.

A Midsummer Night's Dream
Act V, Scene 1

Part One

The Antecedents

one

The Symbolists and the Naturalists

"Peindre, non la chose, mais l'effet qu'elle produit."

Mallarmé

With the death of Byron in 1824 and the end of the Romantic era in England, the stage was set for new artistic battles. Victorian bourgeois reformists replaced the fiery imagination of the previous generation of Romantic poets, and virtually destroyed their radical thrust. Repression, thrift, law and order, and a fierce imperialism were to dominate England for more than a century. Although the liberal teachings of Mill, Browning, Huxley, and Arnold were popular, conservatism rather than radicalism triumphed. As for the furthering of the radical aesthetic, this was left to the French; it was the French Symbolists who became the heirs of the Romantic movement; and the French Naturalists, the antithesis of everything the Romantics represented.

The Romantics had left their mark on their progeny; they had encouraged the cult of the Self, an extolling of the ego which expressed itself through revolutionary activities. But the Romantics had also stimulated an interest in the mysterious and the occult, the beautiful and the absolute. And it was these concepts—steeped in Idealism—that intrigued French poets of the mid-century and precipitated the making of the Symbolist movement and eventually the Symbolist theatre. Aware of their anti-rationalist and to some extent anti-intellectual heritage, Symbolist poets reinterpreted aspects of romanticism to suit their own needs. They developed the art of the Self to new heights: they dramatized their dreams and unconscious life, they glamorized their decadence, justified their drug addiction, elegized their mystical obsessions, allegorized their sexual aberrations, and opted for a life of solitude and a "career of evil." In fact, some (like Baudelaire) believed that evil could produce flowers of beauty and, through their poems, suggested that the bizarre, the scabrous, and the vulgar were as beautiful as their opposites.

It has often been said that Baudelaire is the link between the Romantics, the Symbolists, and the Surrealists, and that his aesthetics and life style had a decisive influence on later avant-gardists, who adored and emulated his bohemian spirit and erratic personal life. A child of the Romantics, he adapted their basic tenets in his search for absolute beauty; unlike them, he wondered if beauty were not emblematic of evil rather than of good. Yes, decadence, drunkenness, and debauchery were evil, he argued, but were they not also pleasurable and intrinsically beautiful? And like Sade and Poe, he reversed the acceptable measurements for beauty and declared that suffering, horror, sexual violence, and sadism were not only beautiful but appropriate subject matters for art. The first of the French Symbolists to poeticize the demi-world in which evil and decadence flowered, Baudelaire set the tone for the century.

As a youth, Baudelaire was true to the spirit of Byron; he cultivated a persona. The life of the dandy—with its self-dramatization, smart clothes, and artificial mask—appealed to him. Although he was later to reject this pose, he was the epitome of the artistocratic, spoiled bourgeois. But he was a man of many faces; on the one hand, his dandyism was typically romantic, but, as Wallace Fowlie has pointed out:

> . . . Baudelaire's dandyism was the artist's heroism of concentration, the almost fatal need to adorn himself in so special and personal a way that he will be separated from all other men. The artist must be unique, or he has failed. He must discover the costume and the words which will mark him off from all other modes of attraction and communication. Dandyism is the effort to suppress all instinctive impulses and to forge a studied personality, to show to the world only the reflective and the critical thoughts. Originality has to be cultivated and prepared before it can be exhibited. The dandy is the aristocrat of the spirit because he is really the actor playing the role of critic.[1]

Still, Baudelaire's real self was tired of acting. In his dingy solitude, he wrote his poems of death and suffering, sexual pleasure and sexual impotence, wine and lesbos, beauty and exotica, the ideal and the ugly. But the lack of recognition and the bleakness of life caused him chronic anguish, and he advocated continued drunkenness. His "*Enivriez-vous*" begins with the cry, "Always be drunk"; sober, life was unbearable. A forerunner of our contemporary drug cultists, Baudelaire believed "that it was through dreaming that man entered into communication with the rich dark world which surrounds him."[2] To evoke the world of dreams and a language to match its elusiveness, he ate opium and smoked hashish, hoping that drugs would release repression. To be sure, he was not alone in this. Several Romantic writers had already experimented with the effects of drugs: Gautier, De Quincey, Poe were all users. But as time went on, neither drugs, wine, nor debauchery soothed Baudelaire; deeply in debt, he suffered intense poverty.

By 1848, he was living the life of a bohemian. A friend of Courbet, Proudhon, and, later, Manet, he became involved with the 1848 uprisings. He and his fellow revolutionists (all outcasts) would meet at their favorite cafés and there they would speak of art, life, and politics. (They even founded a revolutionary paper, *Le Salut Publique*.) But after the defeat of their political dreams with the repression of the revolution and the ascendancy of Louis Napoleon, Baudelaire sank further into despair, and wrote his death poems. He recovered somewhat when, reading Edgar Allan Poe in English, he determined to translate Poe's poetry into French. Shortly he was ready to publish his own collection, *Les Fleurs du Mal* (1857), for which he was tried for obscenity, fined 3,000 francs, and six of the poems were suppressed.[3] But aside from the merits of his own work and personal style, his legacy to future trends in verse—which later found a voice in theatre as well—rested on his theory of correspondences in sensory images (the symbolic association of colors, scents, and sounds), based on the perceptions of the Swedish philosopher, Swedenborg.

Everything in nature corresponds to a spiritual reality, Baudelaire claimed: one's senses and states of being also corresponded to such a reality, and could be expressed interchangeably through symbolic images. Thus Baudelaire wrote in clusters of sound, color, and taste, in smell and sight associations, using sensory symbols to express one sensation in terms of another, and to juxtapose disparate emotions. All through the work, Arthur Symons notes, there is "a deliberate science of sensual and sexual perversity which has something curious in its accentuation of vice with horror, in its passionate devotion to passions. Baudelaire brings every complication of taste, the exasperation of perfumes, the irritant of cruelty, the very odours and colours of corruption, to the creation and adornment of a sort of religion, in which an Eternal Mass is served before a veiled altar."[4]

Baudelaire made no immediate imprint upon the theatre, but his work and theories signaled a new aesthetic which future avant-gardists eventually utilized. His search for "*le mot juste,*" his use of juxtaposition and metaphor, his exaltation of the inseparability of beauty and "evil," and his advocating the felt experience as a foundation for poetry became indelibly stamped in the minds and aspirations of future artists.

Baudelaire's influence was particularly felt by the young Rimbaud, who, between the ages of sixteen and twenty-one, wrote some of the most brilliant French poetry of the century. After five years of debauchery, a tempestuous love affair with the poet Paul Verlaine, and a life of poverty, illness, and disillusionment, Arthur Rimbaud disappeared, and never again wrote another line of verse.

Even before *A Season in Hell,* Rimbaud's poetic images were macabre, obscene, and scatological. At the age of fifteen he formulated his doctrine of the visionary, setting down the pattern for future Surrealists. In his famous "*Les Lettres du Voyant,*" he speaks of his determination to become a seer, a "*savant,*" to be one with God, to see His divine image, and to know the mysteries of the universe. As a visionary, he hoped to transcend daily banalities and to capture through poetry the "inexpressible." For this he advocated a life of a dissolute—in which one could experience "all forms of love, suffering and madness." Through debauchery, he thought he could discover his true Self, release the language of dreams, hear the voice of God, experience abstractions of sound, evoke the "color" of words.

But to "forge this monstrous soul," one also needed magic, and he turned, according to Enid Starkie,[5] to the Cabala, which has heavily influenced mystic thinkers who believe it can unfold the mystery of creation. He did not, however, embrace the asceticism associated with many other mystics; instead, debauchery became his guiding principle. "*Faire l'âme monstreuse*" became his cry; magic, depravity, and decadence became his means. He wanted to test his spirit and mind, to break down reason and repression, to experience suffering and self-degradation. And thus his drug addiction, his masochistic-sadistic homosexual relationship with Paul Verlaine, his constant orgies in the quarters they shared, his poverty and filth, his scandals and scenes, his participation in every kind of orgiastic sensation was, as Starkie has indicated, inevitable.

"Rimbaud . . . who had much of the puritan in his composition, considered debauch a necessary aesthetic and spiritual discipline, and for him it was no self-indulgence. It became, on the contrary, in his inverted asceticism, a form of self-maceration, a form of self-flagellation. . . . Debauch was for him a doctrine, a religious aim. . . ."[6] So were dreams and drugs: ". . . alcohol, even hunger, thirst and fatigue, all served to loosen the cramping grip of conscious thought, and they quickly brought on the state of semi-hallucination which he found most fruitful for composition. . . ."[7]

In this state, Rimbaud wrote his "magic" poems. As an occultist, he believed he could capture the dream world as Baudelaire had done, and create a new language to express the word and the idea simultaneously: ". . . a new language not bound by logic, nor by grammar or syntax."[8] He hoped to find the "magic" in the word (a concept derived from primitive cultures) and the "color of vowels."[9] In "*Alchemie du Verbe*" he imagined that he had already done this: *A* was black; *E*, white; *I*, red; *O*, blue; *U*, green. In *Age of Surrealism,* Wallace Fowlie writes that Rimbaud believed that words themselves were myths and are

> more real than the objects or the ideas which they signify. Words then are the reality, and not the things which they describe. To create a poem is therefore equivalent to rearranging words, to fixing words in new unaccustomed juxtapositions so that they will show different aspects and colors of their myth. Rimbaud and the surrealists and modern poets in general will not try, in their poems, to explain experience. . . . All that they are interested in doing is to show a kaleidoscope view of life, a new *arrangement of signs,* an unexpected set of formations which may cast new lights and shadows on life but without thereby deciphering it [emphasis added].[10]

Rimbaud's quest for the meaning of language, which was initiated by Baudelaire (though earlier poets had also been drawn to the problem), purified by Mallarmé, and adopted by the Symbolists and the Surrealists, is a continuing quest that also finds a voice in today's theatre. (As we shall discuss in subsequent chapters, the Polish avant-garde director Jerzy Grotowski has been experimenting for years with new ways of using his native language, and in 1971 the British poet Ted Hughes and the director Peter Brook experimented with an entirely new language, created by Hughes, which they believed could be understood universally.) In addition, Rimbaud's life style—his irreverence for established social beliefs and customs, his unyielding youthful arrogance toward those who rejected and ostracized him—led generations of youth to emulate his behavior and the visionary aspects of his poetics. Mysticism and poetry, heightened by debauchery and the elevation of the irrational—all this was compellingly attractive to certain future avant-gardists, and adaptable to their purposes.

Rimbaud's spontaneous outpourings, and his flouting of the conventions, sharply contrasted with the quiet, uneventful life of Mallarmé, who shared with Rimbaud an obsessional search for the quintessence of poetry.

Mallarmé was an aesthete who, determined to find the purity of the word, founded theories on the work of Baudelaire and Poe, and, like his models, believed that poetry need not be didactic, nor socially relevant: in effect, he believed in art for its own sake. He revolted "against the oratorical lushness of romanticism," as Fowlie states it, and felt that the power of poetry "is not in its moving rhetoric, not in its precise images, but rather in its suggestiveness."[11] At twenty-two, fascinated by the process of creation more than by the work created, Mallarmé put down the sentence that became the basic precept for impressionism, surrealism, and Happenings: "*Peindre, non la chose, mais l'effet qu'elle produit*"—To paint, not the thing, but the effect it produces[12] became the theoretical motto that dominated his entire creative life. Like Rimbaud, Mallarmé believed in artists as magicians, in the sacredness of the poet's calling, and in poetry as a means of apprehending mystery. *L'image juste* became his goal; analogy and structure his cause, the sound and sensual value of words, his *idée fixe.* His subject matter, like Baudelaire's, dealt with sex, crime, violence, and impotence, as well as the attainment of absolute beauty through death (a typical Romantic preoccupation). In fact, he linked poetry to the beautiful and the beautiful to dreaming and death and hoped for a language of dreams, quietude, and silence.

Early in his career, Mallarmé was interested in the theatre as well as in poetry. His long poem "*Hérodiade*" was begun as a drama, and though the work was never staged, Mallarmé developed his own theatrical aesthetics, which made a substantial contribution to the Symbolist theatre.[13] He envisioned a theatrical language freed of syntax, in which gesture and image would symbolically express the complexity of man's inner life within the context of poetic drama. Such a language—in which poets would learn from music, particularly Wagner, and would not depend on intelligibility in the usual sense—would closely reflect not only dreams, reverie, and silence, but would evoke an atmosphere of mystery. "*Remplacez Vaudeville par Mystère*," he argued,[14] for in his mind the fusion of mystery and metaphysics—a neo-Romantic ideal—could be the basis for transcendental art. Besides, he despised vaudeville, a euphemism for boulevard theatre. To this end, he envisioned a purified, ceremonial, uncluttered *mise-en-scène* conveyed through a language so pure it would become "silent poetry."

Mallarmé's search for a viable theatrical language, and his desire to revive ritual and ceremonial theatre, were his most significant contributions to the Symbolist theatre. He was certain that drama need not be narrative or literal—a belief he shared with Wagner. Through Wagner, he recognized that ritual drama could be a means of evoking mystical sensations and nuances, and through Wagner's ideas on artistic synthesis, Mallarmé came to believe that theatre utilizing dance and mime, and "silent poetry," could probe man's inner depths.[15] Most important, writes Haskell Block: ". . . Mallarmé's vision of what the drama can become represents a total transformation of the theatre, a return to the rudimentary elements of the drama in their pristine simplicity"[16]—a vision later shared by avant-garde theatre artists.

By 1886, symbolism had become a "school." Philosophically it kept alive all the basic tenets of German Idealism, while contributing to the glorification of decadence. And although some Symbolists dissociated themselves from the label "decadent," the works of Baudelaire, Rimbaud, and Mallarmé had clearly led the way to a decadent aesthetic. In describing the literature of the time, Arthur Symons writes that "it was a restless curiosity in research . . . a spiritual and moral perversity . . . a new and beautiful and interesting disease . . . a *maladie fin de siècle*. . . . Healthy, we cannot call it, and healthy it does not wish to be considered. . . ."[17]

Decadent symbolism produced amazing techniques. It encouraged the use of analogy, unconventional grammar, bizarre juxtapositions, violent and paradoxical images, associative words and sounds, and non-literal metaphors. Decadence meant stripping away the outer level of consciousness to convey through symbols a Self revelatory of erotica, dreams, nightmares, fantasies. Decadent symbolism supported the belief in art as a subjective, personal act practiced for its own sake to describe and attain the beautiful. Finally, decadence furthered the drug cult and the cult of the alienated artist whose odd and ineffable images were frequently adjudged to be "mad." But madness, mystery, and depravity were indicative of the temperament of the artists.

While the Symbolists were formulating principles that were to influence future theatrical experiments, a collaborator (but not acutally a part) of the Symbolist decadent movement was developing his own independent doctrines. Alfred Jarry (1873–1907) wrote only two plays in his short lifetime. The first, *Ubu Roi*, opened in Paris on December 11, 1896. It was a stinging attack on the puritanical inhibitions of the public as well as on the stultifying stage presentations of the time, and it made Jarry notorious at the age of twenty-three. In *The Banquet Years,* Roger Shattuck describes the opening of Jarry's *Ubu Roi* as though Shattuck were there; it is worth repeating:

> Before the curtain went up, a crude table was brought out, covered with a piece of old sacking. Jarry appeared, looking dead white, for he had made himself up like a streetwalker to face the

> footlights. Nervously sipping from a glass, he spoke in his flattest, most clipped tones. For ten minutes, he sat in front of the explosive crowd, thanking the people who had helped in the production, referring briefly to the traditions of the Guignol theatre, and mentioning the masks the actors would wear and the fact that the first three acts would be performed without intermission. He concluded in a more properly Ubuesque vein. [Shattuck then quotes Jarry:]
>
> "In any case, we have a perfect *décor*, for just as one good way of setting a play in Eternity is to have revolvers shot off in the year 1000, you will see doors open on fields of snow under blue skies, fireplaces furnished with clocks and swinging wide to serve as doors, and palm trees growing at the foot of a bed so that little elephants standing on bookshelves can browse on them.
>
> "As to the orchestra, there is none. Only its volume and timbre will be missed, for various pianos and percussion will execute Ubuesque themes from backstage. The action, which is about to begin, takes place in Poland, that is to say: Nowhere."[18]

Then Jarry vanished from the stage and Gémier, the actor, appeared. Walking down to the apron of the stage, he delivered his first line: "*Merde* [shit]." Nothing of this sort had taken place on the stage before. Instant fistfights, boos, hoots, catcalls, and epithets topping the one uttered on the stage, erupted. The following morning the critics reviled Jarry, while his coterie of admirers, including Yeats and Symons, who were in the audience opening night, defended the play. *Ubu Roi* is a play about power. Reminiscent of *Macbeth,* Ubu is egged on by his domineering wife to murder his king and thereby to attain the throne himself. Though a mere plot outline sounds less than shocking, it was the texture of the play that scandalized the French. Scatology, grotesque humor, allusions to the stupidity and rapaciousness of men and monarchs, were radical departures from the formal theatre of the time.

Some critics have viewed Jarry as an "anomaly,"[19] but actually he was an offshoot of the French Symbolist poets. Like Baudelaire, he chose a life of vice so that he could explore visions and hallucinations. Like Rimbaud, he saw the world in terms of its irrationality and himself as a character in his play; like Mallarmé, he envisioned language in terms of dreams and fantasies. But while Mallarmé labored to discover the precise meaning of a word, Jarry worked for ambiguity and grotesquerie. In *Ubu,* Jarry found his persona. He addressed himself as Ubu, signed his letters "Père Ubu," spoke in the language of his plays, and held court as if he were King Ubu. His eccentricity was unlimited; he carried loaded pistols, wore painted India ink ties, old trousers tucked into his socks, and kept on his mantle an erect phallus covered with a little velvet hat.[20] Jarry in life was as much a character expressing the world of absurdity as Byron was a romantic hero. In fact, more than anyone else, Jarry extended the Self in art. The Self in art: the lack of differentiation between the artist and the work, the melding of art and reality—the roots of which are to be found among the Romantics—were perpetuated by Jarry and his descendents, who dedicated themselves to keeping this concept alive.

But Jarry's persona could not survive without his illusions, or as Shattuck says, his "hallucinations." And for this he needed drink. No doubt he believed that drink (like drugs) would release irrational patterns and secure for him the bizarre, zany, hallucinatory visions he craved. Self-destructive, a fierce nihilist and philosophical rebel, though never committed to any movement, Jarry was a precursor of Artaud. With the exception of Ibsen's *Peer Gynt,* he loathed the contemporary theatre, especially the theatrical conventions that inhibited the actors and forced them to conform to the dogmas of realism. In *Ubu Roi*, he wanted the actors to use "the universal gesture"[21] in place of mere words, masks instead of makeup, and signs or placards instead of elaborate changes of settings. For *Ubu Roi*, he envisioned a set that would evoke a child's world and designed it himself, aided by Bonnard, Vuillard, and Toulouse-Lautrec. Commenting on Jarry's set, Arthur Symons wrote:

> . . . the scenery was painted to represent, by a child's conventions, indoors and out of doors, and even the torrid, temperate, and arctic zones at once. Opposite you, at the back of the stage, you saw apple trees in bloom, under a blue sky, and against the

> sky a small closed window and a fireplace . . . through the very midst of which . . . trooped in and out the clamorous and sanguinary persons of the drama. On the left was painted a bed, and at the foot of the bed a bare tree and snow falling. On the right there were palm trees . . . beside the door a skeleton dangled. . . .[22]

Jarry's unconventional setting revealed him to be a powerful comic satirist. The setting, the tone, and the content of the play so affected the young Yeats that, following the performance, he wondered, after this, after Mallarmé, Verlaine, and others in that vein, "what more is possible? After us the Savage God."[23]

To be sure, Jarry's world view was savage. Determined to depict the lunacy of the world through his personal antics as well as through his plays, he developed his own metaphysics, which he called "pataphysics": "Pataphysics is the science of the realm beyond metaphysics," he wrote, "the science of imaginary solutions, which symbolically attributes the properties of objects, described by their virtuality, to their lineaments."[24] He sought to attain a consciousness that was unattainable, and he tried to apprehend "the laws which govern exceptions and will explain the universe supplementary to this one; or less ambitiously, it will describe a universe which one can see—must see perhaps—instead of the traditional one, for the laws discovered in the traditional universe are themselves correlated exceptions, even though frequent, or in any case accidental facts which, reduced to scarcely exceptional exceptions, don't even have the advantage of singularity."[25]

These desires, despite Jarry's involuted expression of them, were the desires of all visionaries, but "what distinguishes Jarry's career from an entire tradition of visionary writers . . ." writes Shattuck, "is first of all, his quasi-suicidal attempt to achieve a new level of existence through literary mimesis, fusing his life and his art . . ."[26] This attempt, according to Shattuck, was the beginning of Jarry's mental deterioration in so far as it "violated his own identity and exceeded the limits of literature";[27] nevertheless, it exerted a strong influence on Surrealists, on anti-art movements, and on the extremes of the counterculture theatre movement later on.

During the last half of the nineteenth century, two distinct camps were developing. "Art for art's sake" was the rallying cry of the Symbolists and their followers. At the same time, the Naturalist movement was gaining momentum. These two strands were destined to dominate the intellectual and artistic life of Europe for the next hundred years. Although they were sometimes viewed as irreconcilable opposites, in actuality aspects of each were to merge and interchange. Early in the century, for example, one group of Romantics glorified revolution and the common man; another, German Idealism, with its mysticism and cult of the hermetic. As romanticism ran its course, radicals in the middle of the century accepted certain aspects of romanticism and repudiated others. They viewed Idealism (and the concentration on the subjective) as bourgeois and reactionary, and they considered social issues and scientific investigation progressive and valid subject matter for art. Still, there were those who believed in *both* social reform and Romantic Idealism. For the majority of radicals, however, romanticism had become totally identified with Idealism and as such was entirely rejected.

Materialism was on the march by 1844. Marx had already met Engels in Paris. Four years later they had issued their "Communist Manifesto"; that same year the workers of France had mounted the barricades, only to be summarily shot down. Past the mid-century, Darwin's *Origin of Species* was followed by *Das Kapital.* The intense interest in materialist philosophy and scientific experimentation was reflected in social and political protest. There were great outcries against the slaughter of the workers in the Revolution of 1848 and the Commune of 1871. Fierce social inequities perpetrated by an avaricious bourgeoisie were the subject of graphic portraits in Balzac, of biting caricatures of Daumier, of stinging depictions in Zola. Political repression and economic deprivation prompted artists and intellectuals to demand new solutions, if not new sensibilities.

There arose a whole school of socially-minded critics and writers whose artistic concepts were rooted in a belief that character is an outgrowth of heredity and environment, and that art should be dedicated to the eradication of social evils. These artists—Dickens and Thackeray in England; Balzac, Flaubert, and Zola in France; Tolstoy and Turgenev in Russia—rejected the growing revival of what they considered the worst aspects of romanticism, German Idealism, French Symbolism and the entire art-for-art's-sake movement. They became chroniclers of the social scene, defenders of liberty and egalitarianism, sympathizers with the working class, supporters of science, enemies of the *haute bourgeoisie.* At the same time that their ideas and approach gained prominence, the opposite trend continued to flourish: the Symbolists who deplored the confusion of art and politics and the lesser practitioners of a now diluted Byronism, as well as sentimental writers of comedy and domestic tragedy.

To give concrete voice to the adherents of his position, Emile Zola, then an influential drama critic and outspoken political radical, formulated a historic aesthetic doctrine attacking what he considered outmoded decadent romanticism. Able to take advantage of his considerable position as a critic, he focused his attack on the established theatre, which at the time was particularly flaccid. Productions were superficial and significant playwrights rare (although the young Ibsen, Hebbel, and Büchner had already written unconventional plays). In fact, dramatic literature had been steadily declining, while the novel was being steadily revitalized. In England, even during the febrile Romantic period, no important playwrights appeared (the plays Shelley and Byron had written were essentially closet dramas).

In Germany, the theatre during the Romantic movement had been influenced heavily by *Sturm und Drang* drama. After Lessing had published his Hamburg Dramaturgy (*Hamburgische Dramaturgie*), attacking classical French tragedy and calling for "real tragedy," Schiller and Goethe became exponents of *Sturm und*

Drang plays (those dealing with epic heroes, the fate of nations, and cataclysmic emotions) in contrast to the formal tragedy of eighteenth-century playwrights like Racine. But as *Sturm und Drang* developed and spread over the continent, it became vulgarized, and playwrights continued to hack out melodramas in the name of a dead romanticism. This was the situation that led Zola to write his famous essay "Naturalism in the Theatre."

Zola maintained that art should be regarded as a science in order to achieve a greater fidelity to real life. He advocated the application of the scientific method to dramaturgy: the use of observation and analysis of data. He believed that the playwright, making use of the advances of science, need only report and record the facts in the interests of objectivity. "Naturalism in literature . . . is the return to nature and to man, direct observation, correct anatomy, the acceptance and the depiction of that which *is*. The task is the same for the scientist as for the writer. Both have to abandon abstractions for realities, ready-made formulas for rigorous analysis. . . ."[28]

Zola believed that literature should be socially oriented, and he urged dramatists to reflect the social and economic evils of their times with greater verisimilitude. The milieu of a character determined his inner life, claimed Zola, not mystical abstractions of beauty. He believed that if playwrights were similarly "scientific" in their methods, they could achieve strict fidelity to real life. Fully aware of the danger of treating art like a mathematical problem, Zola was nevertheless adamant in his convictions; he was dedicated to breaking down the clichés and stereotypes that characterized Victor Hugo's historical drama, for example. He recognized however that Hugo was part of the heritage of the romantic rebellion which had at one time been a liberalizing force in France. But, for Zola, Hugo's work was no longer relevant.[29] He deplored "romantic" artists, once a bulwark against the status quo, who were now enjoying the privileges of status and money while attempting to appear radical. As to romantic literary style, this had degenerated into verbosity and artificial "heroic" prose.[30]

In France, Zola's arguments were taken up by André Antoine,

who, with a group of amateurs in 1887, formed the first free theatre in Paris. His Théâtre Libre was subsidized by subscription, and the actors, in order to support themselves, held down ordinary jobs all day. Eventually the theatre became so well established (Zola supported Antoine unequivocally) that Ibsen as well as Strindberg allowed Antoine to be the first to introduce their plays to France. Antoine's theatre was devoted to naturalism. To authenticate their characterizations, his actors copied speech and body movements, and manners and habits from living people. In place of the customary declamatory style, the actors based their speech on stammers, hesitations, and silences. Determined to make contact with one another rather than to speak directly to the audience, the actors were obliged to speak directly to each other when performing, to avoid cliché stances and postures, and to handle props and furniture as they would in real life. In Germany at about the same time, the Duke of Saxe-Meiningen organized a similar company. His first "realistic" ensemble toured Europe, and on reaching Russia had an important influence on Stanislavsky. In addition, a free theatre in Germany, the *Freie Bühne,* and one in London under Beerbohm Tree were established. The radicalizing effect of naturalism on the theatre had gained significant ground.

Nevertheless, various artists, still imbued with romantic philosophy, channeled their ideas into other movements. Wagner believed that the utilization of mythic archetypes expressed through corresponding music and stage design, if directed toward the senses and not the intellect, would result in a transcendent theatrical experience (a foreshadowing of the twentieth century's consecration of the felt experience and mythic metaphor). But his productions never matched his vision, and it remained for the scenic designer Adolphe Appia to merge the physical elements of Wagnerian production with the "soul" of the music. Appia, striving to find the proper relationship between space, lights, setting, and music, was determined to subordinate all theatrical elements—except lighting—to the totality of the musical experience. He abandoned one-dimensional flat scenery and stationary lights, and inaugurated new lighting methods, which he believed were central to expressing the inner world of music. At about the same time, Gordon Craig, the revolutionary scenic designer, finding all schools of theatrical production restricting, formulated his own theories. Craig saw the director, not the actor or playwright, as the prime mover of a production. Most important, he separated the art of the theatre from the art of literature. He wrote:

> . . . A dramatic poem is to be read. A drama is not to be read, but to be seen upon the stage. Therefore gesture is a necessity to a drama, and it is useless to a dramatic poem. It is absurd to talk of these two things, gesture and poetry, as having anything to do with one another . . . you must not confound the dramatic poem with the drama, neither must you confound the dramatic poet with the dramatist. The first writes for the reader, or listener, the second writes for the audience of a theatre. . . . the dramatist made his first piece by using action, words, line, colour and rhythm, and making his appeal to our eyes and ears by a dexterous use of these five factors. . . . [31]

In an imaginary conversation with a playgoer, Craig went on to say that the early dramatists were certain that all action on the stage was meant primarily to be seen, because sight was the swiftest and most appealing of the senses. The theatre is action, he maintains. Prose action is gesture; poetry action is dance. Later in the "conversation," he argues that no dramatic piece is complete unless it is actually performed. Further, "the theatre *must not forever rely upon having a play to perform, but must in time perform pieces of its own art* [emphasis added]."[32] Decades later, Peter Brook and Peter Hall staged Shakespeare in England bearing in mind Craig's predictions.

Both the Symbolist movement and Wagner's influence were spreading. In 1890 in Paris, Paul Fort, a poet dedicated to the basic principles of symbolism, established the Théâtre Mixte (later called the Théâtre d'Art). Here, the works of Flemish playwright Maurice Maeterlinck were first produced (Lugné-Poë, a friend and colleague of Mallarmé, directed the famous *Pelléas et Mélisande*).

Fort's theatre in Montparnasse was short-lived, but Maeterlinck's early themes of the Beautiful and the Mysterious and of lovers in the grip of destiny took hold, and his style and vision of impending doom, perceived as an extension of the Symbolist movement, captured the imagination of the generation preceding World War I.

The revolt against naturalism took yet another form. Late nineteenth- and early twentieth-century German painters and dramatists, rejecting both the Naturalist and Symbolist schools, approached art not from the perspective of any rational philosophy, but as an expression of themselves, and were appropriately called Expressionists. As Gerald E. Weales has pointed out, expressionism "was the most completely self-centered art form ever evolved. The expressionist writer takes the whole human race and the entire cosmos as his province, but he shows it to us as it is seen through the eyes of one character, invariably an alter ego for himself."[33] Further, the artist imposes his own description of reality on the outside world, rather than the outside world imposing its reality on the artist.[34]

In painting, Expressionist artists exaggerated and distorted the realities of color, form, objects, and space, and changed thereby an optical reality into personal vision.[35] In drama, their characters were unidentifiable individuals; they were bizarre, idiosyncratic, and distorted archetypes intentionally made ugly and perverse in order to devaluate the neo-romantic concept of the beautiful. Expressionist dramatists rejected psychological motivations to show only the inner essence of things, and to penetrate beneath illusion and dissect and rearrange nature.[36]

The early Expressionist dramatists were primarily interested in a single theme—the family—which for them symbolized the worst aspects of German life: authoritarianism and parochialism. Their fury against the family unit was conveyed in some plays by fathers imprisoning sons, sons raping mothers, and children killing their parents. Incest, orgy, patricide, and matricide were common themes. Other Expressionist playwrights, however, wrote about ecstasy and the glory of suffering, self-sacrifice and redemption.

But the majority wanted to give form to their violent, wild, demonic feelings, which had all too long been repressed by a stultifying familial and military hierarchy. They attacked the German bourgeoisie with a vengeance; they used scathing language, strident speech, and a texture and tone of writing that was characterized as the "*Schrei*"—the scream—an uninhibited, unmerciful howl that exemplifed and expressed their agonized vision.[37]

Whereas Naturalists depicted life based on their observation of the objective world (in part, on their materialist outlook, as well), and neo-romantics and Symbolists tried to describe the ineffable and the beautiful, the Expressionists wanted to express, not depict, the ugly, the bizarre, and the decadent—without regard for empirical truth. Ironically, their dependence on intuition rather than on rational analysis as an approach to art furthered the romantic ideal; in fact, expressionism was an outgrowth of the more "primitive" *Sturm und Drang*.[38] But perhaps the movement was equally influenced by Rimbaud's "*le poète maudit*" and his contemplation of the "monstrous soul" as well as his obsessiveness with dreams and nightmares.

For example, in art, James Ensor's *Die Masken und der Tod*, painted in 1897, expresses the artist's nightmare: skeletons and masks, distorted lips, noses, and eyes are the subject of his work. Max Beckmann's 1919 lithograph *Die Nacht* is a nightmare murder scene—bandaged heads, garroted necks, bare buttocks, elongated hands and feet, all "screaming" in agony while being hacked to death by a vicious-looking bunch of gangsters—a work, incidentally, which seems to foreshadow the Living Theatre's 1968 production of *Frankenstein*. In drama, playwrights followed similar patterns: they chose the visual rather than the verbal. But the visual was presented disjointedly, as in a dream or nightmare without a frame of reference, detached from a specific naturalistic context, thus making indistinguishable a character's inner reality and the outside world.[39] In Expressionist drama, the only reality was that of the central character's—a reality that dramatists never objectified. Naturalists and realists may also have utilized a "central intelligence'' as the focus for making the artist's perceptions comprehensible and giving them a unity of form. The Expressionist dramatists, instead, tried to evoke feelings that were below the surface of their audience's awareness by reaching for a new synthesis of emotion through fragmentation of reality and stream of consciousness.

In their attempt to find new forms to break through conventional and ''objective'' concepts of reality, Expressionists developed some important and adaptable techniques. They disregarded plot and chose to work with imagistic, episodic scenes; they understood the effectiveness of music, dance, and odd, exaggerated gesture for communicating their perceptions; they elaborated the method of dissociation to enhance the elements of dream and nightmare in their work. If they seemed at times shrill and hysterical, they could also produce a razor-edged intensity. Undoubtedly they influenced German art and drama for decades, but it was not only the Germans who were affected by them. In Russia, Vakhtangov's concept of ''fantastic reality'' had much in common with expressionism; later the Polish director Jerzy Grotowski's production of *Akropolis* also used Expressionist techniques (heightened by the fact that *Akropolis* takes place in a German concentration camp), as did Peter Brook in his production of the *Marat/Sade*. More important, expressionism advanced the transmission of extremes of inner feelings—without regard for nature or versimilitude—as a legitimate subject for art. In this sense, expressionism was significant in shaping the consciousness of future experimentalists who were to justify a very intuitive and sometimes a very distorted art.

At the end of the century, naturalism and symbolism were in a struggle for supremacy. Naturalism was considered the more politically radical, in that its adherents' work reflected the evils of the political and social ambiance. The Symbolists, decried by some as reactionary and decadent, represented the concept of art as personal vision. Despite avowed ideological differences, in actuality ideas from one movement spilled over to the other. The writing of William James and Freud in psychology, and the existential philosophy of Kierkegaard, complicated the intellectual climate. Freud's work with dreams nurtured the Symbolists, while his scientific analysis of personality gave concrete substance to the work of the Naturalists. But several artists no longer supported any one "ism" over the other. Strindberg and Ibsen, as if torn between the current theories, were writing both naturalistic and symbolic plays. Strindberg's *Dream Play* was a symbolistic rendition of internal emotion, but *Miss Julie* was stimulated (perhaps inadvertently) by class struggle and Freudian discoveries in its relentless exposure of the heroine's inner conflicts. Ibsen's *Ghosts, Hedda Gabler*, and *The Wild Duck* mingled naturalism (with its skeptical view of bourgeois values) and rudimentary elements of symbolism.

These contradictory aesthetics represented the artists' struggles, not only with form, but with changing critical perceptions. Since the time of the Romantic revolution, the world seemed to have become .more fragmented and, despite the advances in science, man's social dilemmas more complex. Uncertainty about man's place in the hierarchy of the universe, despair about his ability to reform his social, political, and economic institutions, and unsettling concepts of his psychological nature characterized the transition from one century to the next. All the same, by the time the famed Moscow Art Theatre was to mature, the basic tenets of Zola's naturalism were far changed. Naturalism continued to dominate the thought and practice of the theatre. Still lingering in the background, however, were the Symbolists—their philosphy and techniques destined to reappear in other forms, in other movements, in other times.

two

The Russians Take Over

Naturalism as a radical aesthetic was to reach its ultimate development when Constantin Stanislavsky, then an actor, and his friend Vladimir Nemirovich-Danchenko, a director and producer, met in the back room of a restaurant in 1898 and engaged in the famous conversation that launched the Moscow Art Theatre. In Russia, conventional bourgeois theatre had sunk to its lowest point; the Russian adaptations of French boulevard plays were as unimaginative as their originals. Acting relied on the clichés of the "grand" tradition: tears were expressed by elaborately dabbing a handkerchief to a dry eye; anger, by stamping a foot; anguish, by tearing of the hair; sorrow, by beating one's breast. Antoine (with his Théâtre Libre) in France, Appia in Germany and Craig in England had already made inroads against this tradition, but the Russians were still committed to "stagey" sets, dreary plots, and stereotyped acting. When Stanislavsky finally founded the Moscow Art Theatre and replaced the star system with ensemble acting which demanded authentic emotion on stage, he was extending and enlarging upon naturalistic principles; unintentionally, he was rekindling romantic characteristics as well. Like the Romantics who rebelled against artificial standards in poetry, Stanislavsky rebelled against fustian declamations and pretentious classical acting, and, like the Romantics, he elevated the individual as a subject for art. But his directorial approach was strongly influenced by the Naturalists' insistence that performance be based on fidelity to real life and on detailed delineation of character. Doggedly, he searched for practical techniques that could express both his artistic philosophy and his commitment to ensemble work. And doggedly he trained the actor to probe and identify with the complete inner life of the character he was portraying. What emerged was a new acting method that broke all existing patterns in its successful innovations with the natural use of voice and gesture.

While Stanislavsky was creating and developing his aesthetics, he educated the audience as well. Audiences could not be seated after curtain time, they could not expect the usual bows at intermission, they had to accustom themselves to the actor's new, unexaggerated gestures and way of speaking, and most important, they were forced to relinquish their concept of commercial theatre, for Stanislavsky saw the theatre as a temple.[1]

In the fall of 1898 Stanislavsky and Nemirovich-Danchenko opened the doors of the Moscow Art Theatre with a production of Alexei Tolstoy's *Tsar Fyodor Ivanovich*. Like the Parisian audience that two years earlier had been shocked by *Ubu Roi's* "*merde*," the spectators in Moscow were equally stunned. A new theatrical speech was being presented to them; actors spoke in natural rhythms, unconventional intonations, and hushed tones; sometimes they sat silent, their backs to the audience. For the first time, everything on stage was "real": costumes, settings, and furniture were specifically and thoroughly researched and authentically reproduced.[2]

Tsar Fyodor inaugurated the Moscow Art, but it was later, through the collaboration of Chekhov and Stanislavsky, that the Theatre achieved the perfection of its art. Despite some disagreement on interpretation, Stanislavsky had found in Chekhov the ideal playwright for the development of his company. At the height of its power, the Moscow Art supported over one hundred actors, technicians, and stagehands. It had a varied repertory and played to good houses; in fact, the Theatre was becoming renowned. Nonetheless, there were internal grumblings.

It was the eve of the 1905 Revolution, a period of intensified rebelliousness and social ferment. Stanislavsky's naturalism (by then called realism) was the philosophical and aesthetic mainstay of his theatre, but young and energetic experimentalists within his company were becoming involved with the growing Symbolist movement in Russia whose ideas ran counter to Stanislavsky's theories and methods. In Russian intellectual circles, arguments raged about the merits of socialism, about new and audacious artistic movements. Artists everywhere, including those from the Moscow Art, yearned for new forms. The spirit of Rimbaud and Mallarmé haunted the naturalistic theatre; the plays of Wedekind and Strindberg touched the sensibilities of the youth, and even Max Reinhardt's conception of theatre as pageantry was accepted as a rebellion against naturalism.[3] In keeping with this movement, the Moscow Art produced (in 1901–02) Ibsen's *Wild Duck*, followed by a somewhat symbolistic interpretation of Ostrovsky's *Snow Maiden*; in the 1904–05 season, Stanislavsky himself staged Maeterlinck's *The Intruder, Interim,* and *The Blind,* and later directed his *Blue Bird* as well as Ibsen's *Ghosts* and *Peer Gynt.* Stanislavsky also encouraged Gordon Craig's symbolistic production of *Hamlet* at the Moscow Art, while he, Stanislavsky, continued his own search for new techniques to express the growing interest in metaphysical theatre. In his production of Andreyev's *The Life of Man* (1907), Stanislavsky directed the play against a black velvet background, and even the stagehands wore black velvet overalls, slippers, and gloves so that they would merge with the stage.[4] But aside from imaginative settings and costumes, Stanislavsky introduced no new directorial concepts or acting methods to express abstract ideas. Depicting dreams, images, and symbolic visions were basically antithetical to Stanislavsky's theories, inasmuch as the foundations of his acting and directing methods depended on exactitude and specificity. Besides, his emphasis was always on the psychology of the characters, so that stylization based on metaphysical or abstract concepts was alien to his form and it did not reflect the aspirations of experimentalists who sought to work with techniques other than his. As a result, by 1905 Stanislavsky had established the First Studio, for purposes of experimentation, under the leadership of one of their most brilliant pupils, Vsevelod Meyerhold.

Meyerhold, an actor with the Stanislavsky company since its inception, had left it in 1902, but returned in 1905, deeply affected by the French and (to some extent) Russian Symbolist writers who were then coming into prominence. Meyerhold seemed the most likely person therefore to head the First Studio. But his views conflicted with those of Stanislavsky, and he was soon replaced. He then went to work at the Kommissarzhevskaya Theatre in St. Petersburg and later formed his own company. Over the years, he became the leader of the Russian avant-garde, ultimately provoking the Soviet authorities to such an extent that they finally silenced him.

Meyerhold's main complaint against the Moscow Art was its unequivocal dedication to Chekhov, which, as Meyerhold saw it, prevented the Theatre from producing anything but "Chekhovian" naturalism. Acknowledging Stanislavsky's genius, Meyerhold nevertheless admonished him: he criticized Stanislavsky for developing a naturalism which, denying the "physical," led to passivity. A Stanislavsky actor, he claimed, depended upon inactive verbal psychologizing and over-intellectualized emotions, while disregarding the body as a tool for concretizing feeling:

> There is a whole range of questions to which psychology is incapable of supplying the answers. A theatre built on psychological foundations is as certain to collapse as a house built on sand. On the other hand, a theatre which relies on *physical elements* is at the very least assured of clarity. All psychological states are determined by specific physiological processes. By correctly resolving the nature of his state physically, the actor reaches the point where he experiences the *excitation* which

> communicates itself to the spectator, and induces him to share in the actor's performance. . . .[5]

That the physical aspects of acting were a more important means of conveying emotion than the psychological was a belief that began early in Meyerhold's career. As a young man, influenced by Maeterlinck's aesthetics, he felt that a theatrical experience should convey an "internal mystical vibration"[?] expressed by the actor's "eyes, the lips, the sound and manner of delivery,"[6] rather than through traditional stereotyped movements and cliché voice patterns, and he seized upon the idea of "plasticity" for transcending naturalistic techniques: "Plasticity itself is not new," he wrote, "but the form which I have in mind is new. Before, it corresponded closely to the spoken dialogue, but I am speaking of a *plasticity which does not correspond to the words.*"[7]

"Plasticity," as Meyerhold conceived it, was a means of revealing the inexpressible and ineffable mystery of a character's life, not through words in the text, which he felt were inadequate to convey the "inner dialogue," but through "plastic movement," which finds expression through "gestures, poses, glances, and silences and through a *pattern* of movement."[8] Plasticity need not exclude the word, but must convey the meaning *beneath* the word, the hidden relationships that words alone cannot express. Such plasticity, in Meyerhold's opinion, could add a new dimension to the text, as well as contradict or be entirely unrelated to the text. Plasticity then was a physical means of capturing the unspoken life of the character, his unconscious feelings and perceptions—his inner dialogue:

> . . . Words catch the ear, plasticity—the eye. Thus the spectator's imagination is exposed to two stimuli: the oral and the visual. The difference between the old theatre and the new is that in the new theatre speech and plasticity are each subordinated to their own separate rhythms and the two do not necessarily coincide. However, it does not follow that plasticity has always to contradict speech; a phrase may be supported by a wholly appropriate

> movement, but this is no more natural than the coincidence of the logical and the poetic stress in verse.[9]

Meyerhold was always searching for new styles to achieve the plasticity which he thought would overcome the rigidity of naturalism. At one point, he worked with distorted, exaggerated depictions of character, and then with Oriental dance movements, gymnastics, boxing, and fencing. He experimented with the Italian *commedia dell'arte* acrobatics, and with the comedy and mime of the ancient Romans. Sometimes he would experiment with scenery and rehearse only with a canvas backdrop, plain drapes, or panels; sometimes he would discard all preconceived notions entirely. Plasticity became the central word in the Meyerhold vocabulary; he even studied the movements of animals, who he believed outlasted humans in their retention of innate plasticity. Subsequently, he created a series of body exercises based on the movement of the cat, which, when applied to the actor, afforded him maximum economy and sontrol. The "cat" exercises (later adopted by the avant-garde Polish director, Jerzy Grotowski, as well as by others) aimed at developing the spine as the central support of the body, while at the same time maximizing the fluidity and suppleness of other parts of the anatomy.[10] Eventually this led Meyerhold to a theory that presupposed the body to be an engine, or a machine, and therefore could be understood, controlled, and managed like one: "Since the art of the actor is the art of plastic forms in space he must study the mechanics of his body. This is essential because any manifestation of a force (including the living organism) is subject to constant laws of mechanics. . . ."[11] Thus Meyerhold claimed the actor must develop the ability to respond to outside stimuli, to coordinate his reaction to these stimuli through the mechanics of the body, and to transmit his reaction in theatrical form. The actor's object was to find a rhythm or a gesture for each part of his body so as to identify a character's dominant psychological trait. This necessitated a specific training system: actors were to become as adept as acrobats and as quick as cats. To this system of acting and training, which, for Meyerhold represented the ultimate in plasticity, he gave the name "biomechanics."

The training of the actor was based on three principles, which he called intention, realization, and reaction: "*The intention* is the intellectual assimilation of a task prescribed externally by the dramatist, the director or the initiative of the performer. *The realization* is the cycle of volitional, mimetic, and vocal reflexes. *The reaction* is the attenuation of the volitional reflex as it is realized mimetically and vocally in preparation for the reception of a new intention (the transition to a new acting cycle). . . ."[12]

Some of Meyerhold's students kept notes during the 1920's. Erast Garin, a member of his theatre, recollects an exercise called "Shooting a Bow":

> An imaginary bow is held in the left hand. The student advances with the left shoulder forward. When he spots the gadget he stops, balanced equally on both feet. The right hand describes an arch in order to reach an arrow in an imaginary belt behind his back. The movement of the hand affects the whole body, causing the balance to shift to the back foot.
>
> The hand draws the arrow and loads the bow. The balance is transferred to the front foot. He aims. The bow is drawn with the balance shifting again to the back foot. The arrow is fired and the exercise completed with a leap and a cry. Through this, one of the earliest exercises, the pupil begins to comprehend himself in spatial terms, acquires physical self-control, develops elasticity and balance, realizes that the merest gesture—say with the hand—resounds throughout the entire body, and gains practice in the so-called "refusal." Thus, in this exercise the "pre-gesture," the "refusal," is the hand reaching back for the arrow. The étude is an example of the "acting sequence" which comprises intention, realization and reaction.[13]

Another actor recalls: ". . . from the exercise 'Shooting a bow' there developed the étude, 'The Hunt,' and then a whole pantomime which was used to train every 'generation' in the Studio. A whole series of exercises and études became 'classics' and were used later in the teaching of biomechanics."[14]

Meyerhold's productions reflected his theories. He discarded conventional scenery, costumes, and elaborate accoutrements; he believed that the literary values of a play were secondary to the actor's plasticity and to the audience's responses; hence no play was sacrosanct. In fact, he had to ". . . determine whether the play in hand was one which could be comprehended by the contemporary spectator through the prism of his own time, or whether it would convey its idea only when the conditions and the atmosphere surrounding the original players and playhouse and audience are reproduced. . . ."[15] He was the first in Russia to abolish the curtain and the proscenium arch, and to keep all the lights on. He even conceived of the actor standing "bare" on the stage, committed to audience participation, or to a sort of supercommunication between actors and spectators, and he once redecorated a theatre into a tavern in which the actors mingled freely with the audience. In what is known as his "constructivist" period (the use of architectural methods and materials rather than flats and furniture), he built ramps and platforms, designed abstract planks, staircases, geometric cubes, mobile scaffoldings, crossbars, and catwalks, the latter asymmetrically built on an open stage. Whereas Stanislavsky never broke "the fourth wall," Meyerhold pretended there never was one in the first place. The "new" theatre, he predicted, must rid itself of the box stage; scenes should be staged rapidly, like montages; plays should last no longer than one hour; platforms could be constructed to move in any direction, and seating arrangements for the audience should be totally changed. Clearly the avant-garde theatre directors of the 1960's had read their Meyerhold.

By 1920, Meyerhold was a substantial and compelling force in the theatre. He had become director of his own state-subsidized company in Moscow and despite criticism from supporters of naturalistic art, he was at first free to produce and develop his theories. Meyerhold had been a Marxist for some time and had unequivocally supported the 1918 Bolshevik position. He tended, like most Soviet artists, to idealize the skilled worker. He romanticized their work rhythms and claimed that their gestures—economy of movement and balance—were as beautiful, precise, and defined as a dancer's. But despite his accolades to the proletariat, the Soviet authorities hounded him. As art became more and more a concern of the state, Meyerhold refused to acquiesce to the Commissars' dictums, thus incurring their wrath. By 1928 the period of tolerance in the arts came to an end, and party hacks accused Meyerhold of being arbitrary with the actors, frivolous with the classics, egocentric as a director, and an "alien" to proletarian art: in short, a detriment to the spirit of the Revolution. In response, Meyerhold claimed to deplore Stanislavsky's belief in a character's "soul" as well as the romanticized idealistic notion of ecstasy as a prerequisite to art; he thus considered himself a scientific materialist in his approach to aesthetics.

Continuing to defend his avant-gardism, Meyerhold and his staff were to become victims of artistic repression. In 1930 his closest collaborator, the poet and playwright Mayakovsky, accused of formalism, killed himself. Then Meyerhold's theatre was closed for repairs, and he was forced to move to another, only to discover that the new theatre was more dilapidated than the original one. In the meantime, Party conferences and "Workers in the Arts" meetings attacked the "formalists." And Meyerhold, the defender of experimentation and innovation, repelled by socialist realism (though still a member of the Bolshevik party), was a target for the philistines. An excerpt from an article in *Pravda,* entitled "An Alien Theatre," reads as follows (December 17, 1937):

> On the occasion of the twentieth anniversary of the Great Socialist Revolution, only one out of the 700 Soviet professional theatres was without a special production to commemorate the October revolution and without a Soviet repertoire. That theatre was the Meyerhold theatre. . . .
>
> Almost his entire theatrical career before the October Revolution amounted to a struggle against the realistic theatre on behalf of the stylized, mystical, formalist theatre of the aesthetes, that is, a theatre which shunned real life. . . .
>
> [In its production of Verhaeren's *Dawn*] his theatre made a hero

> out of a Menshevik traitor to the working class. . . . *The Government Inspector* was treated not in the style of the realistic theatre, but in the spirit of the White émigré, Merezhkovsky's book, *Gogol and the Devil.*
>
> It has become absolutely clear that Meyerhold cannot (and, apparently, will not) comprehend Soviet reality or depict the problems which concern every Soviet citizen. . . .
>
> For several years [he] stubbornly tried to stage the play, *I Want a Child,* by the enemy of the people, Tretyakov, which was a hostile slur on the Soviet family. . . .
>
> The systematic deviation from Soviet reality, the political distortion of that reality, and hostile slanders against our way of life have brought the theatre to total ideological and artistic ruin, to shameful bankruptcy. . . . Do Soviet art and the Soviet public really need such a theatre?[16]

Plainly Meyerhold's career in the Soviet Union was finished. In 1939, when an All-Union Congress of stage directors met, Meyerhold's fate was sealed. There are contradictory reports as to whether he recanted, reasserted his principles, or even appeared at all. In any case, "immediately after the Congress, Meyerhold was arrested," writes Edward Braun. Later, "[his wife's] mutilated body had been discovered in their Moscow flat," and on February 2, 1940, continues Braun, "[Meyerhold] is believed to have been shot in a Moscow prison. . . ."[17]

The virtually uninterrupted repression in the arts that hardened after 1928 affected all experimentalists and anti-socialist realists. Among the avant-garde theatre directors, some were able to flee abroad, carrying the fruits of their experience with them into exile; others, like Alexander Tairov, were forced to remain and fared badly.

Tairov, founder in 1914 of a chamber theatre, the Kamerny, was a pupil of Meyerhold but rejected his former teacher's theories and practices. He believed that Meyerhold's actors were subservient to the director's will, that Meyerhold used theatrical effects as an end in themselves, and that Meyerhold's concentration on the body was excessive. On the other hand, he deplored the controlled realism of the Moscow Art Theatre, whose psychologizing and generalized emotion, he maintained, forced the actors into a rigid mold. Attempting to create a theatre somewhere between that of Stanislavsky and Meyerhold, Tairov founded a small, intimate theatre that would attract a celebrated and elitist audience. This theatre, the Kamerny, was to blend all the arts—ballet, music, acting, costuming, scenic design—into one, and was to utilize all kinds of artists: actors, dancers, comics, mimes and music-hall performers. Tairov called this the "synthetic theatre"[18]—a concept that foreshadows the "total theatre" of the sixties.

Influenced by the *commedia dell'arte,* Tairov was convinced that it was possible to work without words—hence, his interest in gesture. But unlike Meyerhold, who held similar views, Tairov saw gesture as only *one* means of evoking emotion. In other words, he sought the origins of the impulse *beneath* the gesture, while Meyerhold sought only the gesture itself. In addition, the Kamerny used music as a concomitant rhythmic extension of the actor's gesture rather than as a general underscoring of the dramatic action:

> . . . Tairov's position was even more extreme than Meyerhold's [writes William Kuhlke]. Meyerhold, in spite of his highhanded use of scripts, did maintain that the theatre grew out of literature and would always be in some way dependent on it. Tairov insisted that though he used literature now as raw material, ideally the theatre should create freely, spontaneously, independently—the theatrical collective making its own scenarios and the actors filling in dialogue extemporaneously, except for moments when the emotional content demanded poetic language, in which case, the poet, working along with the collective, would compose the required set speeches.[19]

(Note the startling similarity to contemporary practices in experimental theatre.)

Tairov's productions came into conflict with the authorities. A non-Bolshevik, he could not reconcile his art with their ideology.

He was unequivocally opposed to what he called "communal" theatre (audience participation), which in the 1920's signified the authorities' concept of the most revolutionary approach to theatre. According to his notebooks, merging actors with spectators was related to ritual and religion and, as such, it would undermine or abolish the formal aesthetics that defined the secular theatre. He claimed that "the path suggested by the socialist theatre is the same path to restoration of *pre*-classical theatre [that is, when the theatre was as yet unformed as an independent art] only with different ideological content."[20]

All the same, Tairov tried to adjust to the regime, but he did not abandon either his quest for experimentation or his predilection for presenting satire, a form the authorities despised. One season he staged G. K. Chesterton's *The Man Who Was Thursday* and Bulgakov's *The Purple Island*, which attacked the Soviet interference in art. But his production of Bedy's *Heroes* in 1936, which the authorities interpreted as a slur against Russian heroes, lost him the directorship of his theatre. Soon after, a committee took over his company and produced works that reflected official policy.[21] Tairov regained control in 1939, but he could not produce in a manner satisfactory to the Soviet government. During the war, the Kamerny Theatre was removed to various outlying regions of Siberia. For the next few years his career zigzagged. At the end of World War II, the regime saw fit to award him the order of Lenin. But the following year, a new "hard line" in the arts led Tairov to make a last, unsuccessful effort to reconcile his work with official doctrine. In 1950, the Kamerny was shut down for good. That same year, Tairov died.

Yevgeny Vakhtangov, an experimentalist widely accepted by the authorities, died before the repression set in. Early in his life he was influenced by the Cubist and Futurist movements in France and Italy, and despite his consciousness of the limitations of naturalism, he became a favorite pupil of Stanislavsky, replacing Meyerhold as head of the First Studio. In 1918, he produced Ibsen's *Rosmersholm*; in 1921, Strindberg's *Erik XIV*; and in 1922,

Ansky's *The Dybbuk* and Carl Gozzi's *Turandot*. The latter two, his greatest pieces, successfully fused the styles of Stanislavsky and Meyerhold. To this fusion, he gave the name "fantastic realism."[22]

"Fantastic realism" was based on the aesthetic principle of "creative distortion," according to which the artist utilizes devices and techniques to convey, not a replica of life, but an image of it as apprehended by the artist's consciousness. "Fantastic realism" implied that the actor's participation in the creative process was equal to that of the director, for the actor's vision (as well as the director's) was essential to the finished production, whereas in Meyerhold's theatre it was only the director's vision that counted.[23]

Stylistically, Vakhtangov preserved Stanislavsky's fundamental techniques, but his approach was fluid, so that he could incorporate other, more contradictory styles. For example, he directed traditional plays, but he reinterpreted their meanings in terms of Soviet problems. Productions were sprinkled with the actors' ironic asides and sarcastic by-plays juxtaposed with the regular text of the play. In *Turandot*, an actor delivered an emotional speech and shed real tears and, as a comment on realism, another actor came forward from the wings to catch the tears in a bowl. In another instance, an actor ate an orange sitting stage front, while the regular action of the play continued upstage. Actors talked intermittently and unperturbedly to the audience and then resumed their roles. Often the ironic undercutting served as a dialectic between the text of the play and the sensibility of Soviet audiences (a technique later used by many avant-gardists); it also served to convey the actors' and director's attitude to the "message" of the play without destroying the cohesiveness of the production.

Vakhtangov's untimely death prevented further experimentation, but his aims and accomplishments are particularly relevant today. Looking for a style that would transcend, though not abolish, naturalism, that would still be communicable to his audiences, Vakhtangov struggled all his life for artistic eclecticism. He worked with the Cubist painter I. Nivinsky to design *Turandot* so that the sets (as well as the actors) expressed the irony of his productions. He advocated exaggerated makeup, yet insisted that the actors penetrate the inner realistic core of the character; he experimented doggedly to find the right prop, gesture, and stance that would be indicative of his concept of the fantastic and the real. In short, his work gave plausibility to mixed styles, and his importance lies in his extraordinary ability to extract and focus on abstract essences and combine them with realistic details. Perhaps his updating the playwright's text, while remaining faithful to its inner content, and his belief in the actor's ability to convey his personal feelings and those of the character's simultaneously, are his most recognizable contributions to our contemporary scene—aspects that were to stir the greatest controversy when practitioners in the non-literary theatre movement of the 1960's followed in Vakhtangov's footsteps.

Stanislavsky, Meyerhold, Vakhtangov, and Tairov were all theatrical revolutionaries in an atmosphere which, during the early period of the Russian Revolution, was alive with the old and the new. But a decade after the Bolshevik victory, revolutionaries appeared reactionary; radical theories like those of Stanislavsky were soon co-opted by the authorities, and Stanislavsky's theatre became official. Stanislavsky himself had encouraged experimentalists, but considering the Commissars' war against the avant-garde, it is understandable that the Moscow Art Theatre became static, a bastion against artistic experimentation. In fact, as socialist realism became more deeply entrenched and polemics against "formalism" more vitriolic, virtually no theatre other than the naturalistic was tolerated. By the end of the thirties and the forties, the experimental theatres of the Soviet Union were nonexistent; records of the experimentalists' work were very difficult to obtain and, with the exception of Vakhtangov, the name of Stanislavsky and the Moscow Art Theatre alone had become the paradigm of naturalism and bore the stamp of official approval. Only with the end of Stalinism and the beginning of the "thaw" did contributions of other theatre directors surface. Meyerhold's name and reputation were vindicated, and access to his and Tairov's notebooks became available. Naturalism, disguised as socialist realism, had been enforced by the Stalinist government while the avant-garde theories of the "formalists" (read experimentalists) were deliberately obliterated. Despite the short-lived "thaw," the death of Stalin changed little in the arts. The use of unconventional or eclectic forms, for which Russian artists were ostracized and even murdered, was never totally eradicated. Ironically, the revolution that brought the Soviets to power eventually sounded the deathknell of revolution in the arts in socialist Russia, while in capitalist France a new kind of art, born out of French decadence and French romantic leftism, had already emerged and was to influence all of Western culture.

three

The Surrealists

If one studies the events of the fifty years that preceded the ushering in of the twentieth century, particularly as they affected France, it would be all too easy to assume that dissent, dissatisfaction, and despair deeply pervaded all of French life, that political commitment to new "isms" (syndicalism, anarchism, socialism, Marxism) was the rule of the day, that a desire to find new modes of artistic expression prevailed, and that the entire country was aflame with the torch of revolution. In actuality, the period was one in which capitalism continued to assert its strength. Competition for money and markets, the rigid stratification of class structures, and the merciless exploitation of the lower classes remained unabated. In France, where twice in one century workers had mounted the barricades only to be summarily defeated, a return to "normalcy" had been advocated by the population at large, and by 1900 the atmosphere was apathetic and depressive. The bourgeoisie was far from unhappy with things as they were, the civil service or *fonctionnaires* had neatly absorbed the political shock-waves and kept the country functioning without any major changes in the rhythm of bureaucratic routine, and the peasants retained their traditional hostility toward change. Though the world was slouching toward war, it was not to be a conflagration of ideologies, but of nations and alliances intent on gaining the lion's share of profits to be made from plundering the wealth of Africa and Asia. When World War I came, the enthusiasm with which it was greeted on both sides—even among the "advanced" leftist German working class—indicated how easily discontent can be submerged by patriotism.

At the opening of the century, artists and poets in Paris—many of them bitter, cynical, nihilistic—felt displaced by the placidity and complacency of established values and taste. They formed their own "counterculture," disdained money (which was hard to come by, anyhow), and ridiculed the bourgeoisie and upper classes. Choosing not to identify with the official salons, the Parisian bohemians organized their own way of life. As French artists and writers had done in earlier periods, they took to the cafés and cabarets, where they could mingle with one another and find a certain amount of freedom to express their alternative life style.

In Lapin Agile, La Closerie des Lilas, and Deux Magots, one could hear intelligent and witty conversations. The artists' heated arguments on politics and art, along with their general lively spirits, made cafés a vital part of Parisian intellectual life. There one could easily meet new people, hear about new movements, and discuss new forms. There one could find the young Picasso, Braque, Matisse, and Guillaume Apollinaire. It was Apollinaire who introduced the word "surrealism," first in the production in 1917 of Jean Cocteau's *Parade*, and again a month later, when his own play, *The Breasts of Tiresias* (actually written in 1903) was produced with the subtitle: *drame surréaliste*. But before the word "surrealism" caught on and became an artistic movement, another new and strange word was on everyone's tongue, a word which was shortly to lead to the emergence of surrealism, but of which Apollinaire had only a vague notion. The word was Dada.

In April 1916, a year before Apollinaire's surrealistic drama appeared in France, three friends—a German poet, a German painter, and a Hungarian poet—sat in a café in Zurich casually discussing the nature of art. Disgusted with the cultural ambiance, they decided to form their own movement. Looking for a suitable name, they rushed to the encyclopedia and adopted the first word they saw: dada—"hobbyhorse" in French; "yes, yes" in Russian. That year the same three gave a performance in Zurich to demonstrate dada. The following happened: "On the stage, keys and boxes were pounded to provide the music, until the infuriated public protested. . . . A voice, under a huge hat in the shape of a sugar-loaf, recited poems by Arp. Huelsenbeck screamed his poems louder and louder, while Tzara beat out the same rhythm *crescendo* on a big drum. Huelsenbeck and Tzara danced around grunting like bear cubs, or in sacks with top hats waddled around in an exercise called *noir cacadou.*"[1]

To Tristan Tzara, Hans Arp, and Richard Huelsenbeck, the three who had participated in that historic meeting in Zurich, and had later performed their happening, dada meant anti-art, anti-reason, anti-thought. Nihilistic from the very beginning, the Dadaists classified all literature as nothing, denigrated all masters of the past, and abandoned all values of the present. In his famous manifesto of 1918, Tzara said:

> Every product of disgust capable of becoming a negation of the family is Dada; a protest with the fists of its whole being engaged in destructive action: Dada; knowledge of all the means rejected up until now by the shamefaced sex of comfortable compromise and good manners: Dada; abolition of logic, which is the dance of those impotent to create: Dada; of every social hierarchy and equation set up for the sake of values by our valets: Dada; every object, all objects, sentiments, obscurities, apparitions and the precise clash of parallel lines are weapons for the fight: Dada; abolition of memory: Dada; abolition of archaeology: Dada; abolition of prophets: Dada; abolition of the future: Dada; absolute and unquestionable faith in every god that is the immediate product of spontaneity.[2]

In the meantime, the young André Breton came home from war, and, with Louis Aragon and Philippe Soupault, started a review called *Littérature*. Shortly after, Apollinaire showed Breton the Dadaist bulletin. Breton, stimulated by its inflammatory language, suggested that Tzara be on the editorial board of *Littérature*. From this union, the Dadaist group grew into a full-fledged movement. They issued manifestos, exhibited art—and participated in performances in which they themselves became the leading actors-provocateurs. Describing what happened at an exhibition of Max Ernst collages, d'Esparbès, then a leading journalist and an enemy of the Dadaists, wrote:

> With characteristic bad taste, the Dadas have now resorted to terrorism. The stage was in the cellar, and all the lights in the shop were out; groans rose from a trap-door. Another joker hidden behind a wardrobe insulted the persons present . . . the Dadas, without ties and wearing white gloves, passed back and forth . . . André Breton chewed up matches, Ribemont-Dessaignes kept screaming: "It's raining on a skull," Aragon caterwauled, Philippe Soupault played hide-and-seek with Tzara, while Benjamin Péret and Charchoune shook hands every other minute. On the doorstep, Jacques Rigaut counted aloud the automobiles and the pearls of the lady visitors. . . . [3]

The Dadaists ridiculed every event, attacked every bourgeois convention, and created a scandal whenever possible. For the Dadaists, nothing was sacrosanct; they protested every formal occasion that pretended to have meaning. At an invitational salon one day, Tzara spoofed the idea of a poetry reading. ". . . [He] read a newspaper article, accompanied by an inferno of bells and rattles. The audience could stand no more and began whistling and booing."[4] Picabia's paintings were then exhibited; one had the initials LHOOQ, which meant "she has hot pants."[5] At another meeting, where Dadaists read manifestoes, the audience was pelted with coins, later with rotten eggs. The madness reached its climax when Marcel Duchamps painted Mona Lisa with a mustache, Schwitters collected garbage to use for paint and sculpture, and Hans Richter painted at night so that he could not distinguish colors. On one occasion, when Man Ray consented to have an exhibition of his paintings under the auspices of the Dadaists, "the room was full of toy balloons, which completely hid the paintings. At a given signal, the organizers, with yells of 'Hurrah,' burst the balloons with their cigarettes."[6] Another time, Tzara organized an exhibition in which he asked painters to show their poems and poets to show their paintings. Inscriptions all over the wall of the exhibition room read: "This summer elephants will be wearing moustaches; what about you?"[7] At a premiere of Cocteau's play *Les Mariés de la Tour Eiffel* (1921), the Dadaists burst into the theatre and shouted "Viva dada." At a lecture given by the Futurist Marinetti, they created a similar scene. Breaking up their opponents' meetings and gatherings, invading theatres and exhibitions, and fighting in cafés, salons, and theatres were plainly *de rigueur.*

The Dadaists grew out of the "madness of the age," writes Hans Arp. The artists were demanding fundamental change, and their tactics sprang from "range and grief at the suffering and humiliation of mankind."[8] Though the dada movement has since been downgraded, even devaluated, it played an important role in introducing nonsense literature, in exposing and attacking pretentious rhetoric, in abolishing the literal word, and in developing grotesque symbolism. In fact, Dadaists were the first to use "contrapuntal recitative [a collage poetry], in which three or more voices speak, sing, or whistle simultaneously in such a way that the resulting combinations account for the total effect of the work, elegiac, funny, or bizarre,"[9] certainly an important contribution to later theatre experimentalists.

By 1922, the Dadaist movement began to pale. Breton, who became dissatisfied with the Dadaists' continual attempts to shock the bourgeoisie, decided to break with Tzara, but not before he was beaten up publicly while demonstrating at a performance of Tzara's *Coeur à gaz* (July 1923). At the same event ". . . Pierre de Massot escaped with a broken arm, and Eluard, after having fallen into the scenery, received a bailiff's note demanding 8,000 francs damages."[10] After that, Breton issued his famous *Lâchez tout!*

("Let Go of Everything"), in which he implored artists to abjure dadaism. In 1923, he founded a new group, naming it "surrealism" in honor of Apollinaire, who had died in 1918.

Breton was a former medical student who had forsaken medicine for the arts. In 1921, having corresponded with Freud, he met the master in Vienna; upon returning to Paris, he became disgusted with the dada movement, which had developed no clear revolutionary program, he believed, but capitalized on notoriety for its own sake. Although the Dadaists staged imaginative confrontations, Breton felt that dadaism posed no serious threat to the status quo. Inspired by his contact with Freud, Breton believed that Freud's theory of dreams and the unconscious, if applied to the arts, could be more creative, more productive, and more revolutionary than dadaism. Freud's theories were having their effects; André Gide had already declared that the liberation of the Self was the mark of a true artist, and, in their psychological novels, Henry James and D. H. Lawrence in very different ways, were depicting man's unconscious relationships. What the poets and novelists of the second half of the nineteenth century had intuitively longed for—a means of apprehending the total Self through a new language—was ironically afforded them by science: Freud gave fresh impetus to the concepts and techniques of portraying the Self in art.

Sensitive to the needs of the time, Breton seized the right moment: in 1924 he issued his first *Le Manifeste du surréalisme*, formulating principles that were to radicalize intellectual and artistic thought for decades, and over which Breton was to reign supreme for more than thirty years:

> SURREALISM: noun, masc., Pure psychic automatism by which it is intended to express, either verbally or in writing, the true function of thought. Thought dictated in the absence of all control exerted by reason and outside all aesthetic or moral preoccupations.
>
> ENCYCL. *Philos.* Surrealism is based on the belief in the superior reality of certain forms of association heretofore neglected, in the

> omnipotence of the dream, and in the disinterested play of thought. It leads to the permanent destruction of all other psychic mechanisms and to its substitution for them in the solution of the principal problems of life.[11]

Breton's break with the Dadaists and his organizing the Surrealists (Eluard, Aragon, Masson, Artaud, Péret, Picabia) into a "revolutionary" movement not only pushed to an extreme the literature of the Self, but broadened the possibilities of attaining Rimbaud's "visionary transcendence." The early Romantics had used descriptive and often rhetorical, rather than concrete, language; Rimbaud and Mallarmé were primarily intuitive, but André Breton and the Surrealists sought to express the unconscious through a totally conscious technique. This goal, a synthesis of the basic tenets of nineteenth-century romanticism and twentieth-century scientific naturalism, became a social and literary aesthetic, applicable to painting and sculpture, poetry and prose, and eventually theatre and cinema. Further, surrealism was to become a way of life: it was to find its own means of changing feeling and transforming or rejecting the world.

Specifically Breton—like his predecessors Baudelaire, Mallarmé, and Rimbaud—envisioned a literature of dreams and nightmare, of trance and sleep, and he worked out a technique to apprehend personal and fragmented associations. He called this technique "automatism": "the dictation of thought without control of the mind." He saw automatism as a device, not only to evoke, but to transform the artist's unconscious imagination. He advised poets to write quickly and instinctively,to rely on chance in order to get the best flow, and then systematically to record their reactions:

> . . . Have someone bring you writing materials after getting settled in a place as favorable as possible to your mind's concentration on itself. Put yourself in the most passive, or receptive, state you can. Forget about your genius, your talents, and those of everyone else. Tell yourself that literature is the saddest path that leads to everything. Write quickly, without a preconceived subject, fast enough not to remember and not to be tempted to

read over what you have written. The first sentence will come all by itself. . . .[12]

"Automatism" prompted writers to conduct experiments with trance, hypnosis, and hallucination, hoping thereby to unlock repressed images. Louis Aragon writes that during this period he had "experienced the full strength of these images. We had lost the power to manipulate them [the images]. We had become their domain, their subjects. In bed, just before falling asleep, in the street, with eyes wide open with all the machinery of terror, we held out our hands to phantoms. . . . We saw, for example, a written image which first presented itself with the characteristic of the fortuitous, the arbitrary, reach our senses, lose its verbal aspect to assume those fixed phenomenological realities which we had always believed impossible to provoke."[13]

Similar experiments took place in painting. As if in a trance, André Masson drew his sketches and "used what were known as support words: while he worked he would say aloud words like 'attraction,' 'transmutation,' 'fall,' 'whirling.' At other times he sang. If one of his canvases failed to satisfy him, he flung himself at it and slashed savagely with a knife. 'One must get some physical idea of revolution,' he told his friends. His disorder and anarchy became legendary. . . . When he was painting *Horses Devouring the Birds*, he announced wildly: 'I will make the birds bleed.'"[14]

Miró showed the same kind of violence. He wanted "to express precisely all the golden sparks of our soul.' . . . He played a wild, distracted game with signs which he scattered on monochrome backgrounds of grey, blue or white. A dotted line and a blob were enough for him to create astonishing effects. . . . He painted on black paper, on glass paper, on card, on wood, on sacking, on copper, on masonite. He used egg tempera, pastel colour, either powdered or mixed with indian ink; he made poem-pictures, picture-objects, drawing-collages and wooden constructions."[15] Max Ernst arranged dissociated collages of leaves, titles, threads from a spool, or pieces of wood. He left to "chance" form and composition.

Convinced that automatism was a solution to unleashing their creative powers, artists constantly proselytized and practiced. Robert Desnos fell asleep in cafés and reproduced trances at will,[16] while Breton, Eluard, and Picabia played games and conducted word associations in public. Breton believed that automatism could apprehend and penetrate "the absolute reality of man's surreality"—that area where the dream and the objective world commingle, where beauty and horror, sex and sadism, exaltation and depression exist side by side despite their conflicting force. Further, he maintained that if one surrendered oneself to dreams and self-invoked trances, one could control and unite those contradictions. ". . . there exists a certain point in the mind," Breton wrote in his second manifesto in 1929, "at which life and death, real and imaginary, past and future, communicable and incommunicable, high and low, cease to be perceived in terms of contradictions."[17]

> ". . . When the time comes when . . . we succeed in realizing the dream in its entirety . . . when the dream's curve is developed with an unequaled breadth and regularity, then we can hope that mysteries which are not really mysteries will give way to the great Mystery. I believe in the future resolution of those two states—outwardly so contradictory—which are dream and reality, into a sort of absolute reality, a *surreality*, so to speak."[18]

Breton's desire for expanded consciousness was a desire to transcend the mysteries and attain the "Marvelous," but the Marvelous did not preclude preaching Revolution of a certain kind. In a Declaration of January 27, 1925, Surrealists maintained that their movement was a "means of total liberation of the mind and of all that resembles it . . . We are determined to make a Revolution. . . . We have joined the word *surrealism* to the word *revolution* solely to show the disinterested, detached and even entirely desperate character of this revolution. . . . We hurl this formal warning to Society: Beware of your deviations and *faux-pas*, we shall not miss a single one. . . . We are specialists in Revolt. There is no means of action which we are not capable, when necessary, of employing."[19] Whenever the occasion presented itself, they attacked the bourgeoisie and condemned it to oblivion.

Aragon wrote: "We shall triumph over everything. And first of all we'll destroy this civilization that is so dear to you, in which you are caught like fossils in shale. Western world, you are condemned to death. We are Europe's defeatists. . . . Let the Orient, your terror, answer our voice at last! We shall waken everywhere the seeds of confusion and discomfort. We are the mind's agitators. . . . Let distant America's white buildings crumble among her ridiculous prohibitions."[20] And Paul Eluard wrote: "There is no total revolution, there is only perpetual *Revolution,* real life, like love, dazzling at every moment. There is no revolutionary order, there is only disorder and madness. 'The war for freedom must be waged with anger' and waged without ceasing by all those who do not accept. . . ."[21]

In politics, the Surrealists followed the Dadaists' style: they disrupted meetings, screamed down opponents, used profane language, and confronted their adversaries with shocking and violent behavior. Primarily, artists had joined the Surrealists to find a revolutionary aesthetic (perhaps secondarily, to make the revolution) and create a new life style corresponding to that aesthetic. This, the art-in-life movement—the artist's self-dramatization in life, as well as in art—captured their needs. Artists had often regarded themselves as personas or heroes in their own works; but role-playing, already evident in Rousseau and Byron, and developed by Jarry and the Dadaists, became an integral part of surrealist principles. Despite their obvious comic acting, Surrealist artists were ruled by a sense of tragedy and dominated by feelings of despair. Perceiving the world as an empty wasteland, they expressed their consternation through defiance, through manifestoes and fist fights, and through a steadfast contempt and excoriating savage sense of humor. According to Patrick Waldberg:

> Philippe Soupault, looking somewhat haggard, would ring doorbells and ask the concierges "if Philippe Soupault did not live

> there." Benjamin Péret would insult priests on the street. Paul Eluard, without warning, sailed for the Orient, where he was soon joined by Max Ernst. Robert Desnos went into trances at Breton's house. Georges Limbour, famished and simulating Desnos's trance, would get down on all fours, bark, and eat the dog's food. Louis Aragon sang softly: "No, I won't go home." Jacques Prévert, at night dressed as a hooligan, would lead astray the innocent passer-by in the bourgeois quarters. Tanguy captured spiders, which he ate alive to terrify the neighborhood. Dali, whose moustache was still young, gave lectures at the Sorbonne with his bare right foot soaking in a pan of milk. From time to time they would strike a critic.[22]

Here is a report of Surrealist antics written in the *Journal Littéraire* on June 13, 1925. The occasion was a performance of a play by Aragon preceded by a lecture by "a certain M. Aron on 'the average Frenchman.'" A critic who had been in the audience wrote:

> . . . I had heard no more than twenty words . . . when a tall joker sitting behind me began talking louder than the lecturer. The latter waited patiently for him to be finished, in order to continue his remarks, but eight seats to my right, another gentlemen began speaking. Replies flew through the air. And suddenly from various parts of the hall echoed a word that was quite familiar but worthier of the Napoleonic armies than of a respectable assemblage. Unfortunately this word was emphasized until it became the only thing one could hear. [M. Aron tried to regain the floor.] Interrupters appeared in every corner. One voice proclaimed: "We will not let you speak. Signed: the surrealists." Then things grew nastier . . . the police intervened . . . Philippe Soupault leaped onto the stage and stood there, arms folded, defying anyone to remove him save at bayonet-point . . . Robert Desnos violently harangued the crowd, striding up and down the stage. . . . Meanwhile the gentle poet Eluard had been punched; Vitrac dashed forward to defend him . . . the whole house was standing, and threats and insults flew through the air.[23]

A scandal that typified the era took place at a banquet when, during the feast, the poet Rachilde, whom the Surrealists considered reactionary, said she thought "no Frenchwoman could ever marry a German." Breton took the remark as an offense to his friend Max Ernst, one of the guests. Pandemonium broke out: amidst shouts of "Long Live Germany," flying fruit, and crashing china, Philippe Soupault was seen swinging from the chandeliers. Rachilde claimed that she had been kicked in the stomach. Hoots of "Down with France" mixed with other curses. When the police arrived on the scene, the mob resumed the battle in the streets. The next day, the press suggested that the Surrealists be quarantined.[24]

Surrealism had reached its peak as the world-wide economic depression struck, and in the early thirties factions began to develop and split the movement. Some artists (including Antonin Artaud) questioned the validity of the rising Communist orientation then introduced by Breton and Aragon. But in 1935, when Aragon alone joined the Communist Party and Breton remained unaffiliated, the split became absolute; reconciliation between the idealist philosophy of surrealism and the materialist philosophy of communism seemed hopeless. Consequently, Aragon broke entirely with the Surrealists and Breton broke entirely with the Communists. In 1928, when Breton met Trotsky and Diego Rivera in Mexico, together they issued another manifesto that placed Breton and the Surrealist movement outside the orbit of the Party. Anticipating Communist control of artists, Breton reiterated that neither he nor the movement would ever defer their art to what they considered an incompatible discipline.

By World War II, artists once again needed to define themselves. Clearly the Surrealists had neither transformed the system, nor human consciousness; the advent of Fascism in Italy and Spain, and of Nazism in Germany, proved that the revolution was a failure and that mankind was capable of unleashing a hatred and barbarity heretofore unmatched. From 1940 to 1945, many Surrealists fled the Nazi invaders and became artists in exile. But the end of the war found them secure and established (they had a large exhibition in New York in 1942 and in Paris in 1947). Nonetheless, the movement had lost its verve, though not its mark. Surrealism had advanced a personal and subjective aesthetic rather than one based on naturalistic verisimilitude. Surrealism found no topic sacred, no institution holy; no event sacrilegious; it apprehended the fantasies of childhood as well as the dreams of perverts; it supported blatant eroticism as well as delicate and fragile sensibilities; it thrived on intoxication, hallucination, and on a super-reality that united dreams with politics, sex with innocence, art with life. Surrealism explored new forms to express a new aesthetic consciousness—a consciousness that juxtaposed montage and collage, that perceived divergent elements simultaneously, and that demanded artists abandon rationalism. Finally Surrealism encouraged the extremes of anti-rationalism and the cult of the Self so that an artist considered his life style as important as his finished work, and his finished work as the extension of his quintessential Self. And this cult of the anti-rational and the Self—begun by the Romantics, advanced by the Symbolists, and developed by the Surrealists—would find new theatrical expression at the beginning of the 1960's.

four

Artaud's Plague

Although surrealism had left its indelible impression on Western art, Western artists in the aftermath of World War II were in no mood to *épater le bourgeois*. Worn out and drained, and reeling from the bitter experiences of the war, artists were suffering from psychic shock. The millions dead in gas ovens, concentration camps, and on battlefields, the terrors of the bombings, and the physical torture endured under the Nazi invaders were grim memories stamped on the consciousness of the artists. Once again they turned to self-reflection. "*Qui suis-je?,*" the question that haunted every generation from Rousseau to Rimbaud, still haunted writers and intellectuals who had lived through the holocaust: Sartre, Camus, Beckett. Only Bertolt Brecht in East Germany appeared optimistic; hoping to find answers through the class struggle, he went immediately to work to build a Marxist-oriented theatre in an ambiance that would be conducive to his needs. For others in the West, the task was not as simple. In France, where artists returning from the war had to live in a society that had betrayed its own people, it was *déjà vu*. There the mood was somber, sad, and quiet. Camus wrote: "A world that can be explained even with bad reasons is a familiar world. But, on the other hand, in a universe suddenly divested of illusions and lights, man feels an alien, a stranger. His exile is without remedy since he is deprived of the memory of a lost home or the hope of a promised land. This divorce between man and his life, the actor and his setting, is properly the feeling of absurdity."[1]

Shortly "the feeling of absurdity" became a powerful expression that described the emptiness of man's existence, his estrangement from society, and the futility of seeking rational answers to life. Along with the term existentialism, absurdity became a catch-all, not only for a state of mind, but for a philosophic movement and a concomitant school of literature: Absurdist playwrights sprang up all over the Western world. The style and content of Absurdist literature—influenced by the Dadaists and the Surrealists—dominated the literature and the drama of the fifties and opened the door to the non-verbal theatre of the sixties.

Ionesco's work was scathing: his comedies were composed of no-sense language; people in his plays turned into rhinoceroses before one's eyes, or were condemned for life to be strapped into a pair of chairs. Beckett's plays recalled the stark, bleak canvas of Dali's *The Persistence of Memory* (1931), as well as the lonely, empty, and poetic ones of Yves Tanguy (*Four Hours of Summer; Hope*). Beckett's characters, existing only in their own memories, were tortured by a futile present and an excruciating past. Waiting for events that never occur, they lived out their lives on roads, in wheelchairs, and in ashcans as a comment on the human condition. Both Ionesco and Beckett utilized metaphor and symbol, disconnected thoughts, pauses and monosyllables to express their sense of the existential void. They derided language—even devalued it—sometimes unrecognizably, and they invented archetypal characters unidentifiable on a naturalistic level but identifiable by their pain and human foibles. Theirs was a writing that went beyond the questioning of philosophical existence. Theirs was a writing that silenced all questioning—one that foreshadowed the next phase in the development of the avant-garde: the abandonment of language entirely.

The Absurdists reigned through the 1950's and the early 1960's, creating discussion and controversy. They produced an important body of literature and became known all over the Western world, but suddenly their popularity waned, and some of them even stopped writing entirely. In America in the early sixties, "new" playwrights, under the leadership of the indomitable Ellen Stewart (known as La Mama), had begun to surface. But no new body of theatrical technique had emerged: naturalism dominated the American theatre; the domestic drama, and the smart little comedy were still the bill of fare.[2]

Into this atmosphere came a sharp sting to the senses which temporarily resuscitated the theatre. In December of 1965, Peter Brook arrived in New York with his production of Peter Weiss's *The Persecution and Assassination of Marat as Performed by the Inmates of the Asylum of Charenton under the Direction of the Marquis de Sade*, and gave the New York theatre establishment a lesson in innovation. Soon *Marat/Sade* was on everyone's tongue; it became daily fodder for TV consumption, and a feast for the tastemakers. The words "Theatre of Cruelty" appeared in cultural pages of magazines and newspapers. The nude behind of Ian Richardson, who played Marat, clearly exposed and brightly lit on stage, made spicy cocktail conversation. Weiss's and Brook's techniques were discussed nonstop; some intellectuals theorized that Brook was a sensationalist who, with startling theatricalities, had ruined Weiss's text; others maintained that Weiss's play was a thesis-ridden bore that would not have had a chance without Brook's innovations.[3]

Marat/Sade had a long and successful run, and Brook returned to London for more experiments, Weiss to Sweden to write more plays, and Broadway went back to sleep. But what accounted for the phenomenon of *Marat/Sade* was not only Weiss's and Brook's creativity, but an event in 1896 in Marseilles: the birth of Antonin Artaud.

Antonin Artaud was born into the culture that had inherited the ideas of Baudelaire, Rimbaud, and Mallarmé. At an early age, he resisted the shackles of conventional bourgeois life by refusing to go into his family's business, throwing himself into the intellectual life of Paris. In school he devoured his favorites: Baudelaire and Poe. At the same time he began to write poetry and to draw—two activities he was to engage in for the rest of his life. By the time he was eighteen, he was already plagued by headaches and fits of depression, and his parents were advised to send him away for a "rest cure." Although he quickly recovered from this early breakdown, he was later to suffer continuously from head pains, and was eventually diagnosed as schizophrenic. But in 1920, he was fit and energetic, and his parents did not prevent him from seeking his fortune in Paris. There he continued to write poetry, and found it therapeutic. But soon writing had become an insufficient outlet for his drives, and he sought greater and more spectacular experiences. And so he chose, as his real métier, the theatre.[4]

The Parisian theatre was in a state of flux. Boulevard theatre still catered to the low tastes of the bourgeoisie and the classical theatre still produced classics in the traditional manner. Newcomers like Louis Jouvet, who introduced such playwrights as Giraudoux and Charles Dullin, organizer of Le Théâtre de l'Atelier, were considered innovators. Dullin attracted Artaud, who became a member of Dullin's Atelier.[5] There Artaud came into contact with art, rather than entertainment, and grew to worship Dullin's pristine dignity and craftsmanship and to loathe the shallow superficiality of the boulevard theatre. But Dullin could not hold Artaud for long, for Dullin's theatre was based on realism, while Artaud sought transcendence. Besides, Artaud was not considered a good actor. After a year at the Atelier, during which time he had neglected his poetry, Artaud began to write again. He submitted a group of poems to the editor of the *Nouvelle Revue Française*, Jacques Rivière, who did not immediately accept them; but the contact led to a remarkable friendship and to a more remarkable correspondence. In the exchange with Rivière, Artaud tried to describe his reactions and sensations in the process of writing a word or the course of his thought *before* he came to a particular word. He discussed how he found the exact word for the exact sensation, and how he could relate it to a concrete or plastic image. Artaud saw this method as an avenue for a new kind of "poetry in space," proliferated images mounted on stage in clusters, some complementing and some juxtaposed against the other. In the meantime, Artaud watched and described his emotional reactions. He observed that he did not receive an idea rationally, but as a visual image transmitted to him via the senses. Hence, to re-create this inner life was to re-create visually.[6]

Artaud did nothing to synthesize his new ideas. Instead, he joined the Surrealist movement, and in 1925 published several articles in the journal *La Révolution Surréaliste.* After a few years of acting in Surrealist films and writing for the movement's journals (and a few falling-outs with André Breton and Louis Aragon), Artaud left the movement and started his own theatre, the Alfred Jarry Theatre, in honor of the man he acknowledged as his true antecedent. The company opened in 1927 with Artaud's one-act play, *Burned Stokach or the Mad Mother*, and several other one-act plays. He produced there for one year and was denounced by the critics—as was to be expected. Not completely discouraged, he presented in 1928 Strindberg's *A Dream Play*, sponsored by members and friends of the Swedish colony in Paris. That, too, proved a disaster. The Surrealists, angered by what they considered Artaud's "sell-out" because he had accepted a subsidy from the bourgeois Swedes, managed to renumber the front rows of seats in the house and to grab the best ones for themselves, thereby creating a confrontation between the players and the audience. With the failure of the Jarry Theatre, Artaud's depression increased, until in 1931 the Balinese Theatre Company opened in Paris.

The Balinese Theatre epitomized for Artaud the differences between Western and Oriental cultures. One was realistic, the other mystical; one relied on dialogue and words; the other on gestures and signs. The Balinese used the stage for ritual and transcendence; the Westerners, for ethics and morality. The Balinese actors, a meticulously trained group which worshipped theatre as religion, appeared on stage as if in a hallucination: characters had no relationship to plot; instead, they represented metaphysical states. Action consisted of fragments and pieces presented simultaneously but enjoyed as an entity; no rational continuity was expected and the fragments produced multi-actions that were both self-contained and conclusive. The Balinese Theatre's goal—to transcend reality, to contact the inner self, to strip off the masks so as to reach the subconscious—was for the performers the only reality on the stage. In contrast to the Western theatre, which generally maintains its "realist" illusion, the Oriental theatre deliberately abandons illusion. Actors use platforms, not standard sets; sound or rhythms, not speech; and the audience, rather than being carried away by the "truth," knows the actors are acting; it accepts this beforehand.

The Balinese company that Artaud saw eliminated verbal language, replacing it by sounds and gestures which, together with various physical configurations and ritualized signs, formed a hieroglyphic picture. The *mise-en-scène* was the focus of the production, rather than the development of character or the unraveling of a plot. Since the language of the company was based upon a learned system of gestures known only to trained and sophisticated theatre-goers, others were meant to understand the language intuitively. But this, according to Artaud, proved no hardship for the uninitiated, because the gestures were based on various states of being which could be easily felt. A movement of the eyes, a turn of the head or the shoulder, the raising of a leg or a hand, the pointing of a finger in a certain direction—conveyed, according to Artaud, a greater psychological or emotional force than words. Though some of the gestures were purely muscular, others were accompanied by sounds—cries, incantations, rhythmic intonations—and sometimes by musical instruments. The stage appeared to be a labyrinth in which the movements of the actors were perfectly synthesized: no transition was necessary, gestures and sounds, executed simultaneously and effortlessly, flowed into one another . For Artaud, the actors were "animated hieroglyphs," enough to make him "forget the habit of speech."[7]

The appearance of the Balinese Theatre confirmed Artaud's basic convictions: that the theatre must be magical and the director, the shaman. The actor must discover his real Self, and be aware that he has a double—himself reflected through a mirror. Conscious that he is of two shadings, the actor must enter the metaphysical realm to discover his authentic Self, his real psychic force. He must be able to renew this search continually, to understand its origins, and to re-create its form, because it is this process that breathes life into a role. While unleashing his inhibitions and repressions that restrict the real Self, the actor exorcises the audience's collective unconscious, thus producing an interaction that transforms the audience as well as the actor.

"The theatre, like the plague," Artaud wrote, "is a delirium and is communicative . . . not only because it affects important collectivities and upsets them in an identical way. In the theatre as in the plague there is something both victorious and vengeful. . . . The plague takes images that are dormant, a latent disorder, and suddenly extends them into the most *extreme gestures* [emphasis added]; the theatre also takes gestures and pushes them as far as they will go; like the plague it reforges the chain between what is and what is not, between the virtuality of the possible and what already exists in materialized nature."[8]

Accordingly, he compared the actors and the audience to victims of a great fire, "signaling through the flames," shrieking out in delirium, confronting their hallucinations, acting out their pain, screaming out their frenzy, wandering through space among corpses and lunatics. The plague signifies man's disharmonious split between the physical and spiritual forces, and is a vivid metaphor for the theatre "not because it is contagious, but because like the plague it is the revelation, the bringing forth, the exteriorization of a depth of latent cruelty by means of which all the perverse possibilities of the mind, whether of an individual or a people, are localized."

". . . The action of theatre, like that of plague, is [also] beneficial, for, impelling men to see themselves as they are, it causes the mask to fall, reveals the lie, the slackness, baseness, and hypocrisy of our world; it shakes off the asphyxiating inertia of matter which invades even the clearest testimony of the senses; . . . it invites them to take . . . a superior and heroic attitude they would never have assumed without it."[9]

The odd analogy of the plague set the tone for Artaud's Theatre of Cruelty; it presumed that man was beset by a grotesque illness from which neither the audience nor the actors were exempted, and that the audience came to the theatre to undergo a violent therapy in hopes of being transformed. The actors, whose job it was to serve as a "force of the epidemic which attacks the feelings and bodies of the population, would carry the contagious epidemic all through the theatre," thereby releasing the violent disorder and latent cruelty of man. Once the overwhelming disease was exposed and exorcised and the hated Self released, the audience, spiritually cleansed, presumably would find its real Self.

In 1936, Artaud issued his first manifesto. He called for a Theatre of Cruelty "to create a metaphysics of speech, gesture, and expression . . ."[10] "to elicit the guilt of the audience, to make them feel as cruel as what they see portrayed on the stage . . . to make the audience leave the theatre in a state of . . . irritation and hostility . . . shaken and irritated by the internal dynamism of the spectacle, and this dynamism will bear a direct relation to the anguish and preoccupations of his whole life."[11] He hoped to "treat the spectators like the snakecharmer's subjects and conduct them *by means of their organisms* to an apprehension of the subtlest notions . . ."[12] and to bring to the surface "those energies which ultimately create order and increase the value of life. . . ."[13]

"I am not one of those who believe that civilization has to change in order for the theatre to change; but I do believe that the theatre, utilized in the highest and most difficult sense possible, has the power to influence the aspect and formation of things. . . ."[14]

Although he believed that theatre affected behavior, Artaud

eschewed a political theatre. What he envisioned instead was a ritual theatre, of psychotherapy and spiritual transformation. "I propose to bring back into the theatre this elementary magical idea, taken up by modern psychoanalysis, which consists in effecting a patient's cure by making him assume the apparent and exterior attitudes of the desired condition."[15]

"We go to the theatre to get away from ourselves . . . to rediscover not so much the best of oneself but the purest part, the part most marked with suffering . . . we seek an emotion on the stage in which the most secret movements of the heart will be exposed . . . the audience should come face to face with his taste for crime, his erotic obsessions, his chimeras, his utopian sense of life and matter, even his cannibalism . . ."[16]

In theatrical terms, this meant unifying sound, gesture, and action into rich, imagistic, harmonious patterns. It meant utilizing gestures derived from Oriental rituals, non-verbalized sounds, or broken speech, balletic techniques, grotesque masks, shocking costumes, images evocative of Hieronymus Bosch and El Greco.[17] In short, Artaud's intent was to unleash upon the audience objects that would elicit violent reactions, leading to catharsis: "Every spectacle will contain a physical and objective element, perceptible to all. Cries, groans, apparitions, surprises, theatricalities of all kinds, . . . resplendent lighting . . . sudden changes of lights . . . masks, effigies yards high. . . ."[18]

With intentions such as these, it was logical that Artaud should want to abandon the use of literary masterpieces for the theatre—perhaps the most controversial aspect of his theories. As early as 1937, Artaud questioned the relevance of past literature as a foundation for theatrical presentations. He claimed the right to transform, transpose, rewrite, or completely abandon old masterpieces. He foresaw a theatre based on myth, not the Greek and Roman ones, but on new ones that would eventually arise from a modern consciousness. To be sure, myths, in representing our relationship to the universe, have helped us discover aspects of human psychology. They define the archetypal, the symbolic, and the primitive; they tie the human race together by revealing common deeds, dreams, and fantasies; they supply man with an ideal and an anti-ideal; they describe the human condition and the unchanging characteristics of man. For Artaud, however, ancient myths were outmoded unless they could be reinterpreted in light of contemporary experience. For him myths represented not only a clearly defined order, but a sensibility very different from his own. Western myth represented everything conservative, staid, and aristocratic; he regarded his world as romantic, fluid, and revolutionary.

Artaud hoped to choose subjects and themes that corresponded to the agitation and inner personal unrest characteristic of his own era: "The theatre must make itself the equal of life," he wrote in a letter to a friend in 1932. ". . . the true purpose of the theatre is to create Myths, to express life in its immense, universal aspect, and from that life to extract images in which we find pleasure in discovering ourselves."[19]

He proposed the following program of theatre works:

> THE PROGRAM: We shall stage, without regard for text:
> 1. An adaptation of a work from the time of Shakespeare, a work entirely consistent with our present troubled state of mind, whether one of the apocryphal plays of Shakespeare, such as *Arden of Feversham*, or an entirely different play from the same period.
> 2. A play of extreme poetic freedom by Léon-Paul Fargue.
> 3. An extract from the *Zohar*: The Story of Rabbi Simeon, which has the ever present violence and force of a conflagration.
> 4. The story of Bluebeard reconstructed according to the historical records and with a new idea of eroticism and cruelty.
> 5. The Fall of Jerusalem, according to the Bible and history; with the blood-red color that trickles from it and the people's feeling of abandon and panic visible even in the light; and on the other hand the metaphysical disputes of the prophets, the frightful intellectual agitation they create and the repercussions of which physically affect the King, the Temple, the People, and Events themselves.
> 6. A Tale by the Marquis de Sade, in which the eroticism will be transposed, allegorically mounted and figured, to create a violent exteriorization of cruelty, and a dissimulation of the remainder.

> 7. One or more romantic melodramas in which the improbability will become an active and concrete element of poetry.
> 8. Büchner's *Wozzek*, in a spirit of reaction against our principles and as an example of what can be drawn from a formal text in terms of the stage.
> 9. Works from the Elizabethan theatre stripped of their text and retaining only the accouterments of period, situations, characters, and action.[20]

Apparently avant-gardists from the Living Theatre to Jerzy Grotowski to Peter Brook had read this list: many of Artaud's suggested plays were subsequently produced by one or another of them.

Repudiating the masterpieces, Artaud repudiated the theatre of words, proposing instead a theatre of harmonized rhythms, abstract sounds, evocative silences, a language of dreams and nightmares—lean monosyllabic expressions, distorted, dissociated incantations, reverberations of all kinds. What Artaud wanted was a "grammar" of sounds based on breathing—for example, as in the system of breathing described in the Cabala—or an "alphabet of signs" like that used in primitive ritual. He wanted to extend language beyond the word. But if words were to be used, let them be used in their "'magical sense'—for their shape and for their sensuous emanations, not only for their meaning"—so that passion could become material or plastic. ". . . Let words be joined again to the physical motions that gave them birth, and let the discursive, logical aspects of speech disappear beneath its affective physical side, i.e., *let words be heard in their sonority rather than be exclusively taken for what they mean grammatically*, let them be perceived as movements, and let these movements themselves turn into other simple, direct movements as occurs in all the circumstances of life but not sufficiently with actors on the stage, and behold! . . objects themselves begin to speak [emphasis added]."[21]

Artaud claimed that playwrights, especially in France, had come to attach great importance to syntactical meaning, and were addicted to explaining and describing discursively. The word therefore had become defined simplistically, only in its grammatical context. Actors had talked about their feelings, psychologized about their states, and depended only on dialogue, while the Oriental approach, which Artaud was advocating, used silence, gesture, and sound. In the Cabala breathing system, for example, every breath one takes is derived from either a "masculine," "feminine," or "neuter" source, and finds its correlation in certain feelings. If the actor knows the source of each breath and the precise muscle it involves, he can conjure up any desired emotion. Breathing life into one's being is tantamount to finding and uniting one's Self with the Cosmos whose air one breathes.[22]

The non-verbal occupied Artaud's mind incessantly. He maintained that voices alone could create various levels of meaning, that they could be as concrete as décor and lighting, and that random sound could be effectively synchronized with movement. What particularly fascinated him were the possibilities of the fusion of sound, sight, gesture, signs, music, and lights into one inseparable amalgam that might produce a state in which the actor's and the spectator's feelings are transmitted without words. Admonished for encouraging a non-intellectual theatre through his predilection for the non-verbal, he wrote: ". . . it is not a question of whether the physical language of theatre is capable of achieving the same psychological resolutions as the language of words, whether it is able to express feelings and passions as well as words, but whether there are not attitudes in the realm of thought . . . that words are *incapable* of grasping and that gestures and everything partaking of a spatial language attain more precision than they [emphasis added]."[23] Words are not sacrosanct, he argued. The language of painting is paint, it is abstract and based on shapes; the language of film is based on visual images. Why must the language of the theatre be based on words?

As for the theatrical setting itself, Artaud, like the Russians, envisioned a breakdown of space in which the action would virtually impinge upon the audience:

> We abolish the stage and the auditorium and replace them by a single site, without partition or barrier of any kind, which will become the theatre of the action. A direct communication will be re-established between the spectator and the spectacle, between the actor and the spectator, from the fact that the spectator, placed in the middle of the action, is engulfed and physically affected by it. This envelopment results, in part, from the very configuration of the room itself.
>
> Thus, abandoning the architecture of present-day theaters, we shall take some hangar or barn, which we shall have reconstructed according to processes which have culminated in the architecture of certain churches or holy places, and of certain temples in Tibet.
>
> In the interior of this construction special proportions of height and depth will prevail. The hall will be enclosed by four walls, without any kind of ornament, and the public will be seated in the middle of the room, on the ground floor, on mobile chairs which will allow them to follow the spectacle which will take place all around them. In effect, the absence of a stage in the usual sense of the word will provide for the deployment of the action in the four corners of the room.[24]

Clearly, Artaud's later followers took him quite literally.

As early as 1932, observers raised the question of why Artaud had chosen "cruelty" as such an important ingredient in his theatre concepts. He defended his theories by associating cruelty with "an appetite for life"—birth, death, love, ambition, creativity, and power are all contingent on cruelty. Cruelty is the acknowledgment of existential realities, an embodiment of a condition of living, an acknowledgment that we are subject to "darker forces." Suffering and the struggle to overcome suffering is part of the concept of cruelty, but cruelty is not equated with sadism or superficial horror—rather, with man's perennial struggle to live. To overcome evil is "cruelty," and the pain of achievement is "cruelty": "cruelty signifies rigor, implacable intention and decision, irreversible and absolute determination. . . . Cruelty is above all lucid, a kind of rigid control and submission to necessity."[25]

Although Artaud had written many essays on his theories, his practical application of "cruelty" remained critically unsuccessful; he staged only one play, his adaptation of Shelley's *The Cenci*. Mounted under adverse conditions, without adequate funds and with too little rehearsal time, the production incurred the critics' ire. With the failure of *The Cenci*, Artaud left France in 1936 for Mexico, in search of hallucinatory experiences among the Tarahumara Indians. By this time he was a confirmed opium smoker, having become accustomed to the drug at an early age as a cure for his headaches. Justifying his drug habit in terms of a search for "cosmic consciousness," he felt he could gain access to unimaginable images, and attain a complete identity with the Self and the Cosmos. Artaud lived with the Indians for six weeks, eating peyote with them and witnessing their rites, which included the trance. By participating in their rituals, Artaud imagined that he had plunged into the mystery of mysteries—the Creation itself. He watched the Indian sun-worshipping dances, learned the symbols of the culture, and returned to Paris feeling that he had assimilated a new kind of life. But Artaud was never to apply his new knowledge to his work. He spent nine years in asylums, being treated for schizophrenia. Released through the efforts of his friends, including Anaïs Nin, he died of cancer in 1948, at the age of fifty-two.

More than any other theorist of his generation, Artaud set the tone for the radical theatre of the sixties. More than any other, he prophesied the death of naturalism and connected it with a dying bourgeois culture, and more than anyone else, he believed that naturalistic language in the theatre had ceased to have any imagistic value; it had become, in his estimation, inexact, restrictive, and dead.

Artaud's theories were a qualitative demarcation between the old and the new, but they were not entirely original. To place him in proper perspective, we need to relate many of his concepts to the work of Mallarmé and Rimbaud,and to later Symbolists, and to the Surrealists and Dadaists who, as has already been observed, created a new style and sensibility. Artaud's perception of the unconscious and the dream world, his references to the occult and to the primitive, are echos of the early English and German Romantics, as well as of Freud and Jung. His adulation of the Oriental theatre reflects the interests of others who had worked with varying audience arrangements and otherwise had abandoned the literal text—the Russian experimentalists, Meyerhold, Tairov, Vakhtangov, and the Polish neo-Romantics.

Certainly, his body of ideas was bold and brilliant; his vision, shocking and imaginative, but his greatest weakness was his inability to put his theories into practice. It was one thing to imagine stage settings, language, and effects, but Artaud needed practical artists who could execute his ideas, and this proved impossible: the rituals he worshipped had emerged from centuries of tradition; the actors he admired were trained from childhood. The kind of rigorous training methods that would have been necessary to bring Artaud's aesthetics to life would have meant a total revolution in technique. Even today the lack of organic techniques has proved a hindrance: some directors and actors have literally grafted on Artaud's theories without the slightest suggestion of truly assimilating them. The results are productions that are composed of cries, groans, and gyrations that are either meaningless or esoteric.

One of the most important issues Artaud raised was the need to redefine the function of the theatre. The question was not a new one, but few directors in the West today have visualized theatre as a means of exorcising one's demons, or of discovering one's metaphysical self: in short, using theatre as therapy. Artaud's assumption that expressing repressed hostility would result in moral catharsis understandably created controversy. History has shown that the unleashing of mass repression often has had monstrous results: Hilter's storm trooper meetings, lynching parties, mass killings, mob rioting all took place within the framework of gigantic theatrical spectacle, and the effect, rather than to curb barbarism, was to encourage it. But Artaud and some of his orthodox followers actually believed that theatre could transform people, provided that the spectacle forces them to confront their "real" selves. Might it not also reinforce their "real," "bad" selves? What guarantee is there that the "real" Self is the "good" one, and, if so, that it will be released through a catharsis? Even if the "real," "good" Self were revealed, why would a person necessarily change?

Artaud's theories reflected feelings that were already surfacing. Both his life and his thought corresponded to the mood of the younger generation of the sixties: his dreams and visions, his disgust with words, his drug addiction, his involvement with Indian ritual and Oriental philosophy, all merged smoothly with the American Romantic/revolutionary/hip ambiance. Indeed the most outstanding embodiment of Artaud was the Living Theatre of Julian Beck and Judith Malina. Combining Artaud and the Happening with the hippie life style and anarchist politics, the Living Theatre greatly influenced the movement to abolish naturalism, while in Poland Jerzy Grotowski used Artaud's theories—although he denies this—as well as the techniques of Meyerhold and Vakhtangov, together with the philosophy of Polish romanticism. In England, Peter Brook, admittedly influenced by both Brecht and Artaud, and still in love with Shakespeare (and with plays like the *Marat/Sade*), was determined to combine the best of them all: he synthesized Shakespeare, Brecht, and Artaud, and later used Artaud's theories and visions as the basis of experiments with sound and language. Richard Schechner and the Environmentalists used Artaud's theories on stage design, lighting, and the seating of the audience. In France, Beckett and the school of the Absurd can be considered descendants of Artaud insofar as they abandoned naturalism and replaced it with a non-linear anti-plot in which words are minimized and silence reigns.

In fact, by the late 1950's, in literature, words were being challenged. Ihab Hassan says in his book *The Literature of Silence* that silence has developed "as the metaphor of a new attitude that literature has chosen to adopt toward itself. This attitude puts to question the peculiar power, the ancient excellence of literary discourse—and challenges the assumptions of our civilization. . . . It is rather puzzling that this attitude has failed, on the whole, to make an impression on English and American critics. Moreover, anti-literature tends to unsettle critics with a firm humanistic bent and to repel others, Marxists or Socialists, who are committed to a certain idea of realism."[26]

Hassan was writing about novels, but his observations may very well be applied to the drama. An anti-art movement was forming in the theatre, rooted firmly in Artaudian theories. Part of this movement was the trend toward silence; part, the desire to give new meanings to sounds and words. This was to merge into the important anti-art aesthetic of the sixties. The emergence of the happening was the first step, and with it, one felt history repeating itself.

Part Two
The Present

"Art must no longer be illusory because its relation to reality has changed. . . . The revolutions and the defeated and betrayed revolutions which occurred in the wake of the war denounced a reality which had made art an illusion, and inasmuch as art has been an illusion, the new art proclaims itself as anti-art."

Cited in Herbert Marcuse
An Essay on Liberation

five

Happenings

"I was about to speak yesterday on a subject most dear to you all—art. I wanted to speak then about art, but I was unable to begin. . . ."

18 Happenings in 6 Parts

"Art is $hit. . . ."

Jean-Jacques Lebel

In October 1959 in a loft in Greenwich Village, a painter named Allan Kaprow presented an evening of entertainment to which he invited a select audience. By ordinary standards, the evening was bizarre: when the spectators arrived, they saw a series of dividing walls of different sizes covered with collages, Kaprow's paintings, and an assortment of nude photographs. Multicolored spots illuminated an arrangement of chairs (the only furniture in the loft); multicolored slides and transparencies, in which "actors" moved or danced, were projected onto walls.

The guests were handed cards with instructions: they were told to listen for a bell, stand erect, light matches, lie on the floor, change seats, move to other rooms, do the Charleston, get undressed. At intervals, and sometimes simultaneously, lights changed, people switched rooms, sounds blasted from loudspeakers. On the screen, slides of a nude girl paralleled an actual nude girl in the room, while other slides, consisting of splotches and dots, alternated with one on which there was a single word. At various times, the participants played instruments, squeezed oranges, and rhythmically moved through the three rooms. At one point someone recited: "I was about to speak yesterday on a subject most dear to you all—art. I wanted to speak then about art, but I was unable to begin. . . ."[1]

There were six official "actors" in the entertainment, including Kaprow, his artist friends, and a cast of "participants." Some painted all the time while others made specific movements, played instruments, or read aloud. Everyone was given numerous tasks, including the spectators, and all the tasks were performed simultaneously at the ring of a bell. The activities that evening were given a title: *18 Happenings in 6 Parts.*[2]

A year later at the Judson Church a similar "theatrical event" took place. The artist Jim Dine had built a flat with three panels; this was to be his only scenery. His props lay on a table near the flat: three jars of paint and two brushes. The canvas on the flat was white, and Dine was dressed in a long red smock. He took up his brushes and painted "I love what I'm doing." When he got to the word "doing," he said: ". . . I picked up one of the jars and drank the paint, and then I poured the other two jars over my head, quickly, and dove physically through the canvas." Dine said later that "It was like a thirty-second moment of intensity. It was like a drawing. . . ." Dine called the piece *The Smiling Workman.*[3] It was a happening.

By the early sixties, happenings was a familiar word: people had attended them in theatres, lofts, apartments, studios, and in the street; they were occurring all over the world.[4] The young French painter and filmmaker Jean-Jacques Lebel staged a happening in Paris and Venice that lasted for two days and ended with a community shower, while in Japan the Gutai Group had created happenings (as early as 1957) that featured the use of inflatable balloons, collapsible paper screens, and plastic bags filled with smoke. One Japanese artist created a happening by rolling around in a mud pile, another by attaching an array of electric bulbs to her costume; in Finland, Sweden and Czechoslovakia, artists took to beaches, cemeteries and garbage dumps as environments for happenings.

The remarkable thing about these events is that none of these individuals were part of any organized movement, and few had contact with one another; they lived in different cities and came from different backgrounds, and yet they all felt compelled to participate in this strange phenomenon. What made people want to splatter themselves with mud, drink paint, wear absurd clothing, or no clothing at all, and partake in what seemed like eccentric, inconsequential activities? Was there actually meaning to this kind of event, or was it a madness for a mad elite?

When Allan Kaprow, an action painter with a graduate degree in art history, coined the term "happening" in the course of organizing his evening of entertainment, it was unintentional. He was searching, not for a theatre experience, but for another dimension to art. He wanted to keep himself and other people "in" his work, he said, and to keep intact the relationship between the spectator and the creator. For him, the two-dimensional canvas had become limited; what he was searching for was a multi-dimensional experience, attainable through materials besides paint which would be, in actual fact, part of the artist's own environment. This aim was already part of a general movement: painters like Kaprow had used rubber, straw, pots and pans, tinfoil kitchen utensils, and materials from bathrooms and living rooms. As a result, canvases grew larger and larger, but for practical reasons they still remained restricted. To depart further from the confines of space, another movement sprang up: artists began to assemble still larger objects like furniture and massive junk, so that in 1957 Kaprow created a huge "assemblage" called *Mother's Boy* (18½ × 15½ × 12½ feet), which consisted of a large armoire, old mattresses, photos pasted on the furniture, and a collage of weatherbeaten pieces of fabric, including an old college sweater. Others like Jean Follett and George Brecht assembled on canvas, hammers, tools, brushes, nails, playing cards, thermometers, and scrabble games; George Segal did a sculpture of a woman seated in her own kitchen which was actually constructed with the model's table and chairs, and her pots and pans—while the figure itself was plaster. This was called an "Environment." Still others used huge movable panels, mobiles, plastic bags, geometric acrylite, and floating objects. But assemblages and environments created problems. They became impossible to install, much less to keep or store inside a gallery; and once such a show was over, the materials were usually destroyed.

The period of environment and assemblages failed to satisfy artists like Kaprow, who still longed to smash through the walls of the gallery. For him, any limitation on space was a limitation on creativity, and he began to see that only "floating" mobiles could break the space barrier. Meanwhile, he had become very interested in sound. Fascinated by ordinary everyday noises—scraping shoes, whistling trains, honking horns, and buzzing planes—he taped the sounds he heard as he went about his daily tasks. At this point, still in the pre-happening days, he met John Cage, who was conducting a course in avant-garde music at the New School for Social Research.

John Cage was considered one of the most important people in the development of the avant-garde. Credited for starting "simultaneous lectures," Cage had conducted an early "event" in 1952 at Black Mountain College where he lectured on Meister Eckhart, while two of his colleagues (M. C. Richards and Charles Olson), stationed in other parts of the auditorium, chimed in with thoughts of their own. Simultaneously, David Tudor played the piano and projected a movie on the ceiling, while Robert Rauschenberg played records on an old phonograph, and Merce Cunningham, followed by a stray dog, improvised a dance.[5] Cage had left the conventional world of music, had abandoned harmony, had worked with silence, sounds of the street, and had been an early proponent of anti-art theories.

Kaprow enrolled in Cage's course, and soon began to "compose" events or activities that suggested arrangements of noise. He believed that sound was an aesthetic experience as well as an unavoidable element of an environment. Inspired by his work with

Cage, and armed with his knowledge of assemblage, Kaprow was ready for his first happening—the famous event which he staged in 1959.

"Happening" turned out to be a curiously accurate word, for the coinage perfectly describes the essence of the event. Happenings are a juxtaposition of diverse elements and occurrences, performed in any environment by an audience who are at once spectators and participants.[6] Though they grew out of the collage and the giant assemblage, happenings are a departure from the past in that people's *real* life activities are paired not only with painting and sculpture, but with sound, lights, film, and objects, and all are part of the "canvas." In a 1968 interview, Kaprow argued that we live in a society where people perceive sights, sounds, and events with immense speed, simultaneously and/or in a non-logical sequence, and that as they perform their daily activities, they are unaware of the many images that affect their behavior. Daily rituals are frequently at variance with the individual's interior life; tasks are often performed in an alienated, technological atmosphere. One writes a serious letter while listening to rock-and-roll; reads a tragic play and overhears a comedy on TV; studies an esoteric subject against a background of popular advertising; one talks, entertains, or sleeps through the noise of automobiles, trucks, trains, planes, and subways; listens to music from stereo tapes, or transistors, and in the midst of this barrage of communication, one can cook, eat, drink, talk, dress, paint, make love, or give birth. Especially complex is our relation to television. ". . . 17 million people . . . are watching the same thing at the same time—that can create a terrific sense of community," says Kaprow, "or at least provide the underpinning for that sense to build on."[7]

One of the problems of contemporary life is understanding the patterns, shapes, and images that affect our consciousness. Happenings formalize these patterns and images; their creators see them as artistic metaphors for our present modes of communication. Happenings describe popular trends in art and music that are implicit in the environment; they depict modern advertising methods and the function of objects and electronics in a technological age. Asked if his work had any specific social value, Kaprow replied: "Work such as I do has latent social values . . . during times of crisis I sometimes feel that the work is useless. But art cannot be simply topical. I am not able to be indifferent to what's going on in America, and so sometimes my work is embarrassing to me because I can't use it immediately. But then I suppose that most shopkeepers and lawyers who think about it are in the same quandary. . . ."[8]

Although happenings (in America) began as exercises in form, artists, in the process of utilizing materials from daily life and from pop culture, inadvertently commented on society. Jim Dine, Red Grooms, Claes Oldenburg, and others used junk found in gutters, backyards, garbage lots, and trash cans: empty milkbottles, paintboxes, old mattresses, sticks of wood, articles of old clothing of every variety and shape and texture, cellophane wrap, vinyl, pails, rags, mops. They used electrical items, too: buzzers, lights, wires, antennae, radios, transistors, photographs. The disarray, the jagged roughness of the junk, coupled with its rough line composition and arbitrary design, produced complicated collage which, on the surface, was ugly. Yet it was the ugliness with which Beckett's tramps and Ionesco's madmen surround themselves. Beneath the form was a silent condemnation of the contemporary milieu, its penchant for disposables and for collecting junk. Implicit in all of this was the artist's rejection of traditional subject matter: what was heretofore considered unfit for art—debris, trash, junk—was now the essence of art, and a metaphor for the movement. American society had championed junk and ballyhooed the disposable, and artists had turned it into art, also to be disposed after a one-shot showing.

The structure of a happening, as Kaprow had first envisioned it, was many-faceted, but his main interests were space and sound;

later he considered audience participation and response equally important. Since space (or perception) is one of the most fundamental problems of the artist, Kaprow strove to revolutionize spatial arrangements. In conventional theatre, actors are separated from the spectators, and the players respect the demarcation line: space is limited and prescribed. In happenings, action becomes mobile; space is no longer bounded by artificial divisions; scenery ceases to have a rigid function. Scenery can be anything—inanimate objects, painted collage, mobiles, sculptures, free forms, animals, the natural environment, even the actors themselves. In a happening, any space can hold random objects (as they appear in life), and any arrangement of objects is acceptable. In fact, action could be separate and simultaneous, like that of a three-ring circus. Claes Oldenburg believed that people, as well as scenery, could be objects: "The audience is considered an object and its behavior as events, along with the rest. The audience is taken to differ from the players in that its possibilities are not explored as far as that of the players. . . . The place of the audience in the structure is determined by seating and by certain simple provocations."[9]

But the location, Oldenburg maintained, actually determined the quality of the event. Happeners claimed that since space is unlimited, the audience's movements are also unlimited; "real" or material environment could then mix freely with illusionary objects. A real tree could mix with painted flowers, painted portraits with live models, actual cars with replicas. Objects do not convey explicit messages, although their spatial arrangements can imply "stories," and reveal relationships, but happenings have little in common with traditional narratives; they are a non-linear experience geared toward a gut reaction.

A happening script tells the "actors" what their tasks are, and the "play" can be rehearsed very briefly. But the "actors" perform in their own fashion. If an actor's task is to type a letter, he may "choose" to be slow, fast or tired; he may give the typing to someone else, he may get into an argument over it, none of which is indicated in the script. The actor follows the structural pattern of the text and improvises at the same time; besides, "actors" in a happening are really not actors in the traditional sense. They play themselves; they do not attempt characterizations, or "lose" themselves in the performance, nor do they structure their inner lives to conform with a role. Instead, they carry out the events of a happening in a functional manner. Aware of the actor-audience relationship, as a musician and acrobat are aware of their audience, the actor does not superimpose another personality on his own.[10] In fact, in Kaprow's first happening, he used painters as "actors"; they knew Kaprow was interested in problems related to painting and, not being trained actors, they never assumed a theatrical persona.

Audience participation, a key problem in the avant-garde, remained a key problem in happenings. Robert Rauschenberg argues that the audience should be as responsible as the entertainer for making theatre interesting. "I would like people to come home from work, wash up, and go to the theatre as an evening of taking their chances."[11] Rauschenberg assumes that the audience finds theatre essential to its existence. But theatre artists are well aware that popular audiences are scarce and their reactions, varied. Audience response to happenings—whether they took place in lofts, streets, garages, subways, parks, beaches, fields, or lakesides, and whether people were seated on chairs, tables, floors, ladders, scaffolding, or windows—was always unpredictable. Some participated, others simply watched; what they didn't do was as important as what they did do. Silence was as interesting as noise, stillness as significant as movement, and spontaneity as exciting as planned activity.

Kaprow later summarized the essential characteristics of happenings and his points are worth quoting:

> (A) The line between art and life should be kept as fluid, and perhaps indistinct, as possible. . . .
>
> (B) . . . the source of themes, materials, actions, and the rela-

> tionship between them are to be derived from any place or period except from the arts, their derivatives, and their milieu. [Kaprow aimed here to break entirely with past aesthetic criteria.]
>
> (C) The performance of a Happening should take place over several widely spaced, sometimes moving and changing locales. . . . [Kaprow wanted to avoid stereotypes that result from repetition, and from conventional use of theatre space.]
>
> (D) Time which follows closely on space considerations, should be variable and discontinuous. . . . [The objective is to break the barrier between art and life, and to release the artist from conventional arrangements of time-space.]
>
> (E) Happenings should be performed only once.
>
> (F) . . . audiences should be eliminated entirely.
>
> (G) The composition of a Happening proceeds exactly as in Assemblage and Environments, that is, it is evolved as a collage of events in certain spans of time, and in certain spaces.[12]

As happenings continued, it became evident that Kaprow's interests became more rarified. He was intrigued with the way the light shined on a Nedick's sign, the rumble of a subway under his feet, chance occurrences, and the idea of a floating painting.[13] But his work didn't develop. Perhaps this was because Kaprow deliberately chose to describe rather than to comment on the social ambiance: his happenings remained open-ended, uncommitted, and undirected. Further, the form of happenings presented a real problem. The abandonment of the traditional plot, climax, and character, though radical, was not replaced by other elements. The life-like tasks in Kaprow's happenings, detached from their psychological or social meanings, were no substitute for theatrical tension. Without a point of view, and depending entirely on pop culture, the happening became mundane and repetitious. When Kaprow said that happenings express nothing more than the actual moment, but that on another level, the pieces were fantasies derived from life and symbolically suggestive, he voiced the essential contradictions (and failures) of the form. The presentation of the stark details of everyday life provided no meaningful ground for symbolic interpretation. They showed actuality (which

Kaprow calls ritual) without any relation to large issues, and this is precisely what reduced ritual to repetition. One cannot show a man repeatedly drinking coffee; in itself, this activity is banal and artistically insignificant.

Looking back, Kaprow sees the value of the happening as an experience in ordinary communications: "Narrowing the world or expanding its consciousness with the real world at our disposal," he said, "made our sense of what was going on crazier . . . it made us part of a larger design . . . every act related to what someone else was doing, an extension of oneself."[14] Apparently, Kaprow's involvement with pop culture as a force of communication presented a challenge to him, and he tried to understand his relationship to his generation's culture at the same time that he was experiencing it. As for socially relevant art, Kaprow said: "As a matter of fact, I try to make my work as insignificant as possible . . . because the more you force an issue, the less you achieve, the less you pay attention, the more you will achieve, the more you work for enjoyment, what is achieved is often more than what is expected. . . . But a social goal is a paltry goal. . . . I strike for amplitude and wholeness of existence."[15]

While Kaprow was presenting his happenings, the Frenchman Jean-Jacques Lebel was doing similar work, but with a different outlook. In Venice in July 1960, he invited 150 people to a palace for a cocktail party, and asked them to wear formal clothes and bring along white flowers. When they arrived they were shown into a funeral hall where a man killed a body already in a coffin. Simultaneously, a choir sang in Latin. Screams and crying were heard while Lebel read a page from the Marquis de Sade. A eulogy was recited and a man masturbated behind a curtain. The body was carried into the street; passersby thought it was a real funeral. The coffin was carried to a gondola; the people followed in other boats, but the body was thrown into the water amid hymns and singing. Later it became known that the body was a sculpture by

Jean Tinguely. The happening was entitled *Funeral Ceremony of the Anti-Process.*[16]

In another happening, *For Exorcising the Spirit of Catastrophe,* Lebel became more complex. First, he welcomed people to the sound of jazz, then "A large metal sculpture is beaten and broken. Two naked girls start large collage painting on wall. Lebel makes collage (with political headlines) on their bodies. . . . Simultaneously, color slides of bodies and paintings are projected by Ferró [the artist] onto the body of a woman [dressed in] black silk underwear. Ferró paints a picture with an electric drill, phallus sticking out from his pants, dipped into girl." A man comes forward, dressed as a priest, and screaming in Japanese, caresses the audience "with an immense papier-mâché phallus . . . goes into mystic orgasm and then collapses. . . . Lebel as TV man hallucinates in electronic language, waving yin-yang code flags. . . ."[17]

Perhaps Jean-Jacques Lebel's happenings reflect his background (his father was an art collector and the friend of Dadaists and Surrealists) as well as his beginnings as a painter and filmmaker. Like his predecessors, Lebel's aim was to shock the bourgeoisie, stir up their sense of outrage by deliberately working with forbidden images. Thus he introduced into happenings nudity, sex, sadism, and scatology—all forms of eroticism, in fact—and, since the French bourgeoisie ostensibly despised these elements, Lebel relished them. Viewing sexual repression as part of a larger social issue, Lebel believed that "the function of art . . . must be to express, at all costs, what is hidden behind the wall"—a wall that the bourgeoisie erect as a fortress against sex. Apparently, Lebel, following in Artaud's footsteps, aimed to change bourgeois perceptions; for him, ferocious attacks that "unveil" and "violate" bourgeois psychological and political repression are justified.[18] That the bourgeoisie might never see his happenings did not in the least deter Lebel.

Lebel was also involved with the contemplation of dreams, drugs, and myths—subjects which, according to him, also threaten the bourgeoisie as well as suggest answers to their metaphysical and social problems. And it was through the activity of happenings, which included these elements, that Lebel hoped to shake them up. In his work, the mythical and hallucinatory world was juxtaposed with reality, resulting in a myriad of images, as though in a "Collective Dream."[19] The "Collective Dream" is a vehicle to release inhibitions and repressions; it operates under no rules; everything is invented through a continuing creative process in which everyone relies on each other's uncontrolled kinetic responses. And these responses (conscious or unconscious) are synthesized and transformed into an ideograph, a language, a configuration. Like free jazz, notes can be enlarged and developed; a great degree of creativity depends upon the rapport between the players.[20] How this affected the bourgeoisie remains ambiguous, but theoretically the "Collective Dream" was designed to change perceptions, arouse genuine feelings, and expose false social patterns.

The basic difference between Lebel and Kaprow is that Kaprow used the happening for its aesthetic meaning, Lebel for its political effect. Kaprow's disdain for the "System" surely equalled that of Lebel, but Kaprow chose form as a means of rebellion, perhaps inadvertently reflecting the influence of Marshall McLuhan. Lebel was also interested in form, but form in itself was inadequate to convey his disgust with the System or, indeed, with Western civilization as a whole. For Lebel, communication was virtually hopeless in the face of degenerate Western affluence. An avid Marxist (but an enemy of Stalinism, both in the Russian and French versions) he worked closely with Daniel Cohn-Bendit, one of the leaders of the student uprising of 1968 in France. Lebel was reacting to "reversals in art and history," as he said later, and to the madness of his times; in so doing, he responded with his own madness and political fanaticism. But his self-projected image of the paragon of a counterculture artist in revolt was only a duplicate of French romantic revolutionary fervor, sprinkled with surrealistic philosophy, which apparently comes alive with every generation—and with every generation is summarily defeated.

Nonetheless, Lebel searched consciously for "latent myths" to change our conception of life. Influenced by the contemporary drug culture, which he believed was related to new myths, rites, and patterns, Lebel felt that the hallucinogenic experience was not a barometer for artistic criteria, but an attempt at new perceptions that might produce Nirvana. "All art is magic, else it is not art,"[21] he said, and he longed to extract what he thought was the "magic" in drugs and in film and happenings. He believed that his role as artist was first to change man's perceptions and secondly his social condition—not an unusual position among some of the counter-culture youth of the sixties.

By 1968, Lebel had gone through the gamut: after filmmaking in St. Tropez, and happenings on the Continent, he settled down to making the Revolution. In the uprising of 1968 he, together with his Living Theatre compatriots, led in the takeover of the Odéon, and issued the famous anti-art proclamation laying down the dictum that all art happened on the streets or anywhere you see it. He seemed to be coming around to John Cage's position that all life is art, but Lebel went further: he declared: "*Art is $hit.*"[22]

For all its shortcomings, the happening had a decisive influence on the arts, and on the theatre of the sixties in particular. Following the line set down by Artaud and the Surrealists, happenings set the stage for further development. Disorder and disarray became a standard aesthetic criterion; the non-rational became a virtue; experience of the moment, a philosophical quest; the non-verbal response, a sign of probable truth. Artists were sure that the visual and the felt experience were paramount. A gigantic mistrust had set in against logic, against Marxian dialectics, and against humanistic Western traditions. It was humanism, long the mainstay of capitalist culture, that was considered by artists—and by youth in general—to have brought Western civilization to the brink of decay, deceit, and depravity. And large segments of American and European youth, dismayed by the discrepancies between what humanism preached and its application in the West, opted for disorder, disarray, and anarchy. Artists rejected classical tradition as a symbol of bourgeois culture, and considered the happening as their own; happenings coincided with a tone, attitude, style, and ambiance that captured the fragmentation of their lives. A happening apprehended the hallucinogenic experience; it used junk to symbolize a junk society; it adopted technology as material for new art; and it amalgamated all art into one event. In the theatre, happenings broke the stranglehold of narrative and of the proscenium arch, and abolished the separation between audiences and players. Finally, happenings helped usher in the Living Theatre which synthesized the happening, cruelty, and anarchy to make theatrical history.

On the other hand, happenings, as well as Artaud's theories, opened up a Pandora's box in the avant-garde, and for a decade arguments on aesthetics raged. Could the theatre develop its own "poetry in space"? Was it necessary to use the written word as the foundation for theatre? Would the essence of theatre be entirely redefined? And, as Lebel said, was art only $hit—and therefore to be abandoned for revolution?

Other avant-gardists were soon to give their answer.

six

The Living Theatre—The Mother of Them All

The most important American counterculture group to develop an answer to the questions posed by Artaud and the happening was Judith Malina and Julian Beck's Living Theatre. They and their company had given their answer earlier in a New York theatre loft on Fourteenth Street, long before the emergence of happenings and Artaud. In fact, they had a following of liberals and radicals who idolized their productions of Kenneth H. Brown's *The Brig* and Jack Gelber's *The Connection*, and indeed whatever they produced. When, in 1964, the Living Theatre got into trouble with federal tax authorities and went into self-exile in Europe, many of their admirers felt deprived. Reports filtered back that the Living Theatre had developed into a revolutionary anarchistic commune, that the Living Theatre had been instrumental in political events in Milan, Berlin, Paris, that the Living Theatre had led the insurrection at the Odéon during the 1968 May events, and that their "cruelty" techniques were at the center of growing controversy.

The reports were intriguing, and when the Living were invited back to America by Robert Brustein, the prestigious Dean of the Yale Drama School, their return was eagerly awaited. To be sure, their reputation of personal and artistic anarchy had preceded them, yet many people expected that the American invitation would temper their willingness to risk notoriety, and that the years of exile would have mellowed them.

But the Living Theatre remained true to its image. The Becks—husband and wife Julian Beck and Judith Malina—and the forty men, women, and children who comprised their group, opened in September of 1968 at Yale, and proved not only that they could create the stormiest of controversies, but that they were the undisputed leaders of the American avant-garde: their performances were without doubt the most provocative of the 1968–69 season. Four new works were presented in repertory: an adaptation of Mary Shelley's *Frankenstein; Mysteries—and Smaller Pieces; Antigone;* and *Paradise Now*. On the opening night, the Yale audience was crackling with anticipation, but the evening ended with a furor of cheers and boos, frenetic adulation and hostile indignation. After their first performance of *Paradise Now*, the Becks and some members of the audience were arrested for nudity, but Dean Brustein and cartoonist Jules Feiffer came to their defense and those arrested were released. In their spare time at Yale, the Becks "rapped" at student and faculty gatherings, got involved in newspaper controversies, and were the principal participants in antagonistic verbal clashes. Finally, by the end of their stay at Yale, some people were relieved to see them go.

New Haven proved to have been mild in its reception compared to the opening at the Brooklyn Academy of Music, where the Living Theatre settled in for a four-week run. The refurbished Academy (considered an off-off-off-Broadway theatre), drew the establishment from Manhattan's uptown (disguised in their hippie clothes), the real hippies from downtown, and the self-appointed intelligentsia. An audience of admirers, dissenters, poseurs, and some serious theatre critics, were argumentative and adoring, belligerent and supportive. Not generally a place for this kind of controversy, the theatre was all at once alive. Still, it apparently proved too alive for those who left after the second intermission. But those who stayed cheered the Becks for ten minutes.

Most of the established New York critics wrote scathing reviews of the Living Theatre soon after: John Simon of *New York* magazine called them "fascists," Walter Kerr of the *New York Times* dismissed them as "misfits," Harold Clurman of the *Nation* thought them childish, Eric Bentley in the *New York Times* relegated them to "political simpletons," Richard Gilman in the *New Republic* admonished them for arrogance, and Dean Brustein disowned them, first through the grapevine, and then in the *New York Review of Books.* Clive Barnes in the *New York Times* tepidly came to their defense, only to be put down by the professorial tones of Eric Bentley's "I Reject the Living Theatre" *Times* article. Outside the establishment press, the *Village Voice* gave them favorable and abundant coverage.

During the Living Theatre's run at the Brooklyn Academy, half of its audiences, many in a rage, would leave before the end of the performance. In cultural circles, a controversy was on: were you for or against the Living? No middle ground seemed possible. By the end of their engagement, the Living had become the essence of Artaudian plague from which some people retreated, lest they become contaminated. But the Living continued to draw young people to its doors—the hippies, the yippies, the students, and the intellectuals. After a nationwide tour, they finally returned to Europe, leaving mixed feelings as well as severe upheavals. The significance of their work may yet be unclear, but that they were a phenomenon is unquestionable. Surely they threatened, provoked, irritated, and unnerved liberals and radicals as well as traditionalists. For the Living Theatre was the only American company which dared to challenge not only naturalism, but the definition and function of the contemporary theatre; moreover, they suggested that anarchism be the political basis for a theatrical avant-garde.

As early as 1943, Julian Beck and Judith Malina were radicals.

They detested the capitalist money system and "bourgeois" theatre for its stifling limitations on art, and they believed that their work was a way of renouncing this system. So when Beck inherited $6,000 from his aunt in 1951, he and Judith Malina launched the Living Theatre—a theatre devoted to radicalism. First they gave performances of Lorca, Paul Goodman, and Gertrude Stein in their upper West Side apartment until they were able, in 1959, to organize a permanent repertory company on Fourteenth Street. Their big success came with their productions of *The Connection* and *The Brig*; in 1961, they won the Paris Critics Award for the best acting company at an international competition of the Théâtre des Nations. For three years in a row, they also were awarded the *Village Voice* Obie. But neither their artistic recognition nor their good following prevented the 1963 closing down of their theatre; the Becks were forced into exile.

The Living Theatre had always been extremely poor; it had been haunted by debts, suits, creditors, and landlords; it lived from moment to moment, and from hand to mouth. Trying to support a repertory company—moreover an avant-garde one—was virtually impossible in New York. And, the Becks were not the kind of people who could handle large sums of money; they had utter disregard for organizational enterprise, and no matter how successful their productions were, they were still in debt. It was not surprising that since 1959, the Becks simply did not pay the government their taxes; they ran up an enormous bill, plus penalties and interest. When questioned about this later, Julian Beck had a simple answer: he paid the actors $45 a week, he said, five of which were to be given to the government, leaving a sum of $40 to be paid to the actor. Since they had to raise the $40 in the first place (which wasn't easy), they chose to use admission taxes toward the salary in an effort to keep the plays going. For Beck, it was a question of the law versus art, and he chose art. But the United States government didn't see it that way. Neither did the Becks' landlord. In a combined move with the tax agents, the landlord seized the building one night, and shut it down—but not before the company staged a dramatic sit-in.

The Brig was playing—an imaginative drama that depicted the intense cruelty of military punishment—and it was a fitting background for what was to come. Despite the law, the actors wanted the play to continue for another week. The landlord wouldn't hear of it. But the Living Theatre managed to play one more night to an audience that, when barred from admission through the front door, climbed over the roof to get in through the windows. Downstairs, pickets chanted "Save the Living Theatre," while inside *The Brig* was performed. After the play, people milled around in the streets; Judith Malina was interviewed through a window; and the entire company was arrested because they would not leave the theatre.[1]

The illegal performance of *The Brig*, the sit-in, the police bust, the clamor, and the histrionics were not only all acts of civil disobedience, but the foreshadowing of scenes later to be "staged" all over the world. For the Living Theatre believes that theatre, politics, and life are synonymous, and this principle remained central to its gestalt.

The Becks are committed to pacifist anarchism, which postulates that the overthrow of capitalism, the withering away of the state, and the abolition of money can be accomplished through peaceful, massive indoctrination. And, like all anarchists, the Living Theatre disavowed authority of all kinds. The Becks stressed individual freedom, even the individual's right to participate in revolution on his own terms. Like traditional anarchists, they hate party discipline; they reject organized movements, and never force their colleagues to adhere to any particular strategy against their wills. This meant that the Living Theatre could not control the actions of its own members. Historically, lack of discipline in political activity has always precipitated egocentricity and individualistic, anti-social behavior. Ultimately, it was to have the same effect on the Living Theatre.

Anarchism became synonymous with the Living Theatre's brand of revolution. Living the roles of anarchist actors, the members of the company were committed to dramatizing their politics not only on the stage, but in life as well, so that at the time of their arrest and financial bankruptcy, Judith Malina, acting as her own attorney, "played" Portia in the courtroom, while the members of the Living Theatre staged demonstrations, acted out their own individual responses, and made scenes in and out of the courtroom. Regardless of the "show," the Living Theatre was fined and jailed for its failure to pay taxes (sixty days for Beck, thirty for Malina) and the theatre was closed down. It was then that the Becks chose exile.

When they left for Europe in 1964, the Becks took with them a nucleus of the company. There they found fertile ground for their anarchy. The tactics of New Left confrontation were emerging, and the Becks fitted in perfectly; they organized themselves into a commune, traveled in two buses, played France, Italy, Switzerland, and Germany, ate infrequently, shared the work, the decisions and the money. Despite the hardships, the Becks built their repertory, kept their company intact while they picked up foreign actors, and created four new pieces. *Le Living,* as they came to be known in Europe, had grown into a family (there were numerous marriages and children). By now the company had learned, to some extent, how to book theatre engagements, pay bills, and discipline itself, but they still lived in poverty; they had burned their bridges to become a revolutionary theatre.

The company made close alliances with leading intellectual revolutionaries like Jean-Jacques Lebel, then one of its chief chroniclers; the members gave political speeches in France, Italy, and Germany, and attracted thousands of students and intellectuals to their rallies, demonstrations, and performances. In 1968, they were instrumental in shutting down the Odéon theatre; and later they attempted to do the same in Avignon. Wherever they went, they created scenes, arguments, and confrontations. They lived from crisis to crisis, always in the center of political and artistic battles. Although their beads, beards, long hair, hip clothes, and stoned appearances antagonized many people, they developed a large following. Anarchist kids, hippies, students, drop-outs, and "freaks" followed them by the carloads and turned the Living lodgings into a giant crash pad. Their personal and political style added to their charisma. Even as they were ostracized, busted, beaten, and scorned by the establishment, Le Living thrived: hip culture and anarchism successfully merged.

Artaud's theatre of cruelty had been the mainstay of the Living Theatre technique, and the preaching of pacifist anarchy its content. That their anarchy was updated to include Oriental mysticism, Zen, Yoga, confrontation politics, gestalt therapy, Norman O. Brown psychohistorical concepts, and eclecticism of all sorts, did not disguise the influence of nineteenth-century Godwinism—about which, more later. Nonetheless, the Living Theatre was the first international repertory company to combine radical politics with radical theatre techniques.

Emulating Artaud, their pieces were spectacles rather than literary dramas. Enacted in a *mise-en-scène* fugue rather than in a naturalistic linear form, the pieces relied on dense metaphors rather than on plot. The action, sequentially and spatially arranged, was built on juxtaposed physical configurations made with the actors' own bodies (thus carrying out Artaud's concept of expressing abstractions physically). Words were replaced by sounds, grunts, groans, screams, and chants counterpoised by deliberate silences and ritual signaling. The company adopted Artaud's credo, "Between life and theatre there will be no distinct division, but instead a continuity." Even their name, the *Living,* was appropriate, signifying their commitment to abolishing the separation between what is happening on the stage and what is happening in life. The living event, the existential response, was as important to them as a rehearsed play, and therefore an important consideration was the immediate reaction of the audience. The Living provoked audiences into "acting" instead of only watching, and thus the theatrical event melded into a real one, and vice-versa. Sometimes the audience was lectured, as in *Mysteries*, or sometimes the actors intimidated the spectators by glaring at them, as in

Antigone. Audience participation was not only an arbitrary theatrical device; it was rooted in Artaud's philosophy and Kaprow's happenings, adopted to espouse pacifist anarchism.

The Living took its political-psychotherapeutic task seriously. In *Paradise Now*, actors confronted the conventionally dressed members of the audience who, in the eyes of the Living Theatre, were synonymous with, or actually were, agents of the bourgeois state. Such audiences, asserted Beck, were victims of suppressed psychic energy, and could neither free themselves nor anyone else. Such people inhibit trust, prevent sexual freedom (the latter, for him, a sign of real liberation). The Living, taking on the semblance of self-appointed encounter group leaders or self-styled gurus, provoked the public's hostility, bombarded it with noise and chaos, attacked it by frenetic, sometimes mindless activity, shocked it with surprising changes of lights, and assaulted it with sudden images of nightmares and dreams, and with their own personal idiosyncratic behavior. The actors' bizarre dress and gothic make-up, their unrestrained psychic and sexual energy, their air of erotic mysticism, even their arrogant, intense certitude, were thrust into the audience's faces—violently, aggressively, abrasively.

Insisting that they were not mere rebels but paradigms of revolution in art, politics, and sex, they characterized themselves as the most radical organized theatre company in America. They claimed to live outside the capitalist social structure, regardless of economic realities. They disdained money, conventions, and commercial success. They appeared to emulate the zealousness of early Christian pilgrims organized in a religiously oriented commune—whose religion was revolution, whose practical work, theatre. As preachers, the Living Theatre exhorted audiences to adopt their moral values, as in *Antigone* and *Mysteries*; to believe in their concept of human character, as in *Frankenstein*; to commit themselves to the anarchist revolution, as in *Paradise Now*. They hoped the audiences would transcend their capitalist regimentation and attain the final vision: an anarchist community where all men are brothers, lovers, and permanent revolutionists. The repertory as it was performed in New York reflected these concepts.

Perhaps the most theatrically rewarding spectacle in the Living Theatre's repertory is their adaptation of Mary Shelley's *Frankenstein*, an enactment of the discontents of modern civilization. Here the Living Theatre uses Western myths and philosophy to illustrate the monstrousness of our past as well as its hopeful but ambiguous future. Frankenstein, a Faustian figure—scientist, creator, teacher, revolutionist—searches for an "end to human suffering," only to encounter man's character paradoxically corrupted by man's civilization.

Mary Shelley's novel is the springboard for the action. The story is virtually wordless; the *mise-en-scène* is abstract and non-logical and, as in a film, images are more important than the narrative, and are enacted in a montage of quasi-balletic patterns. Noise, silence, exotic effects, gothic and Surrealistic nightmares are intertwined with shadow play and garish lighting, and sometimes merge, as in a dream.

The opening scene of *Frankenstein* finds the actors already on stage, sitting in yoga position, meditating. Dressed in jeans and colored shirts—oranges, reds, greens, and yellows—cross-legged, arranged symmetrically, each actor is inscrutable: their faces are individualistic and beautiful. They sit like Buddhas—a testimony to their powers of yoga concentration; they are extremely themselves. Suddenly, one is aware of the background: a twenty-foot pipe scaffolding, composed of three tiers divided into fifteen cubicle units. These contain pipes, ropes, ladders, and nets. To the side of the stage sits a young woman, calmly broadcasting that the cast is meditating in order to levitate the actress seated in the center. We are told that if she levitates (magic), the play is completed; if not, the play continues. After a countdown, the "girl fails to levitate," but our longing for a magical trip is assuaged by the Living Theatre's play.

Now the beauty of the "meditation" rite in the prologue is over, and a mass killing begins. The cast grabs the unlucky actress, throws a net over her head, and shoves her into a coffin. All together they march down the aisles in a funeral procession: the girl screams, moans, bangs on the lid of the coffin—she refuses to die. Others take up her cry: one yells "No," another follows suit; the procession breaks up. Actors, howling piteously and pleading for their lives, run up and down the aisles until one by one they are captured and put to death. Dragged to the open cubicles in the scaffoldings, the victims beg for their salvation: they howl, cry, scream, pray. But it is useless: they are hanged, shot, gassed, crucified, electrocuted, stabbed, garroted.

As bodies lie dead all over the stage, Dr. Frankenstein enters, and presents the leitmotif: "How can we end human suffering?" He raises up the dead girl, injects her with a needle, drains her blood in a macabre but compelling bit of shadow play, and then, before our eyes, the actors arrange themselves acrobatically and build a scrap-iron laboratory in which Frankenstein is to create the "New Man." A corpse-like actor is strapped to the table, a nurse plugs a dozen colored tubings into different parts of his body, his organs are reflected in multi-colored projections hanging on top of the slab, and in a satiric moment, parodying some of the more ridiculous moments of Dr. Kildare, Frankenstein goes to work.

The scaffolding is now lit up. It becomes the World, and each compartment represents a segment. Intermittently, news is broadcast; the announcer's cool, indifferent tone contradicts the horrors of the day. Each announcement covers an actual current event. As the progress of technology is reported, the largest plank in the scaffolding becomes alive: workers march, capitalists threaten, Marxists argue, generals plot, but the drone of the microphone—technology at its worst—drowns out all other sounds.

Meanwhile, the body does not respond to Frankenstein's "science"; his heart is weak and almost failing. But Freud and Norbert Wiener appear. The latter gives advice on electrodes for the eyes, the former on sexual organs. The Creature begins to stir; he grunts and moans, the doctor works frantically on the plugged-in spaghetti-like wires attached to the body; the colored, slide-projected organs light up, the body moves spastically, and suddenly Frankenstein cries, "Turn the Creature on." Silence. Darkness. The body appears in full form: he is a giant twenty-foot

Monster/Creature—a stunning but horrifying configuration formed from the arrangement of the actors' bodies hanging from the poles of the scaffolding. The creature stands in the center of the World-structure, swaying, moving, the two red eyes in his head blazing. He is us, magnificent, grotesque, pathetic, mysterious; it is he who will create a civilization that will, in turn, menace us.

Act II exposes the creature's Head. The scene opens in the dark; soon red lights change to green, then to blue; they blink on and off like lightning. Suddenly, superimposed against the structure of the scaffolding, is a lit-up plastic tubing of the inside of the giant Head, divided into sections, plainly labeled: Ego, Subconscious, Erotica, Love, Intuition, Wisdom, Knowledge, and so forth. The actors in these cubicles emit strange noises in consonance with the conflicts in the psyche. Meanwhile, the Creature lies strapped to the table; he dreams of the legends of the past. Western mythical archetypes come to life on stage. Ego and Wisdom become Daedalus and Icarus; Love is Persephone; Intuition is Ariadne; Imagination is Theseus. The company moves from role to role in a succession of quick kaleidoscopic actions with a minimum of speech and a maximum of images. (Some enact the myths as if they were recapturing their childhood encounters with ancient mythological heroes; they declaim as if in a child's fairy tale.)

As consciousness of past Western civilization is evoked, Frankenstein teaches the creature the language demanded by technological development: "institution," "organization," "education," "automation." Inside the Head, the functions fight for supremacy and control. Meanwhile, the Creature experiences the agonies of the collective unconscious: cyclones, drownings, disease, starvation, old age, and death. (In the drowning scene, some of the actors enact the boat; some, the swimmers; others do the drowning. In the famine scene, actors wearing shawls assume simple body patterns.) Finally the Creature dreams of an encounter with the Four Horsemen of the Apocalypse, and his trip is ended. Suddenly, the Creature appears as Man. On his feet, he looks human, but is unable to speak; he grunts, stammers, and trembles.

In a painfully moving moment, he exercises a superhuman effort to communicate. He remembers his trip to consciousness and he laments:

> It was dark when I awoke. I felt cold also and half-frightened. I could distinguish nothing; I was a poor, helpless miserable wretch. And feeling pain invade me on all sides, I sat down and wept. . . . I learned that there was but one means to overcome the sensation of pain and that was Death.[2]

In the meantime, the functions have finished their arguments. Ego has won: he has pushed the Man/Creature out into civilization. There Authority takes over, and the oppression of Man begins.

In Act III, the Head has been transformed into a World Prison. Cubicles are covered with hanging rows of black beads, representing the bars of a cell, and ironically they are as beautiful as Japanese calligraphy. Carrying eerie green lanterns, a posse runs up and the down the aisles of the theatre searching the audience for its victims. The fugitives hide all over the theatre, but each is eventually caught. They are charged with being alive:

> Police: Are you Steven Ben Israel?
> Actor: Yes.
> Police: Were you born in Brooklyn?
> Actor: Yes.
> Police: You're under arrest.
> Actor: Yes.
> Police: Are you Carl Einhorn?
> Actor: Yes.
> Police: Are you twenty-nine?
> Actor: Yes.
> Police: You're under arrest.
> Actor: Yes.

A variation of these six lines is repeated as each is arrested, fingerprinted, and put into the first cell. As a new prisoner is taken, a whistle blows, and, like a ritual dance, all the prisoners turn their backs to the audience and shift a cell. Then each in his cubicle acts out his lunatic life, talks gibberish, draws circles in the air, tries to levitate, or behaves as if he is an animal. Some cry, scream, fight, sit catatonically, play with their genitals, or try to fly—all grotesque activities executed simultaneously and rapidly. Once again a whistle blows, the inmates stop their activities, turn their backs to the audience, and move to the next cell. The intention is to experiment with actual, rather than theatrical, time, and to force the audience to experience the exact conditions of the prisoners.

The last to be arrested is Dr. Frankenstein. As a revolutionist plotting the prison break, he tries to make contact with the inmates. He moves from cell to cell; notes are passed, looks are exchanged, instructions are given; finally the guards are attacked, there is a scuffle, the set turns a hideous red: The World is on fire. A brilliant red holds the stage for a few minutes; gradually everything turns gray, then black; then all is silent. In the darkness, the inmates rise from the dead, and with their "charred" bodies create once again the configuration of the Creature. Once more he is a giant, shaky, grotesque, horrifying, but pitifully fragile. A green searchlight shines from his eyes, he peers out accusingly to the audience. Now the Monster/Man raises his arms to the heavens. He "signals through the flames" as a sign of supplication. "Man lives."

It is easy to understand why many critics felt that the Living Theatre's production of *Frankenstein* was the most theatrically satisfying piece in the repertory. Not only did it appeal to those most concerned with structure, but it most clearly exemplified the Living Theatre's philosophical belief at the time. Mary Shelley, the original author of *Frankenstein*, was the daughter of William Godwin (one of the founders of modern anarchism). The Living Theatre's adaptation, though updated, still reflects Godwin's philosophy. Godwin was a radical long before Mary Shelley wrote her gothic novel, and long before her elopement with the famous poet. And although Godwin's anarchism was not a completely new movement (Rousseau and Shaftesbury already having theorized on the innate benevolence of man), he laid down some theoretical foundations which remain the basis for the anarchistic doctrine. Godwin preached that all men were naturally good and all authority was naturally evil. "Remove all these restraints which prevent the human mind from attaining its genuine strength," said Godwin, ". . . positive institution has a tendency to suspend the elasticity and progress of mind . . . each man should be wise enough to govern himself, without the interventions of any compulsory restraint . . . government, even in its best state is an evil . . . we should have as little of it as the general peace of human society will permit."[3]

Godwin believed that man's problem lay in institutional life, the abolition of which would be resolved by the "doctrine of necessity," that is, if educated man saw the truth he would of his own volition overthrow the institutions crippling his economic, social, and political life. This theory supposed that men's self-interests were similar, that reason would force men to chose good, not evil. Godwin's theory ignores the problem that men from different vantage points view good and evil quite differently. Obviously "good" men become part of the "evil" system which they themselves have created, thereby subverting their own "natural goodness." Godwinism, and later the anarchists—and, for that matter, Freud and Jung—have never conclusively defined man's *real* character, while Marx denied that man has a "real" character. The relationship between character as determined culturally and as determined psychically is a matter of continual debate. The Living Theatre's inability to deal seriously with this question was symptomatic of an unrealistic anarchist philosophy disguised as New Leftism, that tended to confuse the production and undermine its intellectual significance.

Another conceptual weakness (as manifest in the production) is the Becks' apparent belief that mind exists before consciousness. Memory, experience, knowledge—mythic and legendary—are part of the innate collective unconscious; only modern words are learned. When the mind functions in the objective world, it creates a prison, and it becomes its own prisoner as well—not only is it restrained by civilization, but by a driving ego. The Becks' claim that ego is the central force, the dominant function; it overtakes the mind, and is responsible for creating the prison. And it is this prison (created by ego), held in check by authority and institutions, that drives men to evil and madness—thus a circuitous argument rather than a progression of ideas. Further, authority is not specifically depicted nor distinctively delineated. If all authority is *a priori* evil, and all men are *a priori* good, why do good men possess such "bad" egos, and create such evil prisons? What, in fact, is the relationship between ego, responsibility, and authority in Western civilization, or in any civilization? Will the ego need radical transformation before man builds a free society? What happens to authority and its institutions in resurrected, revolutionary Man? Is the monster pattern inherent, and will it continually emerge, even though reconstructed, to create new authority, and thus perpetuate a cycle of repression? Arguments that supported ego transformation for the betterment of the collective, rather than for the Self, were a predominant theme during the sixties, and found a voice in the Living Theatre's *Paradise Now*. But as presented in *Frankenstein*, the ego and rebirth themes plainly are an outgrowth of contradictions of nineteenth-century consciousness applied to the 1960's.

If the content of *Frankenstein* did not match the Becks' rhetoric, its aesthetic value was not flawed by the discrepancy. The theatricality of the fire, the creation of the Creature, the configuration of the Man/Creature, were authentically exciting. Especially effective was the massive three-tier compartmental setting, which recalled both Kaprow's and Lebel's work, as well as that of Meyerhold's constructivist days. Lit by multiple colors, the setting facilitated multiple action. One moment the set was a laboratory, the next, a prison, then the frame for the Head, and finally cells for little playlets. Like a giant happening, the action, at first spreading all over the stage, spilled out into the audience and was enhanced by fluttering, gray-green, or blood-red lights, electronic devices, whistles, sirens, bells, and colored slides flickering on and off, punctuated by screams, shrieks, howls, and moans. There was an inordinate beauty in all of this: in the mixing of textures—iron, rope, wood—and in the methodical movements of the prisoners, so hideous in meaning and yet exquisite in form, and in the pathetic beauty of the Creature, struggling to speak poetic prose. The high point of the production was the actors' hanging from the scaffolding to resurrect the Creature, a personal symbol perhaps of the actors' own will to survive despite the real world prison to which they feel subjected. The configuration was a double metaphor, then: not only did Man live in that Creature; the Living Theatre lived as well.

With *Mysteries—and Smaller Pieces* and *Antigone*, the Living Theatre moved away from philosophy to didactic aesthetics. Mysteries, a simple production that combined Oriental ritual with political propaganda, showed four influences: (1) Artaud's theories; (2) medieval theatre; (3) Greek mythology; and (4) Indian philosophy—in particular, Yoga. Early in his life, Artaud wrote a play called *Mysteries of Love*. In a letter to a friend, he claimed that the drama was about "spiritual tenaciousness . . . [that] would give form to the most secret movements of the soul through the simplest, nudest means . . . it would show . . . unexpected aspects in the most usual, banal situations."[4] This statement may have precipitated the Living Theatre's desire to produce *Mysteries*. Yet, on another level, the production seems to be an outgrowth of the medieval Mystery play, which dealt with one topic only—the depiction of good Christians doing sacred deeds for the betterment of Christians. Still another influence: in Greek mythology, the highest state of morality was achieved if one was invited into the Eleusinian Mystery cult. Held in Eleusis outside of Athens, in honor of Demeter and Persephone, the ritual of the mysteries took place each year. The initiation rites were formal; one had to be invited, and only the good were asked to join. It was a great privilege to be initiated into the mystery cult, because it promised, among other things, "life after death as a reward for goodness."[5]

Clearly integrated in *Mysteries* is the Living Theatre's fourth model: Indian philosophy as a solution to Mystery.[6] Influenced by contemporary youth's yearning for Hindu mysticism, the Living had become involved with Yoga—not only with Hatha Yoga's breathing and physical exercises, but with the entire body of yogic philosophy and spirit—as adapted pragmatically by members of the group. (That the Becks are presumably atheists, and the Hindus, religious believers, did not seem abrasive to them.) Traditionally, Yogis are passive; they do not engage in social or political struggles; they believe change is a result of personal revelation, and that inner peace is achieved through mystic sources; they are committed to self-denial, altruism, and to such virtues as cleanliness, self-control, prayer, and meditation. When a Yogi masters all the required principles and rituals, he becomes master of the Self—the highest form of consciousness. Only then may he reach Nirvana, a state of being that mitigates desires for wordly things. Although traditionally Yogis remained aloof from politics, modern radicals have argued that greater consciousness, leading to greater political action, could be achieved by combining certain principles of Eastern philosophy—its qualities of reliance on intuition and its belief in cosmic unity—with R. D. Laing's "politics of experience."

But in *Mysteries,* the Living's attempts to synthesize Western and Indian philosophies missed its mark. *Mysteries* was essentially simplistic; it divided the good and the evil as in a fairy tale. The Living Theatre, as leaders in the Mystery cult, presumably, was the good—there to judge the audience's qualifications for initiation. The audience's first test was to bear witness to an actor's fortitude as he stands on stage in a military stance for a half-hour before the action of the play begins. There, in an undershirt and jeans, his long hair tied with a rubber band, this non-active actor is a study of concentration, a kind of abstract human still life. Apparently, he stands there to test his own and the audience's endurance. (An important trial for a Yogi or a Zen Buddhist is to stand staring at an object or at a wall as a means of developing concentration and calm in a hostile world.) But New York audiences wanted instant play, and the "hostile world" screamed: "Is this what you call the living theatre?" "I want my money back!" "Author, author!" Through it all, the man stands quietly—symbolic passive resistance.

The existential moment for the audience passes or, rather, never takes place; most members of the audience could not bear the thirty minutes of silence imposed by the actor. Stillness and silence, as an antidote to language—another Yoga and Zen characteristic, as well as a deliberate aesthetic then being developed by the avant-garde—were alien to the audience, and they were uncomfortable. The same uneasy shifty restlessness persisted once the stage was empty, and an Indian raga was heard in the darkness. "Non-action" is apparently unnerving.

The ritual of silence and staring done with, the cast dramatizes the "bad" life through a depiction of the military-based cash economy. Responding to the sharp, crisp military orders of a commanding officer, a group of actors jogs up the aisles from the audience onto the stage (recalling *The Brig*). Simultaneously, other actors, shouting the words that appear on dollar bills, also run up and down the aisles. A cacophony of noise rises to a crescendo of people buying and selling dollars, interrupted by military orders, foot drills, stamping, marching, and screaming: a marketplace for the dollar. Finally, a screech: "Yes, sir," and the scene ends. In counterpoint, an Indian raga is heard that signifies a moment of serenity as opposed to the hideousness of the marketplace scenes. Now the offering begins: a procession, carrying tiny incense lights, comes down the aisles and offers the lights to those who wish to be initiated into the Mystery cult. The moment of stillness is intense. Some in the audience are silently meditating, and there is a moment when emotions are inarticulate, but in the next sequence, speech becomes explicit. Julian Beck sits on the stage in a circle of light—a cross-legged guru. Beck gives the Word. "Live: the good life," he teaches. "Stop the War," he chants. "Ban the Bomb," "Free the Blacks," "Change Yourself," "Freedom Now." (These are excerpts from street songs by poet Jackson

MacLow.) Part of the audience joins in, repeating the chants; others are stunned or contemptuous.

The communal chants over, the actors and some members of the audience run up to the stage and form a circle. Their arms locked around each other, their eyes closed, and swaying gently back and forth, they begin a slow, melodious, symphonic humming based on the sound "mmm." It rises to a crescendo, subsides, and fades, leaving a sort of vibrating energy in the air. The initiated have found a connection, one that excludes the uninvolved. But the cult doesn't discriminate; to "join" means simply to make a decision. Remaining in one's seat signifies an unwillingness to become transformed.

When the communal connection is over (the offering having been taken, the Brahmin-guru, Julian Beck, having preached his exemplary actions, and the initiation rites finished), the Living then performs the life of the good cultists: Yoga exercises. Members of the cast, using streams of toilet paper, sit cross-legged on stage, and blow the polluted air out of their noses—the filthy and diseased air of capitalism. This scene exemplifies not only the actors' biological attempts at purity and cleanliness, but the Yogi's attempt to cleanse the Self, the first step to consciousness, for breathing correctly is the key to living correctly. Following are scenes dealing with the freedom, creativity, and humor that attends the Good life. In a series of various *tableaux vivants,* mostly comic—a high point of the group's self-expressiveness—the whole company creates a series of living statues. Later, three persons line up facing one another: one starts an improvised sound and body gesture, and moves to the center of the stage; another imitates him, and, halfway through, the second one invents his own sounds and gestures, which yet another picks up and repeats. The process continues until someone spontaneously ends it. The exercises are not only delightful examples of the liveliness that attend the "good," but the improvisation stresses the dialectical continuum in art: the link to the past is combined with the present to form a new synthesis.

The last part of *Mysteries* serves two purposes. If the first part is a metaphor for life, the last is a metaphor for death, and for Artaud's conception of the threatre as a plague. The whole company "dies" from the plague and is "buried" on the stage in a common pyre. When the lights go up, actors choke, spit, cough, vomit, scream, and writhe. Suddenly, there is a horrendous scream; an actor falls dead. Others also begin to die: they roll off the stage, drop in the aisles, gasp for breath, scream and wail, cackle their death rattles, and try to escape the final horror. Three are left alive to bury the others. Picking up the ruined bodies, they pile the corpses gently on top of each other for a mass burial. Some members of the audience cry, and others run up to the stage to comfort the dying, but some are unconvinced that anything "real" is happening. During a performance in Brussels, however, the late Saul Gottlieb reported in the *Tulane Drama Review* (Summer 1966) that "fifty people elected to die with the actors; in Vienna, the fire department rang down the curtain because twenty Viennese students had joined the dying; in Rome, there were fist fights between anti-Mysteries and pro-Mysteries." In New York, some of the young "died" too, but much of the audience remained perplexed and silent. People have compared the plague scene in *Mysteries* to Auschwitz, Hiroshima, Vietnam, and to the end of the world, but the plague is a warning: be good or die. It is also an enactment of Artaud's metaphor—the attempt to turn the theatre into a living microcosm of a plagued world.

If *Mysteries* was an evocation of Indian and Western morality, the Living Theatre's *Antigone* (Judith Malina's adaptation of Bertolt Brecht's version of Hölderlin's translation of Sophocles) was an attempt to combine morality with Artaudian theatricality, Brechtian dialectics, Greek classicism, and Living Theatre philosophy—a union some critics found inauthentic and incompatible. The Becks' aim was to uncover the ideas in the text, and to stage them in terms of their meaning for contemporaries. They never intended to reproduce an "authentic" Greek tragedy in *Antigone*, but to merge their own colloquial style with "classicism," and, in so doing, to comment ironically on those aspects of classicism that they believe are irrelevant and reactionary.

In *Antigone*, the actors work on a bare stage, wear their own everyday clothing, incant or intone dialogue, substitute a chorus of sounds rather than the traditional verbal recitations, use physical configurations based on grotesque paintings, and create a *mise-en-scène* with balletic movements and kinetic placements. That the acting styles clashed was almost to be expected, but one credits the attempt, as well as the results.

Judith Malina's interpretation of *Antigone* supposes that contemporary colloquial characters on stage are as interesting and noble as classical heroines, a concept that quite intentionally stripped the play of its traditional grandeur and challenged the value of classical tragedy. Comical and self-mocking, Malina's Antigone was an ordinary woman whose personal—as opposed to political—views demand that she bury her brother. Discarding traditional self-conscious heroics, she looked as if she belonged to no distinguishable class or to no particular era; in fact, Malina may have been acting out her own life. She wears her usual black slacks and black blouse; her hair is combed in her usual style; she speaks in her natural voice: a little bit of Yiddish inflection, a little bit of New Yorkese, a little bit of the trained actress. Three times removed from the original manuscript, twenty-five hundred years away from the original event, she accepts the situation as a contemporary reality, and asks the audience to do the same.

Mixing styles, however, presented a problem. The audience saw Judith Malina as supremely herself: small, angry, sad, charming, funny, ridiculous, and imaginative, always strong and certain. Deliberately rejecting the classics, she combined Brechtian techniques with elements of camp and Chinese fairy tale, adding her own individuality to denigrate Western traditional acting—especially the supposed "nobility" of tragedy. But the imprecise stylistic mixtures confused the critics, who did not understand Malina's intentions, and labeled her performance elementary and simplistic.

Classical acting was further denigrated by Julian Beck's Creon. His performance of the king was a paradigm of absurdity, an illustration of a pop cartoon, a melding of the ridiculous and the comically grotesque. Sometimes Beck incanted his lines like a rabbi, or parodied a southern Congressman; sometimes he imitated Lyndon Johnson (who was regarded as a war criminal by much of the Living's audience at the time), or stepped out of the character to narrate the tale. As Creon, he alternated between fear and cruelty, shrewdness and miscalculation, bravery and cowardliness. He gave orders to his henchmen, but feared them, too, and even as he kills Antigone he mourns her death. Contradictory and complicated, he's a man with a thousand faces—every tyrant that ever lived. The faces are changeable from moment to moment, like the rubber ones of a circus clown; sometimes a demonic smile appears on his lips, at other times, a half-insane silly smirk. Petulant, whining, autocratic and foolish, he is anything but graceful; his movements are large, clumsy, elephantine. Carried on the backs of a human pyramid, his hands licked by a sycophantic dog pack who crawl after him on their knees, Beck's Creon may be an ordinary fool, but he is wise enough to attain power, and to recognize when that power is threatened. Beck's portrayal is a reversal of the tradition that maintains that Creon's reign is justifiable except for the single flaw of his stubborness. Beck's Creon reigns, not out of special qualifications, but because he is banal, ordinary, and stupid; he has one quality, however, that supports power: ruthlessness.

An interesting aspect of *Antigone* is the Living Theatre's attitude to the audience, whom they viewed first as victims, and then as persecutors. As we come into the theatre, Creon stands with his henchmen; they peer out at us, nod in our direction and whisper, presumably about us. Intermittently other actors saunter out on stage. One of them regards us with suspicion, another with hostility, defiance, and arrogance. A girl in an Egyptian haircomb appears, wearing a purple satin blouse and black satin pants; a big, thick, round-buckled belt holds in her pelvis; she looks like a

Spanish apache dancer, ready to whip us. Another slinks onto the stage; she is a double for Dracula's wife: she is all in black—black sphinx-like hair, black, black eyebrows slanting upward toward the sky, layer upon layer of different colors on her eyelids. Sleek, shiny, sexy, and menacing, she glares at us.

And so they come on stage, each one more sinister than the last; each in his or her hippie outfit: colorful tops, jeans, beads, and hair—long, gleaming, short curly, thick, frizzled, rubberbanded, or scruffy hair. Their bodies, supple, sculptured, and thin, they form abstract patterns as they arrange themselves kinetically across the stage. They stand for many minutes, confronting us with their bodies, so different from our well-dressed, well-mannered, audience-behavior: we are their enemies; they are ours. We are being scrutinized, analyzed, categorized: our fate is being decided. Suddenly, the tension, which seems unbearable throughout the theatre, is broken by the actors' wails, screams, laments, and by the piercing sounds of sirens. The actors drop to their knees; some run out into the audience, threatening to kill us, first with their hands and then with imaginary knives, swords, guns, and scythes. On stage, a ritual murder begins: Creon emasculates the Elders; one by one he castrates them, unmistakably, repeatedly, as they fall to their knees, screaming with pain. The action is graphic. Meanwhile, the Chorus moans, screams, wails, hums, and groans, a non-verbal symphony that testifies to the agony of the Greeks. Some of the Elders and Chorus translate their thoughts into instantaneous action by creating physical configurations that resemble images from Bosch's *Descent Into Hell*, Goya's *Ravages of War*, Michelangelo's *Last Judgment*. Without using words, the actors turn the stage into pyramids of Hell. These are counterpoised by moving scenes in which Man comments on what he is, what he has become, and what he could have been. Action is suspended for a few instants and the actors, with upraised hands, proceed down the aisles of the theatre to form an architectural, cathedral-like pattern while intoning lines based on the Sophocles/Brecht wailing-wall dirge, *Hymn to Man*.

The poem evokes the Babylonian captivity as well as an instant recognition of the human condition—that, in spite of all man's knowledge, he has become his own enemy. For that instant, victim and victors realize their oneness, and weep. But only for an instant. Soon Antigone is put to death, and the Greeks celebrate with an orgy. This is a brilliantly conceived ritual, executed in time to the clicking of an actor's tongue and the slap of his hand on his thigh. The actors move in a pattern; they attempt to arouse each other by touching their own genitals; they smile, breath heavily, and groan orgiastically, but their fantasies are more promising than reality. Despite the fondling of their bodies, they provoke neither desire nor sensuality; instead, they invoke a death celebration, in which the participants' egotism is the focal point. In sharp contrast with the orgy, Antigone and her lover repeatedly execute powerful and stunning physical images (reminiscent of Picasso's *Guernica*) that dramatize the last moments of their agony and death. After the killings are over, the company take positions across the length of the stage, poised as if to attack the audience. As the group approaches the apron, they glare at us, and suddenly realize that the audience is also an enemy. Slowly they move backward and continue backing up against the wall, some cringing and crouching. Others stand horrified, as though they are about to be machine-gunned. One by one, the actors disappear. The stage becomes empty.

Antigone might have been the Living Theatre's masterpiece. Certainly it had the makings of a masterpiece. But a sloppy approach to aesthetics, typical of the Becks, remained a central problem. If the Becks had been more adept at synthesizing styles, or if they had rectified either badly trained or untrained voices in the company, the production might have been splendid. But the Living Theatre actors lacked plain audibility; they shouted raucously, garbled their words incoherently, or were otherwise difficult or impossible to understand; half the play was incomprehensible. Moreover, some members were permitted to "act" through "non-acting"—ostensibly to parody bourgeois standards of art.

But the Living Theatre's concept of *Antigone* was too sophisticated for crude anti-art techniques, which, in the first place, were inappropriate to the production's over-all design. The work demanded stylistic integration on a high level; the actors should have been *more*, not less, adept. Instead, each actor, trying to repudiate tradition, elected his or her own style, resulting in an amateurish mishmash.

In addition, the handling of dialogue became the Living Theatre's biggest problem. Essentially a non-verbal theatre, the company wanted to give a new sensibility and dimension to language by investing words with sound. But they repeatedly used meaningless incantation or word elongation without any discernible emotional base, so that much of the sound became noise: this contrivance reduced the language to political rhetoric, and thus the dialectic of the play was obscured. Nonetheless, the production was an achievement; it demonstrated that the avant-garde need not "burn" classical or traditional words, but that it was possible to combine new techniques with old masterpieces, provided the new techniques were worked out.

The Living Theatre's final production in New York, and the piece for which they received the most abuse, was *Paradise Now*—their "message to the world." *Paradise*, "a collective creation" by the company, is a long spectacle without a text or story line. It was designed in a non-linear pageant style to express a symbolic trip that lead to the supposedly paradisical state of anarchist revolution. Again, it reflected the influence of Artaud and the happenings, but it was also an attempt at reconciling Hebrew, Indian, and Western philosphies with New Left confrontation politics.

Artaud wrote a poem, "Umbilicus of Limbo," in which man takes an unknown trip to explore primitive existence. Full of rites of passage, initiations, and exorcisms, the journey enables man to expand his consciousness.[7] *Paradise* is a similar trip, except its goal is revolution, which also includes the effects of drugs. Long ago, Julian Beck wrote: "Who says we are mistreating the body with our drugs our opium our marijuana our lysergic acid psylocybin heroin cocaine peyote mescaline, mushrooms hashish kheef amphetamine. We are honoring it [our body] and its ability to change like the moon, like an embryo, like a poem, like a day, like a war."[8]

When asked by the editor of the *Tulane Drama Review* about his relationship to drugs, Beck said: "To the degree that drugs enable one to begin to associate differently in the head, remember differently, learn time differently—that is, for the brain to function on different wave-lengths, in different areas—[drugs] are extremely important for man's development." In the same interview, Judith Malina said that they "get high" when they have two shows to do and are very tired.[9]

Drugs as a means of expanding consciousness became, for the Living Theatre, an important factor in the revolution, and those who were part of the drug culture seemed to experience *Paradise Now* more vividly than those who were not. But since marijuana, LSD, and the rest are illegal, the Becks have avoided discussing this subject to any extent. Nonetheless, observing the performance of *Paradise Now*, it seemed apparent that many of the actors in the company, and many of the participants in the audience, were "high." The result was some unorthodox behavior. Rumors of urination, defecation, and even rape were never denied by the company.

It is important to recognize that the underlying aim of *Paradise Now* was to make a "revolution" on the stage, not to create a theatre piece. This goal coincided with the Becks' participation in the May–June events in 1968 when they, together with Jean-Jacques Lebel and others, took over the Odéon and, in an all-night session, conducted a "revolutionary forum." There, for twenty-four hours a day without sleep, young anarchists argued their positions. That there had been an actual uprising in the streets as a foundation for these talks, and that this forum had not been a rehearsed piece, but life itself, did not seem to deter the Becks. They were determined to use the same "revolutionary forum" as a basis for their play, *Paradise Now*.[10] (Incidentally, Erwin Piscator tried doing the same during the 1920's in Berlin, so the Becks' notion was not entirely without precedent.) In a 1968 letter discussing *Paradise Now*, Julian Beck wrote:

> . . . the subject [*Paradise Now*] is the revolution and the work of the play is not just to propagandize for the revolution, not just to assault the culture and spread the word, but to begin the work, to establish anarchist cells, . . . the cooperatives of free labor, the building of the substructure within the society that will, could, replace the one in which we are now deteriorating . . . if the play succeeds, it will start anarchist cells, potentially, wherever we play; we will enlarge the communications networks between workers, practical work, demonstrations; but more than that, the initiation of vanguard attack to weaken the structure of the society . . . if the play succeeds, it should stimulate the growth and development of newspapers, printing services, news services, green revolution cooperatives, handicraft cooperatives . . . [it will] hasten the steps for the non-violent revolution, the revolution that destroys the economy, that eschews the use of money, that starts the change. . . .[11]

How this was to be accomplished practically in the theatre remained a mystery that the Becks never quite elucidated. Perhaps a description of *Paradise Now* will speak for itself.[12]

Looking at the diagram given out at each performance, we noticed it is like a map that charts the rungs, rites of passage, and directions to Paradise. In reply perhaps to Frankenstein's question: "How to end human suffering?" Paradise is defined as the Permanent Revolution; Paradise is the reconstructed, unrepressed, Dionysian Man, Universal Love, the realized Self, the communal "we" in place of the "I"—a vision of Eden in which the Ego is transformed, and where man can recover his spontaneity and purity.

The "chart" is composed of eight rungs in vertical ascent: (1) the rung of good and evil; (2) the rung of prayer; (3) the rung of teaching; (4) the rung of the Way; (5) the rung of redemption; (6) the rung of love; (7) the rung of heaven and earth; and (8) the rung of God and Man. These eight rungs are ladders to the top, leading to the Permanent Revolution which will unite God and Man. The Permanent Revolution will result from a quantitative series of revolutions in culture, perception, sexuality, and so forth. The eight rungs are further divided into triads, consisting of (1) rites of passage; (2) a corresponding Vision; and (3) a corresponding current event or action. The rungs signify man's contradictions and conflicts: rigidity versus movement, inhibition versus enthusiasm, "hostility resulting from an unsatisfactory life" versus love, fear versus action. (See picture section.) The triads on the rung indicate the specific action along the way and determine the specific scenes to be enacted by both the company and the audience. Erasing all distinctions between actor and spectator, the company encourages the members of the audience to join the "trip"—to come up on the stage and perform. Many in the audience do. "Destroy the power of violence," "demonstrate in the streets," "form anarchist cells," "demand free theatre," are the company's direct exhortations, incitements, suggestions, and appeals to the audience "to act," "to become other than what you are," to execute a "revolutionary act in the theatre here and now." *Paradise Now* is not a play *about* revolutions or discussions about revolution, says Judith Malina, "it's a play that wants to make revolutionaries of people *on the spot.*"[13]

As we approach our seats, the house lights are on full blast; there is, of course, no curtain, and already dozens of hippie-looking kids are sitting on stage—eating, playing guitars, holding hands, necking, and throwing paper airplanes and balloons out into the audience. The theatre is sold out. Hardly so startling today as it was in 1968, word had gotten around that the show is played semi-nude. The audience is composed of all types—hippies, "squares," couples with babies, intellectuals, uptowners, downtowners, and very few blacks. Everyone is in a carnival mood; there is lots of expectation. Anxious to get a rise out of people, the kids on the stage shout to the audience: "You came here tonight to act, well, act!" The audience seems restless, tense. Clapping begins.

"On with the show," "Action, action," "Shut up, you mother," "Up yours!"

Then, out of nowhere, actors appear in the aisles—a long-haired girl in pink pajamas, another in orange and red pants, a third in purple, the boys in jeans, beads, colorful shirts. All of a sudden, someone has my ear and is kneeling close to me, looking me straight in the eye, and touching me. He issues forth a most plaintive whisper: "I'm not allowed to travel without a passport." Before I get a chance to reply to what seems to be a most personal agony, he is off whispering into another ear. I look around; I see spectators are being touched; the actors are speaking quietly, then imploringly. Soon the actors are angry, hostile, ferocious. Now they are all yelling the same slogans, and the noise reaches a crescendo of agonized fury. Suddenly, one gives out a piteous but horrendous orgasmic howl, which is echoed by the entire company: AAAAAAAAA-hhhhhhhhhhhhhh!!!!!! Silence. . . . The audience is startled out of its wits. "I don't know how to stop the war," "You can't live if you don't have money," are first whispered, then become part of the same rising crescendo and the same howl. I see Judith Malina in her black Antigone outfit—black pants and shirt—looking small, thin, haggard, and disheveled. Her eyeballs dilating, her jaw stiff and frozen, she has a wild, frenetic, "stoned" appearance. "I am not allowed to smoke marijuana," she screams over and over again. Suddenly she stops and bends low against the ear of a staid, middle-aged, respectably dressed matron seated on the aisle. Malina's intensity is nerve-shattering: enlarged eyes, hair flying, hands wildly gesturing, the veins in her neck protruding, she irrepressibly repeats the slogan until a state of unbearable tension has been reached. Yet she continues to scream: "I am not allowed to smoke marijuana!" Suddently the woman picks up her purse, as if to smash Malina's face. The face ducks, the hand is restrained; the woman tries again, her handbag flying in the air. The audience, meanwhile, has been watching this encounter, laughing nervously, some shouting approval, and others dismayed. "Let her have it!" "Stop it!" "Calm yourself." "Sit down." "On with the show!" "This is the show." "No violence!" "Call the police!" "Why hit Judith?" "She deserves it." "Control your violence." "Knock her teeth out." "She encouraged it." In the meantime, the woman's male companion has been calming her, and they exchange seats: the man moves to the aisle, and sits impassively. The audience senses the "scene" is over, and applauds; Malina moves quickly up the aisle, a slight smile on her face. The "real" action of the play continues, and other protestations follow, all accompanied by the same howl at the end of the line until they shout: "I am not allowed to take off my clothes," upon which the company actually does take off its clothes and stand semi-nude: the boys in their bare-behind loin cloths, the girls looking sexy or scrawny in tiny bikinis. The audience has now gotten the titillation it wanted. Some spectators follow suit and strip totally naked as a sign of solidarity. Actors and members of the audience now go to the open space on the stage for the first Yoga ritual: The trip to Paradise has begun.

The opening of *Paradise Now*, which has been played entirely in the aisles, is the prologue to the "trip." It explains in symbolistic terms the restrictions on money, travel, and communication and on sex, drugs, clothing, and sensual experience; it dramatizes the pain and suffering of having to live under such taboos. Nudity is the breaking of the first taboo—a prerequisite for the return of man to his original paradisical state. He cannot hope to re-enter Paradise with his civilized accouterments, the badge of his repression. Clothes are the first thing that God demanded of "sinful" Adam and Eve, and clothes therefore separate man from his Self and ultimately from others.

The house lights are now dimmed. Semi-naked and completely naked are all seated in a circle silently gesturing: it is the first part of the triad of the first rung, and the rites of the guerrilla theatre signify solidarity. The part of the audience which has remained in its seats can neither hear nor see, for the others who are now up on stage have completely encircled the company. The second part of the triad follows: it is an acrobatic pyramid constructed from the bodies of the Living, and it resembles an elephantine figure which illustrates the "vision of death and resurrection of the American Indian." Once the company builds the pyramid (which is stunning), it "dies," and, lying prone on the floor, is resurrected as a group of hippies; it is they who "plot" the "trip." Actors chant instructions to the audience to act: "Create the revolution," "Form Anarchist cells," "Be the leaders," "Be whatever the world is," "Enact the culture," "Be the students," "Be the workers, be the capitalists," "Change the system, change, change, change." They remind the audience that "eight million people in the city of New York are living in a state of emergency and need to be liberated." A heated discussion between audience and players follows. The pattern of *Paradise Now* is now clear. It consists of ritual enactments of political and social conflicts, glimpses of the future (Visions), and discursive confrontations between actors and audience. During the first rung, when the action turned out to be a discussion about the "emergency facing New York City," the actors "provoked" the audience to get an argument going: they harangue with slogans, insult with obscenities, shout, sweat, and spit, pile hostility upon hostility, and sometimes bring the audience to a fever pitch of excitement. People respond: they shout, get into arguments with their neighbors, walk out indignantly, spit in the actors' faces, demand their money back, bristle with hostility themselves, and generally behave like an incited mob. All kinds of incidents were possible when the Living Theatre played *Paradise*. For instance, at Yale one night, the SDS kids demanded that the Living Theatre live up to its promise to allow two hundred kids in the theatre free. The local fire department forbade it. The SDS people demanded a "confrontation." The discussion lasted for an hour, and it halted the play, but few realized that that *was* the play.[14]

One of the most "revolutionary" rites performed in *Paradise Now* is that of universal intercourse, commonly known as the "love pile," the "group grope," or the "gang-bang." By the time this scene takes place, the actors and the audience are virtually all on the stage. Everyone is now an actor. Those who have hated the show have left; those who like it are participating, and the others, perhaps neutral, stand around watching, gossiping, arguing, smoking pot, petting in the aisles, exchanging telephone numbers. Many go out for coffee, and some come back. As Richard Schechner has said in *TDR,* Spring 1969, "it's one long Yom Kippur service—whenever you return, the show is still going on." Actually, it is reminiscent of ancient Chinese theatre in which plays are all-night carnivals.

During the "love pile," everyone either gropes or watches. Actors and members of the audience turned actors throw themselves face down on the floor—literally into a pile—so that one doesn't know whose body one might be caressing. The whole point is that it doesn't seem to make any difference. What matters, according to one youthful writer, is the "existential moment":

> I accepted it when I found myself lying on the floor, down in the darkness with all these people, humming and oohing and oming, happily entangled, with some unseen stranger, gently stroking my thighs, and another unseen spectral wench running her fingers through my hair, buried, knotted in this shifting, heaving, humming mass, and I found a boob to fondle with one hand and a bare back to tickle with the other, and nobody knew whose was whose, but nobody cared, because it was all very tender, this anonymous, communal group-grope, and I realized that I'd blown my cool. I wasn't witnessing myself anymore, I was simply touching and being touched at random, and of course it crossed my mind . . . that the back [I was] tickling might be *a man*. But then that didn't matter either, and in fact, when the lights went on, it turned out to be a skinny Jewish kid of about seventeen. But as I say, I wasn't bothered. I was simply pleased to be *eased* into the flow of it all and it all came nat-u--rally.[15]

The rites continue half the night. Money is burned on stage, a trance is induced, an actress stoned on pot is massaged all over her body by three men, violence is presumably exorcised through the use of Tantric techniques, and Vison after Vision is enacted, until, three hours later, the final Vision: Man "flies." In this one, a group stands in the audience, waiting to catch the people who have lined up for the flying experience: "Breathe, breathe, breathe," yells the group. A youngster stretches his hands out as if to swim; he "flies" off the stage, into waiting arms. It's a moment of magic exhilaration for the "hip," a metaphor for Man's free spirit. The final Vision is the procession to the street, presumably to begin action there. Beck and those who are still left in the theatre take members of the audience on their shoulders, and in a spirit of victory and defiance lead them toward the streets, stopping at the lobby exit doors. "If I could turn you on," Beck chants from the now-famous R. D. Laing quotation, "If I could drive you out of your wretched mind. If I could tell you I would let you know. . . ." The "trip" to Paradise is over, and the show is officially finished. Julian Beck never goes into the street; he was forbidden to do so upon threat of arrest; instead, he quite calmly says goodnight to his friends at the threshold.

The debate around the Living Theatre, and, in particular, around *Paradise Now*, raged all that year. Thousands of words were written in attack and in defense. At Yale, the theatre magazine devoted its entire spring edition to stories, comments, critiques, and controversy about the Becks. Joseph Chaikin said: "I love them. In this time where people's attention is most concerned with the comparison of marginal differences, the Living Theatre makes a great explosion and forces its audience back to fundamental questions. At the same time, I'm not a loyal follower, because I think a lot of their cant is bullshit, but I know a lot of it to be the expression of deeply wise, alive, beautiful people."[16]

Anthony Scully said: "George Wallace is the logical successor to Julian Beck as head of the Living Theatre. Imbued with the same Old Testament, Plymouth Rock polarization of good and evil, the same self-righteous notion of his people as the chosen people ready to cleanse the earth with fire and sword, a pure tribe imprisoned in the fleshpots of Egypt. . . . If the distinction between the two is that Beck does not advocate bloody revolution or war, the simplistic ideological thinking process they share will soon, when necessary, erase that distinction."[17]

And George Gaynes said: "Altogether they are thought-provoking, just plain provoking, admirable, appalling, attractive, repulsive, masterful, inept—they are thesis and antithesis—light and dark—hope and despair—and for all I know: Yin *and* Yang."[18]

Whatever the consensus, the Living Theatre had made its mark. Its basic appeal was to the rebellious, alienated youth who dream of commune living, of Nirvana in place of a decadent society. For them, the Living represented a buffer against despair and loneliness, an alternative to the competitiveness and harshness of everyday life, an antidote to political corruption and a means of building a new culture in the middle of the old one. All of this was undoubtedly appealing, but the possibility of the tyranny of the commune was a harsh reality, and one that the Becks and their followers assiduously avoided discussing. The Becks could not refrain from their political self-righteousness and revolutionary saintliness. They had cultivated their positions as counterculture gurus, all the while developing their own tyrannical dogmas. In fact, the theatre became so cultist it eventually became detached from the radical mainstream. Still, such developments are not without tradition. Romantics of the eighteenth and nineteenth centuries also established their own cults: idiosyncratic behavior and manners, self-dramatization, and revolutionary fervor went hand in hand. Educated young rebels followed Jean-Jacques Rousseau's eccentricities in setting themselves apart from the bourgeosie.

True, the Living Theatre seemed a far cry from the nineteenth century; its style, jargon, and political rhetoric were part of the hip counterculture. Beads, beards and hair became their stamp. But underneath the modern rhetoric one detects a rehash of Romantic notions: the Living's eccentricity, as its members became actors in the Revolution (in and out the theatre); its defiance of institutions;[19] its role as artists-revolutionaries; its political martydom and its affinity for mysticism. In addition, the Living Theatre bore the mark of the Symbolists as well: Rimbaud's dreams of magic, Baudelaire's drugs and dandyism, and Mallarmé's ideas of ritual. This is not to say that the Becks were consciously aware of the Romantic tradition when they formulated their politics and created their pieces. The point is that the Romantics' reaction to the discontents of civilization was appearing in new form.

In *Frankenstein*, Man is turned into a repressed monster as payment for civilization; his Apollonian ego had created a world prison. The Becks' answer is to destroy the prison and re-create Man, but how Man was to flourish, unhampered by his driving ego and institutional life, was never raised. In *Paradise Now*, the Becks, influenced by Herbert Marcuse's *Eros and Civilization*, attempt to show Man's ego undergoing a "non-repressive sublimation,"[20] which presumably leads to a free society. In the process, Man supposedly loses his aggressions, and rigidity and replaces these by enthusiasm, energy, love, and revolutionary fervor. But what compels this ego-transformation? Education, class necessity, simple dissatisfaction with society? Is it logical to assume that knowledge and determination alone can result in ego-transformation, and hence in the creation of a non-violent revolution? The Becks' argument was eventually to become a sore point among the left. Most repudiated the ego-transformation theory as non-workable, and rejected the idea of non-violent revolution. The masses, whom the Becks saw as decisive factors in the revolution, depended upon the technological society for their livelihood and were not strong enough politically to overcome the power of the state. And would the ruling classes themselves become so transformed as to relinquish power peacefully, simply because it believes in the progress of mankind?[21] Or (following Godwin and Shelley) does the Living believe that all men, regardless of class, can eventually be influenced by reason and love, and that these alone can overcome evil and transform society? The Becks' arguments make freedom and change possible irrespective of class interests, historical developments, or continuing ego drives; they disregard the theory that violence is a function of state power and of those who support that power. A reading of history will show that when any state is threatened—be it socialist or capitalist—the power elite resort to repression and force. Unconcerned with what appears to be simple political theory, Judith Malina had this to say:

> Our aim is to change all hostile confrontations to loving ones, and at no point do we give up on the possibility of human beings to change. We believe in change because that's what revolutionary means. Revolutionary means to turn the wheel, and if it's a world full of anger, hatred, bitterness, hostility, and hunger, then it's for us to turn it to the other side. . . . What you call "enemies" are ultimately our friends. They might not, at this time, be aware that they're our friends. What we want to do is to make them aware. . . . All those over twenty-five have "enemies" but no one under twenty-five thinks in that direction any longer. Even the kids who are violent have a tremendous capacity for understanding the individual policeman who confronts them. At the moment one is in direct confrontation with the police there is no feeling of personal hostility . . . .[22]

One wonders if the young people who had their heads broken by the "pigs" at the Democratic Convention in Chicago in 1968 would agree.

Caught in the contradictions between romantic idealism, New Leftism, Indian mysticism, and the changing political temper of the times, the Becks emerged as a puzzling conglomerate. Their gestalt therapy techniques—based on eliciting hostility in order to convert it to love—didn't help either, but instead divided the audience between the violently opposed and the violently faithful. Neither side retained its calm, and talk of love was hypocritical; rational conversation was impossible in an atmosphere where people became locked into their positions. And neither the Becks nor their actors refrained from inciting: when they sensed that a member of the audience might be different from themselves, they crudely "assaulted" him, whispering, yelling, screaming, shouting, imploring, insulting. And so, like early fanatical Christians, they came to love the people—so long as they were Christians.

Actually the Living were best appreciated by audiences who were sympathetic to their methods, but sympathetic audiences made poor foils. When the young hip spectators did respond, they did so by yelling out banal repetitions and unoriginal expletives that vitiated the Becks' concept of spontaneity. Ironically, they ruined the show; participation was in danger of becoming a convention. On the other hand, when an audience's response was unrehearsed, it was for the most part hostile—which, for the Living's purposes, was good. But soon that hostility would develop into hatred, and the audience, rather than being converted to revolution, merely left the theatre irate. Hence, as therapeutic revolutionaries, the Becks brought out the worst in people: hostility and violence—dangerous emotions for a radical movement.

Audience confrontations were not taken very seriously by the serious revolutionaries in the audience, because the confrontations were considered theatrical devices, disguised as political debates to create and release tension, rather than ideas. For example, when asked why his company avoided larger issues, like American imperialism, Beck said that his actors were more interested in the "here and the now." Such a reply was not only suspect, but an implicit acknowledgment of the company's limitations as political propagandists. Who were the Living Theatre recruiting for the revolution—those already committed, or the marginal liberals whom they professed to love, but, in practice, treated with contempt. In the confusion, the Becks alienated some of the youth as well. One young man during the performance of *Paradise Now* said: "How can you think this is important? All of you sit around and joke, and people are dying in Vietnam. They put caskets back, and you sit here and take off your goddamn clothes and you think it's goddamn funny. And that's all you can say about the goddamn war. Well, take off your goddamn clothes, all of you."[23]

The Becks and their followers certainly do think what they do is important. They believe that reducing aggression in even one person is worth the enormous effort it may take. Such beliefs testified to their self-appointed roles as therapists as well as artists, but actually the Becks' artistic concepts could be understood only by the sophisticated, since so many of the allusions and metaphors in their work depended upon the occult and the esoteric. In fact, the masses, having already become alienated from left-wing artists because of differences in life styles, never even attended the Living Theatre's performances. In Avignon, in 1968, for example, when the Living Theatre was faced with a police bust, the workers had remained indifferent. During a local rally, they were content to lean out their windows and stare at the long-haired "odd-balls."

In Berkeley, California, the Living Theatre had similar experiences. There, the real struggle was not on the stage, but in the streets. The students had demonstrated their belief that their own fight under the pain of gas and police clubs were the bitter reality—and what the Becks were advocating was naïve illusion. Telling the students how to make the revolution from the comforts of the stage was for the Berkeley students simply ridiculous. In California, the Living Theatre suffered its worst defeat. By the time the Company had reached the West Coast they were not only worn out, broke, and their tour hopelessly mismanaged by friends and foes, but some members of the troupe had come to realize that the discrepancy between the Living Theatre's public ideology and private life could no longer be tolerated. There were arguments, bickerings, and real economic threat; in fact, the Living Theatre in California apparently almost starved to death.[24] No longer a real commune, but a frustrated freaked-out company of actors, they had to stay together to survive. They returned to New York to play for another three weeks, but it was the beginning of the end.

On January 11, 1970, at the *Akademie der Künste* in West Berlin, the Living Theatre, after touring Europe on their return from America, gave its usual performance of *Paradise Now*. It was the last evening of its engagement. On the surface, nothing had changed; the Becks and company had played with their customary intensity, and the Berliners had responded with the customary mixture of rejection and admiration. But backstage, it was another story. Actors who had lived and played together for six years were saying their last farewells, preparing to go their own ways: the Living Theatre and its legend were over.

Months before, as a result of stormy sessions in America and in Morocco, and quiet discussions in Sicily, a decision had been reached: the Living Theatre would split into "cells," and this January evening in Berlin was to be their last stop together. Judith Malina and Julian Beck were to go to Paris, and a group of ten planned to return to America; in Berlin were Steven Ben Israel and Henry Howard, with nine others who expected to remain in Europe; in London, Rufus Collins (with a smaller group) expected to leave for India. A few had left the company entirely.

When news of the Living Theatre's split reached the artistic community of Europe, rumors ran high. Many felt that the Becks had been dethroned by their own company; some felt that *Paradise Now* had exhausted the troupe's creativity. Others maintained that a huge commune of forty-five theatrical personalities with divergent political views, facing financial hardship and nomad existences, inevitably had to fail. Julian Beck insisted that the break was not a break, but an "extension of the logical outcome of what we had been doing for twenty years." For him, a state of emergency existed and, "For the sake of mobility, the Living Theatre is dividing into cells as part of a plan to attack the entire structure from many sides. . . ." He complained that "the press (and others) had automatically interpreted our new move as a sign of our disintegration arising from dissension and conflict instead of an expansion based on what we have learned together through the years. We have found in the past great joys, great pleasures, and we have learned to tune in to our weaknesses, too. And this has given us the strength and knowledge to do what we are doing now."[25] Despite Beck's claims, the severe political and artistic schisms developed over the years made it evident to the entire Living Theatre that its differences could not be resolved. They had had too many bitter experiences. In Morocco they were attacked, beaten, and ostracized for their long hair and hippie appearances; during previous engagements in France, they had had bouts with the French radicals who attempted to shut them down when they played the Maisons de la Culture (state-controlled theatres set up by Malraux, representing the de Gaulle government), and their American experiences were still fresh in their minds. All over Europe, touring conditions had become worse; housing was unsanitary; money was low, and their position among radicals who, unlike the Living Theatre, had moved away from non-violence, was considerably weakened.

In the United States the company had faced its severest crises. Surrounded by the tremendous barrage of publicity and controversy that the Living's appearances had always encouraged, it became clear that "we had become institutionalized," said Julian Beck, "and were trapped by the establishment and dependent upon it for support . . . we were simply selling ourselves and our ideas to the ticket-paying public and we could no longer go on in this manner." Moreover, the Living Theatre began to feel uneasy with its non-violent stance in light of the brutalities of the 1968 Chicago Democratic convention and the violence against students, black and white, that marked the end of the sixties. Radicals continually upbraided them for clinging to their old position in the face of these realities.

Many of these problems were reflected in *Paradise Now.* Schematically brilliant, it failed to radicalize the audiences. It advocated taking over the theatre building, removing authority figures, forming anarchist cells, changing aesthetic values, and abolishing personal repressions—changing one's self. Yet the Living remained unchanged, in that the members still suffered from the same personal hangups as everyone else, and were tied to the system by being dependent upon commercial bookings in commercial houses.

In the course of playing, the company began to question other premises. They could not resolve their "anti-art" aesthetics. Could one perform a play in a theatre and pretend it was an anti-play, and not being performed in a theatre with seats; could one invite audiences to respond to harangues, and insult those that did; could one proselytize for free theatre and then charge admission; could revolutionary theatre raise the slogan "the streets belong to the people" and then, upon pain of arrest, take the audience only as far as the lobby; could a company exist with multi-political views and present to the public one united position; could one mix a theatrical event (formal production) with the real event (the activities of the audience) and maintain that real events on stage—rape, fornication, urination, and defecation—were artistically valid and beautiful?

A number of the members recognized the weakness of *Paradise Now* but the company had no time in America to discuss art and politics at length, though they were to analyze them only later, under the impact of their cool receptions in America and Europe. By that time, the Becks were particularly upset by the French radicals' criticism of the Living Theatre. Julian Beck, a long-time believer in non-violence, could not go along with the growing trend toward violent revolutionary action. He and Judith Malina clung to their beliefs, but they and the company's work had somehow fallen out of date. Their old productions, *Frankenstein* and *Mysteries,* seemed increasingly less relevant. In fact, their whole philosophical and aesthetic approach was in question.

The company wondered if it should take a completely new direction. If political questions could be resolved, how could the answers be translated into artistic form? Did all the members share in the commitment to revolution, violent or non-violent? Could a commune of forty-five persons, including babies, survive the rigors of constant traveling, performing, and self-evaluation? Could the company continue to play commercial engagements and be revolutionary? These and other problems that were raised by *Paradise Now* were discussed in long sessions that revealed irreconcilable differences. Members struggled with their political and artistic inclinations as well as with their egos. The decision to split from the "family" was not without tensions and outbursts: to take a simple, clearly defined position was difficult. Everything was a combination of the personal and the private, the political and the artistic, the emotional and the rational. Above all, choices were painful.

The Becks felt "if we were to find a means of surviving without money [the commercial audience] then it was necessary for us to live like a guerrilla band and that meant that we would have to limit the number of people in that band. A small group could find ways of getting by, of making do, of surviving." Others felt that they should all return to their roots again. Older members of the theatre wanted to strike out on their own. "It became clear to us," said Julian Beck "that we were each yearning for heightened autonomy. And within the old structure functioning as it always had under the administration of Judith and myself, there was automatically a limitation on each of the members of the company; by dividing into cells, it was possible for each cell to be autonomous and grow up without the domination of a matriarch and patriarch . . . the idea of leadership had to be eradicated."

The Becks had a plan. With fewer mouths to feed, they could limit their commercial engagements (or not accept any) and be free to do what they consider their real work: direct political action. The concept of actors as activists, as a means to radicalize audiences, is nothing new for the Becks—theatre as politics has always been their goal—but apparently they were now prepared to emulate the techniques of the most radical theatre groups in America and Europe. They planned to create "scenes" in the midst of real life—what is commonly called guerrilla theatre. In this context—the fusion of art and life—aspects of the 1968 Chicago convention, the Paris uprisings, the Chicago trials, the student sit-ins, the slogans, placards, costumes of the radicals, may be considered theatre, and its participants, actors.

Uncertain what exact form guerrilla activities would take (by definition the form must be somewhat uncertain), the Becks intended to play in factories, parks, subways, and "close to the means of production." They preferred places of unlimited space and flexible seating, and they planned carefully to avoid conventional theatre houses: "Buildings called theatres are an architectural trap," said Julian Beck, "The man in the street will never enter such a building. One, because he can't afford to, because the theatre buildings are property held by the establishment by force of arms. Two, because the life he leads at work and out of work exhausts him, and three, because inside they speak in a code of things which are neither interesting to him nor in his interest. The Living Theatre doesn't want to perform for the privileged elite anymore because all privilege is violence to the underprivileged." By assessing the composition of the audience, the Becks hoped to make their work pertinent to its specific needs. Clearly, working-class communities, college campuses, and black ghettos would require different pieces, so that the new Living Theatre intended to have in its repertory short works: enactments of strikes, or sit-ins, or "action" that the actors impose upon the life of a community. For instance, such an action might consist of simply driving people to work in order to engage them in face-to-face discussion on politics; it might be confronting people in parks, restaurants, or streets and creating a situation that will dramatize political realities. These may be planned out, rehearsed, or improvised—the important thing is that they be designed to produce a certain effect. As Julian Beck put it: "We want to create circumstances that will lead to action, which is the highest form of theatre we know."

The breakup (or expansion) of the Living Theatre was part of a process in which all radical theatre groups were involved in 1970–71: to determine how to function as revolutionary artists, radicalize audiences, and still survive. With these new changes, the Becks have swung full circle, in one sense, and moved forward, in another. More than twenty years ago, they founded their own theatre rather than exist in the established one. Now they claim to have changed their form once again. Whether these plans will eventually affect the theatre world is uncertain, though if one is to judge from the past, the new Living Theatre will no doubt have reverberations. One feels sure they will survive. As Judith Malina said at the time of the breakup of the group; "We don't precisely know what our next moves are, but if we can't solve our problems, we will fall back on that beautiful slogan of the French revolutionary students, 'Imagination Takes Power.'"

Despite all its weaknesses, the Living Theatre were originals—in fact, a metaphor for its times. Not only were its politics and techniques a sharp influence on experimentalists all over the world, but wherever it played, its effect was electric. It released vectors of energy and generated excitement and agitation. Even its threats of violence created a theatrical tension that was intriguing. Robert Brustein was right when he called the Living a cathartic theatre in the Wagnerian sense, for it had co-opted nineteenth-century *Sturm und Drang* to dramatize the political and social issues of our times. That its stance was more or less politically rigid may be less important than that its break with traditional naturalism brought into the theatre young and vital audiences. For the young saw the Living Theatre actors as symbols of an exotic mystique and participants in the shaping of history. With their weird hippie dress, exaggerated hair styles, and crude casual selves (accepted as fashionable now, but considered quite outrageous at the time), the actors were walking advertisements for the counterculture movement, representatives of the here and the now. They symbolized youth's vision of the "good life," regardless of its romance and myths. Most of all, the actors presented an anti-literary, surrealistic theatre picture in which they themselves were the *mise-en-scène*.

The most successful aspects of their work were their Artaudian images: their strange, grotesque, bloodcurdling hells; their vertical pyramids and towers; their geometrically placed bodies and kinetic consciousness; their walking monsters and wailing humans; their supple bodies; sometimes like mobile sculpture and sometimes like still life—these were all beautiful. Even their moments of repose, and their experiments with ritual time, rather than stage time, made for a kind of penetrating beauty; a serenity in which one could evaluate one's inner experience precisely at the moment of theatrical action. Their repose, although infrequent, dramatized an enviable quietude when spirit and body are at the "still point." And this stillness has its own force. It afforded an opportunity to concentrate on the details of an actor's face, hand, and body as things in themselves—in relation to time, movement, space, and shape, and looking in this sense became a special pleasurable experience. Especially compelling was the actors' urgency, the sense of inner commitment that they communicated the moment they came on stage; it gave their work an intense feeling of life lived in its most existential terms.

The Living Theatre represented the most radical goals in the theatre of its time, both politically and aesthetically. They declared that a theatre performance in a proscenium theatre with the audience sitting out front passively watching was an outmoded trap, that theatre as illusion had become part of the despised bourgeois culture, and needed to be revolutionized. Further, the Living saw its duty to art as establishing new perceptions and new standards. In commenting on this, Marcuse understood the need of groups like the Living Theatre for a new aesthetic, and summed up the anti-art argument given in Germany after World War I (an argument Marcuse himself did not accept).

> Aesthetic needs have their own social content: they are the claims of the human organism, mind and body, for a dimension of fulfillment which can be created only in the struggle against the institutions which, by their very functioning, deny and violate these claims. . . . Today's rebels want to see, hear, feel new things in a new way: they link liberation with the dissolution of ordinary and orderly perception. . . . the revolution must . . . be a revolution in perception which will accompany the material and intellectual reconstruction of society, creating the new aesthetic environment. . . . Art must no longer be illusory because its relation to reality has changed. . . . The revolutions and the defeated and betrayed revolutions which occurred in the wake of the war denounced a reality which had made art an illusion, and inasmuch as art has been an illusion, the new art proclaims itself as anti-art. . . .[26]

The anti-art theory (revived once again) presented the Living Theatre and the entire counterculture with a real problem: was it desirable to fuse the theatrical act, based on illusion, with the real, living event, or was the illusion itself to be totally abolished? Or, to put it another way, is all life theatre? The answers were explicitly given by the Living Theatre. It remained for others to challenge or take up the cause.

LUNATICS, LOVERS AND POETS

The contemporary experimental theatre

THE LIVING THEATRE

FRANKENSTEIN

Act I— The Monster Is Created

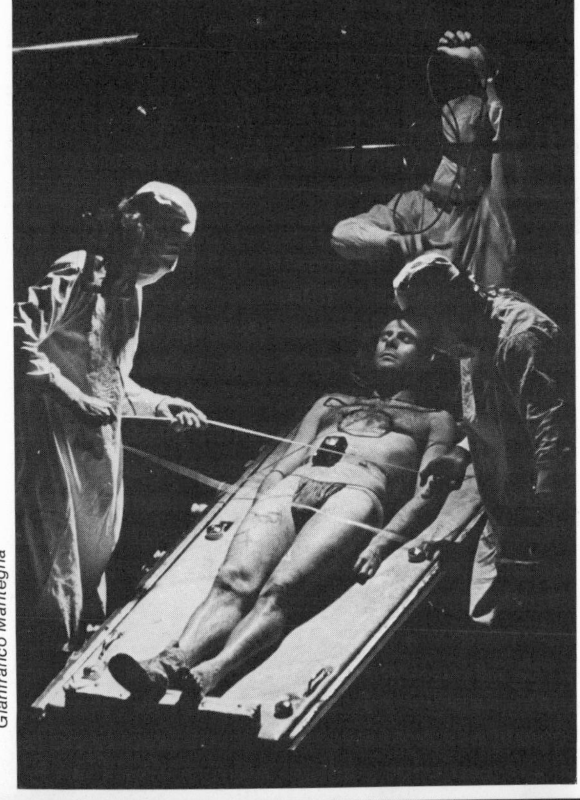

Gianfranco Mantegna

Act II— The Head Comes Alive

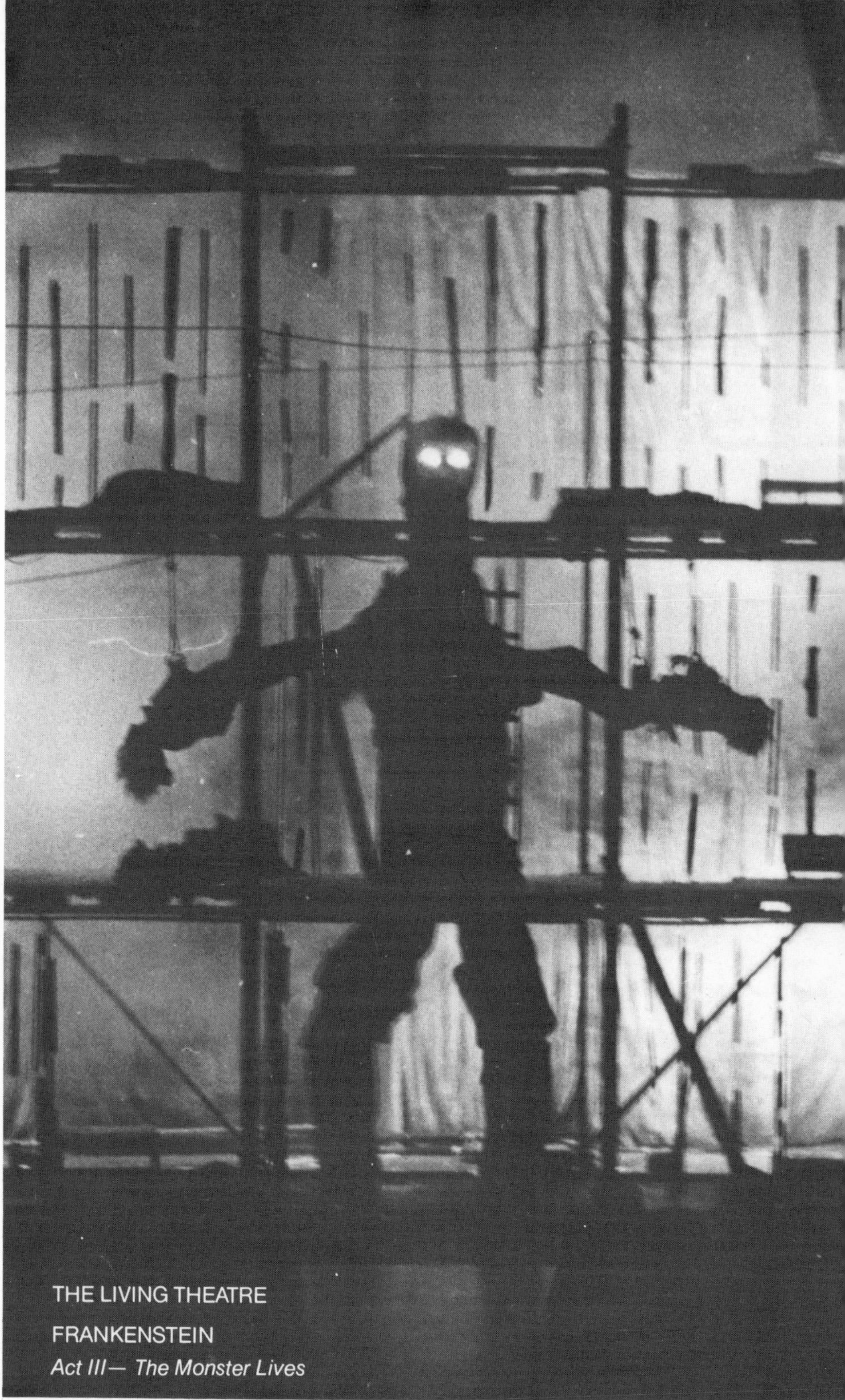

THE LIVING THEATRE

FRANKENSTEIN

Act III— The Monster Lives

Carlo Silvestro

THE LIVING THEATRE

Mysteries and Smaller Pieces

Gianfranco Mantegna

Gianfranco Mantegna

THE LIVING THEATRE

ANTIGONE

Judith Malina and Julian Beck

Gianfranco Mantegna

Gianfranco Mantegna

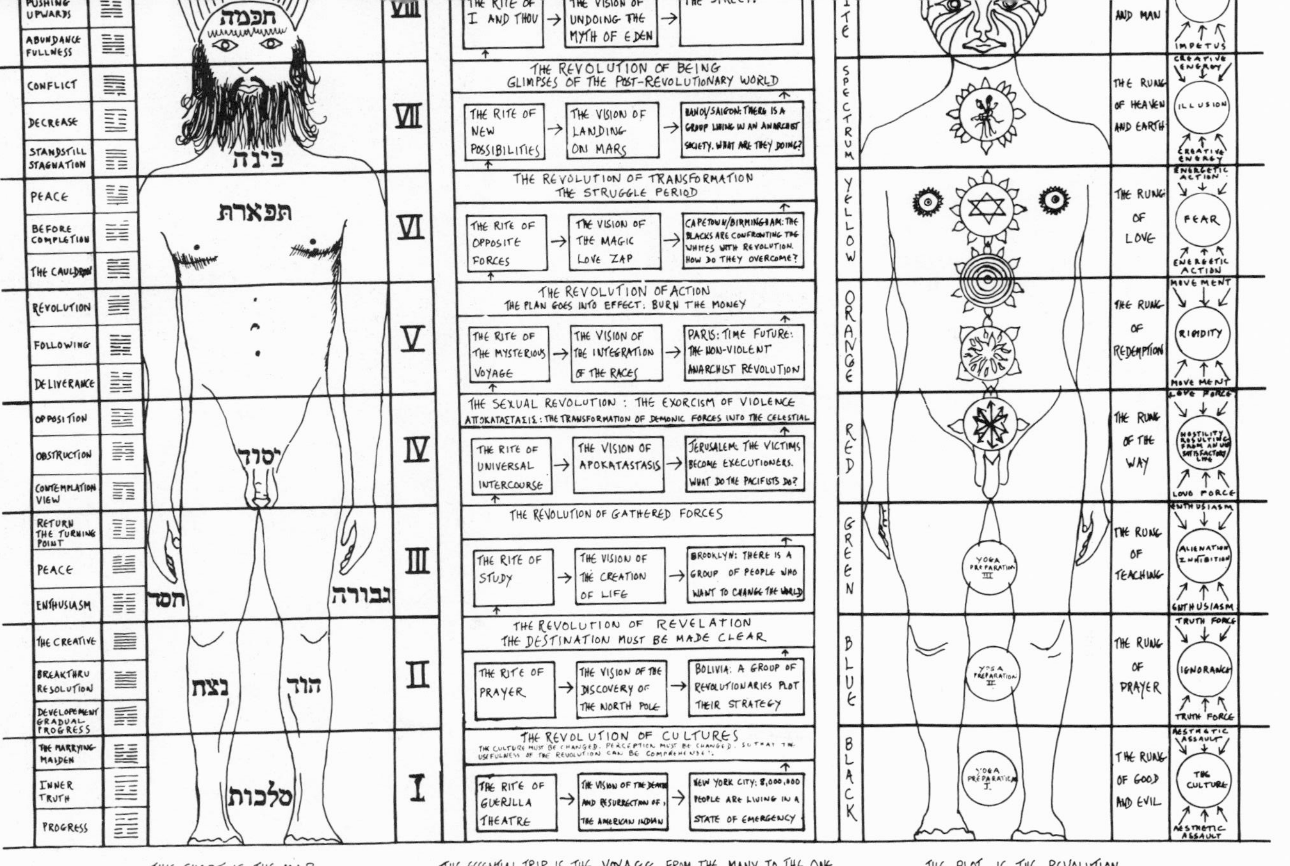

THIS CHART IS THE MAP — THE ESSENTIAL TRIP IS THE VOYAGE FROM THE MANY TO THE ONE — THE PLOT IS THE REVOLUTION

THE LIVING THEATRE — PARADISE NOW — COLLECTIVE CREATION

PARADISE NOW

The Vision of the Death and Resurrection of the American Indian

Gianfranco Mantegna

The Rite of Universal Intercourse

Gianfranco Mantegna

Max Waldman

Ryszard Cieslak in Jerzy Grotowski's The Constant Prince

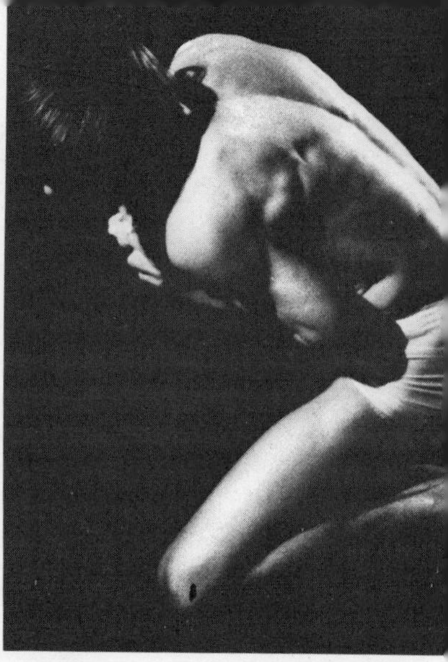

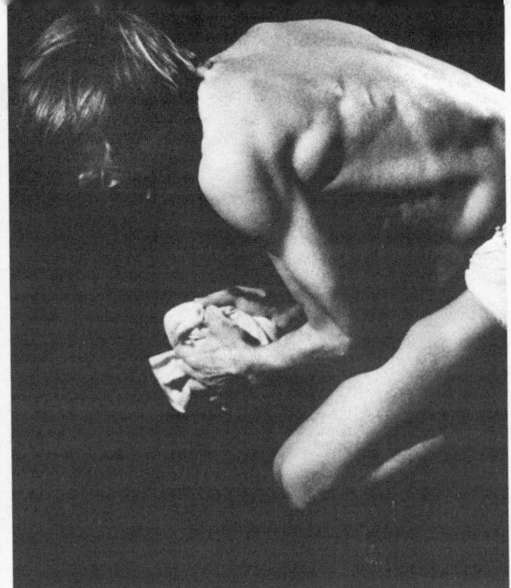

Ryszard Cieslak in The Constant Prince

all photos by Max Waldman

Teatr-Laboratorium

The Prisoners Think They See the Saviour, It Is a Headless Doll

SCENES FROM GROTOWSKI'S AKROPOLIS

Ryszard Cieslak and Rena Mirecka

Douglas Jeffrey

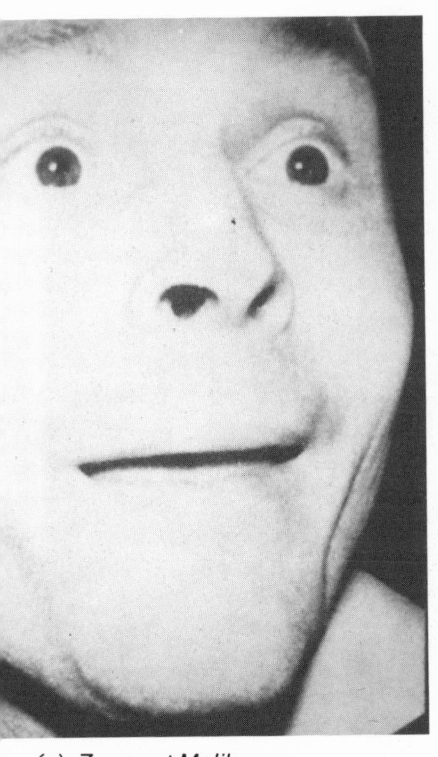

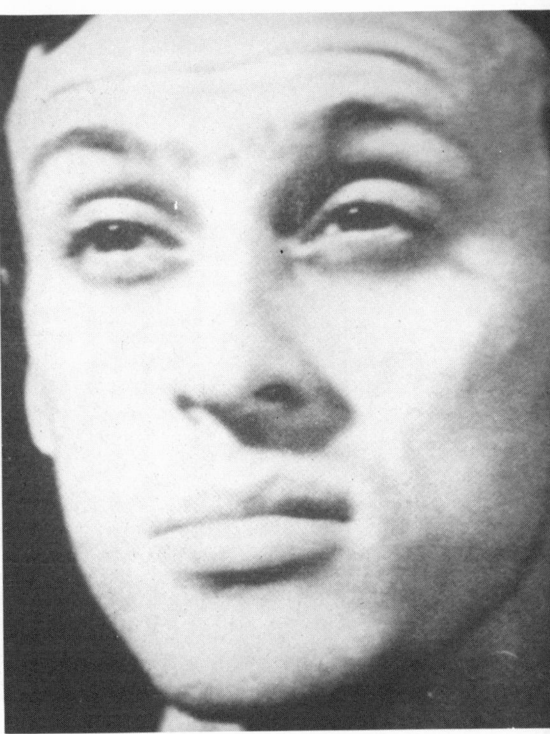

(a) Zygmunt Molik

(b) Zbigniew Cynkutis

ACTORS IN AKROPOLIS *CREATE MASKS FROM THEIR FACIAL MUSCLES*

(c) Zbigniew Cynkutis

(d) Rena Mirecka

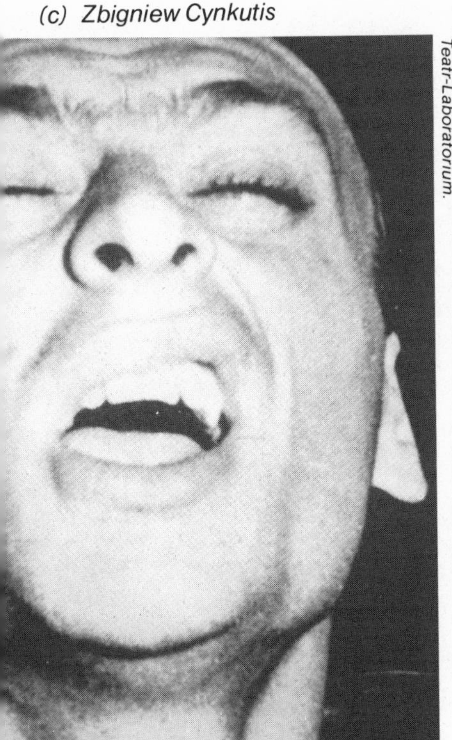

Teatr-Laboratorium.

Karl Bissinger

The Kennedy Assassination

THE OPEN THEATRE IN THE SERPENT

The Company Creating The Serpent

Karl Bissir

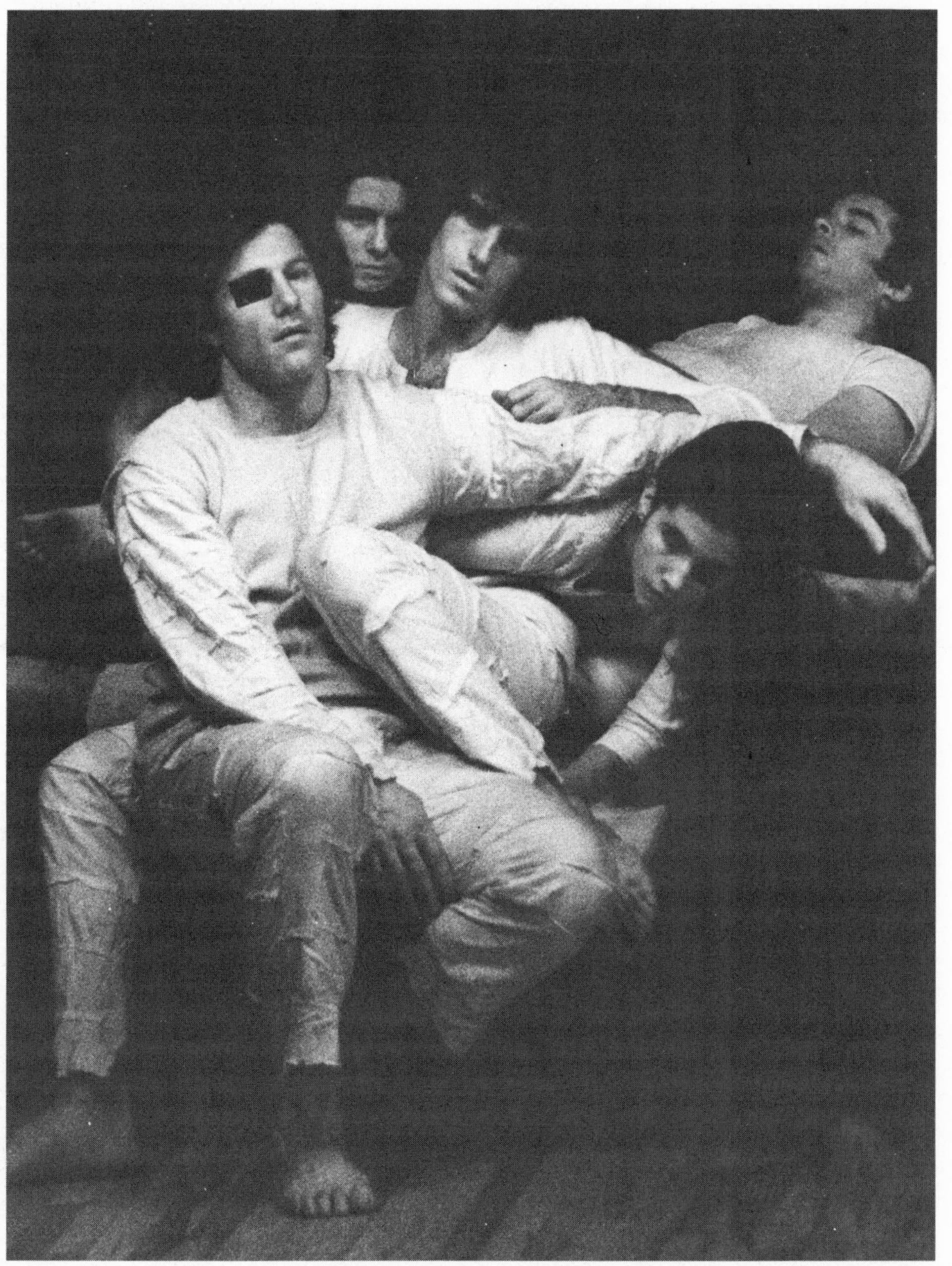

Max Waldman

THE OPEN THEATRE IN TERMINAL

Max Waldm

THE OPEN THEATRE IN TERMINAL

Max Waldm

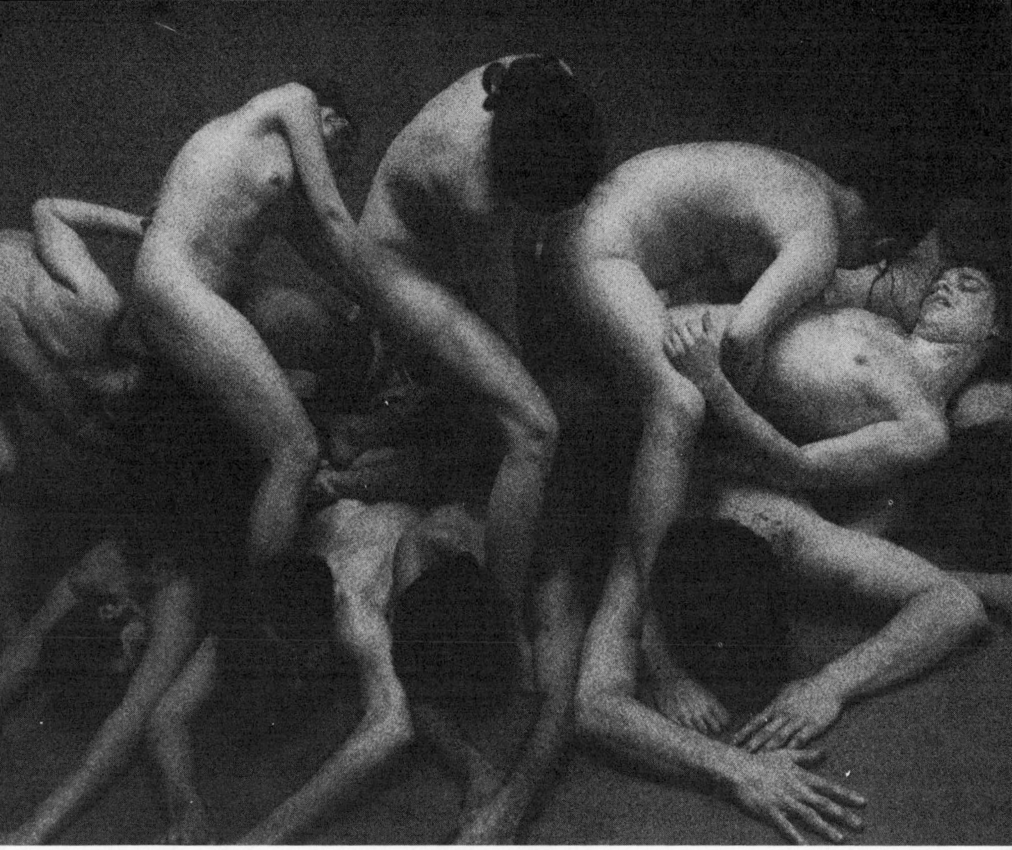

The Birth Ritual *Max Waldman*

THE PERFORMANCE GROUP IN DIONYSUS IN '69

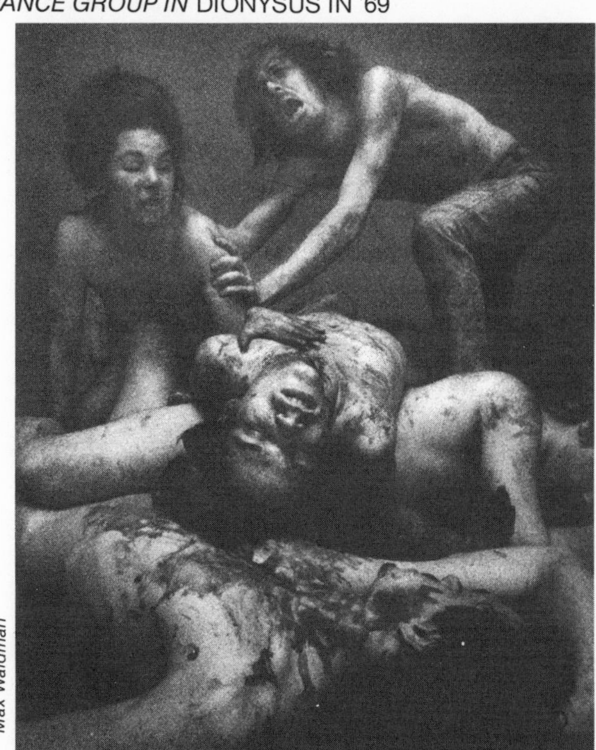

The Death Ritual

Max Waldman

Réanne Rubenstein

The Environmental for Dionysus in '69, *designed by Michael Kirby and Jerry Rojo*

The Environmental for Andre Gregory's Alice in Wonderland *designed by Eugene Lee*

John Chim

Amnon Ben Nomis

John Vacarro's Playhouse of the Ridiculous in the MAGIC SHOW OF DR. MAJICO

Charles Ludlam and the Ridiculous Company in Bluebeard

Max Waldman

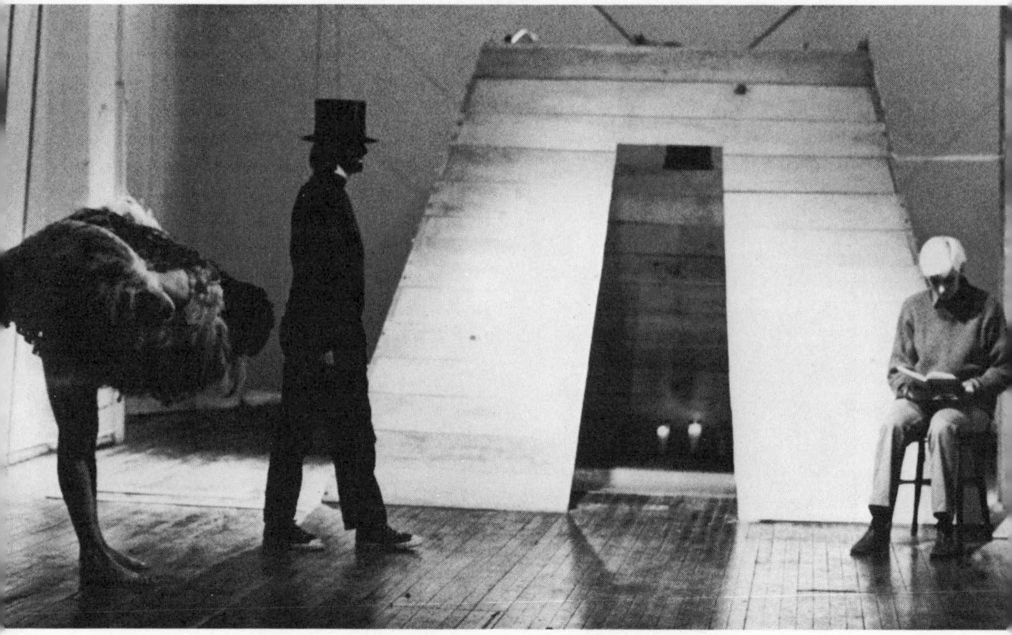

Robert Wilson's Overture to Ka Mountain

Kazuko Osh

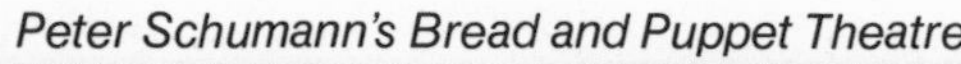

Peter Schumann's Bread and Puppet Theatre

Mason Singer

Max Waldman

PETER BROOK'S MARAT/SADE
Ian Richardson as Marat

MARAT/SADE

Glenda Jackson and Patrick McGee as Charlotte Corday and De Sade

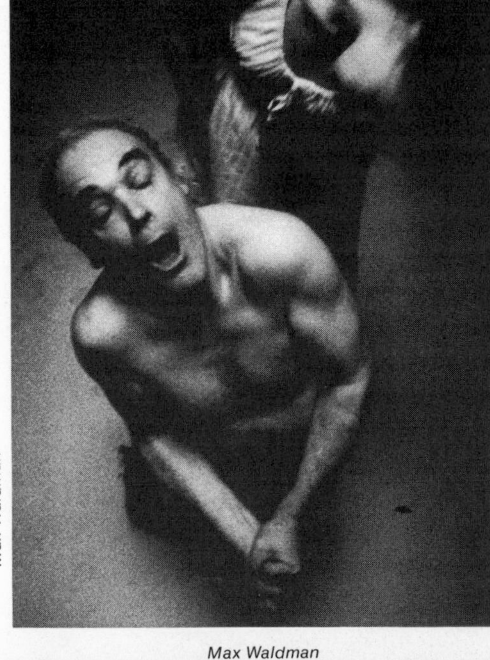

Max Waldman

Charlotte Corday Subdued by the Nuns

Max Waldman

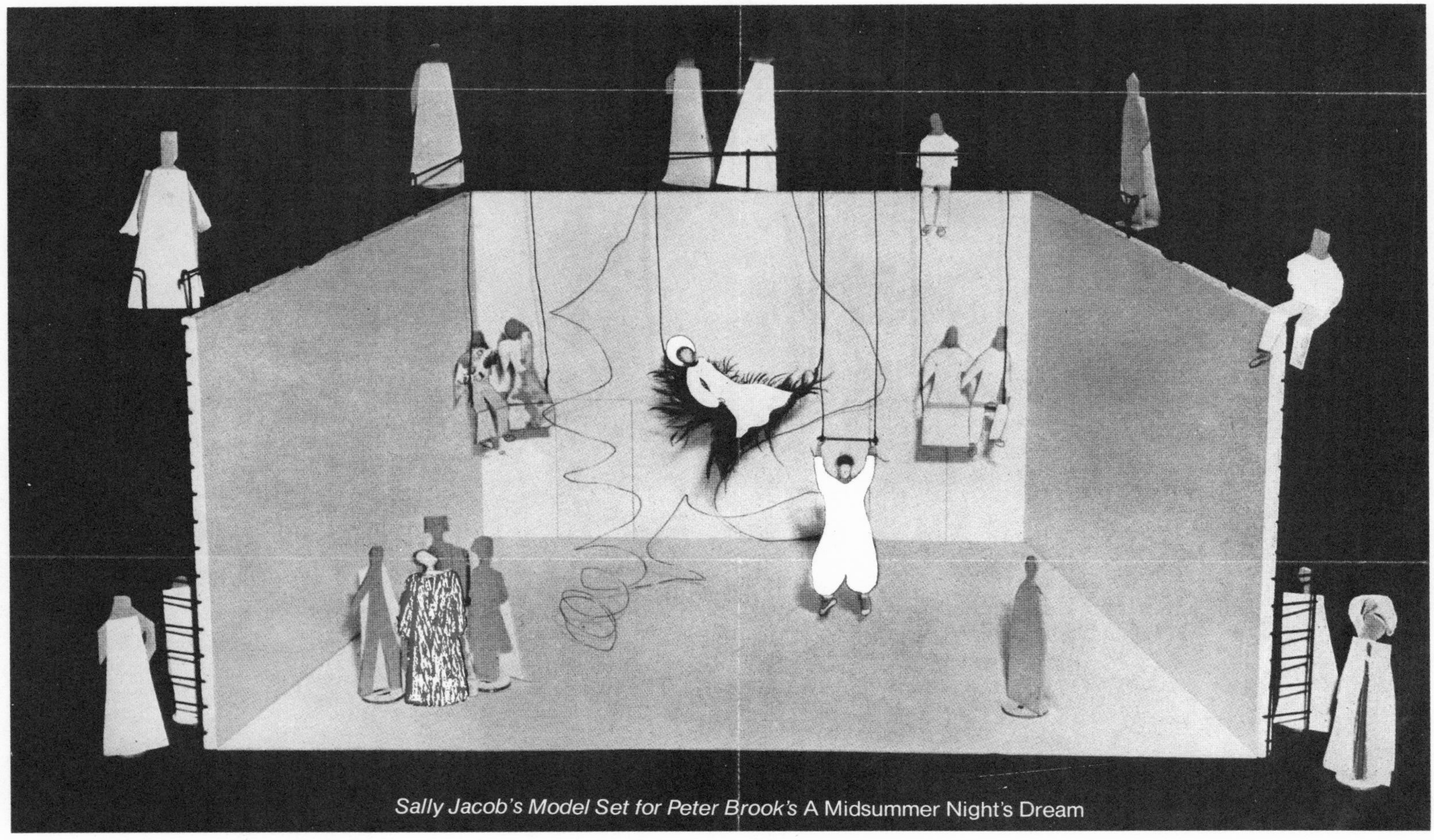

Sally Jacob's Model Set for Peter Brook's A Midsummer Night's Dream

Royal Shakespeare Company, Aldwych Theatre

David Farrell

Titania and the Fairies (Sara Kestelman)

PETER BROOK'S A MIDSUMMER NIGHT'S DREAM

Bottom and the Fairies (David Waller)

David Farrell

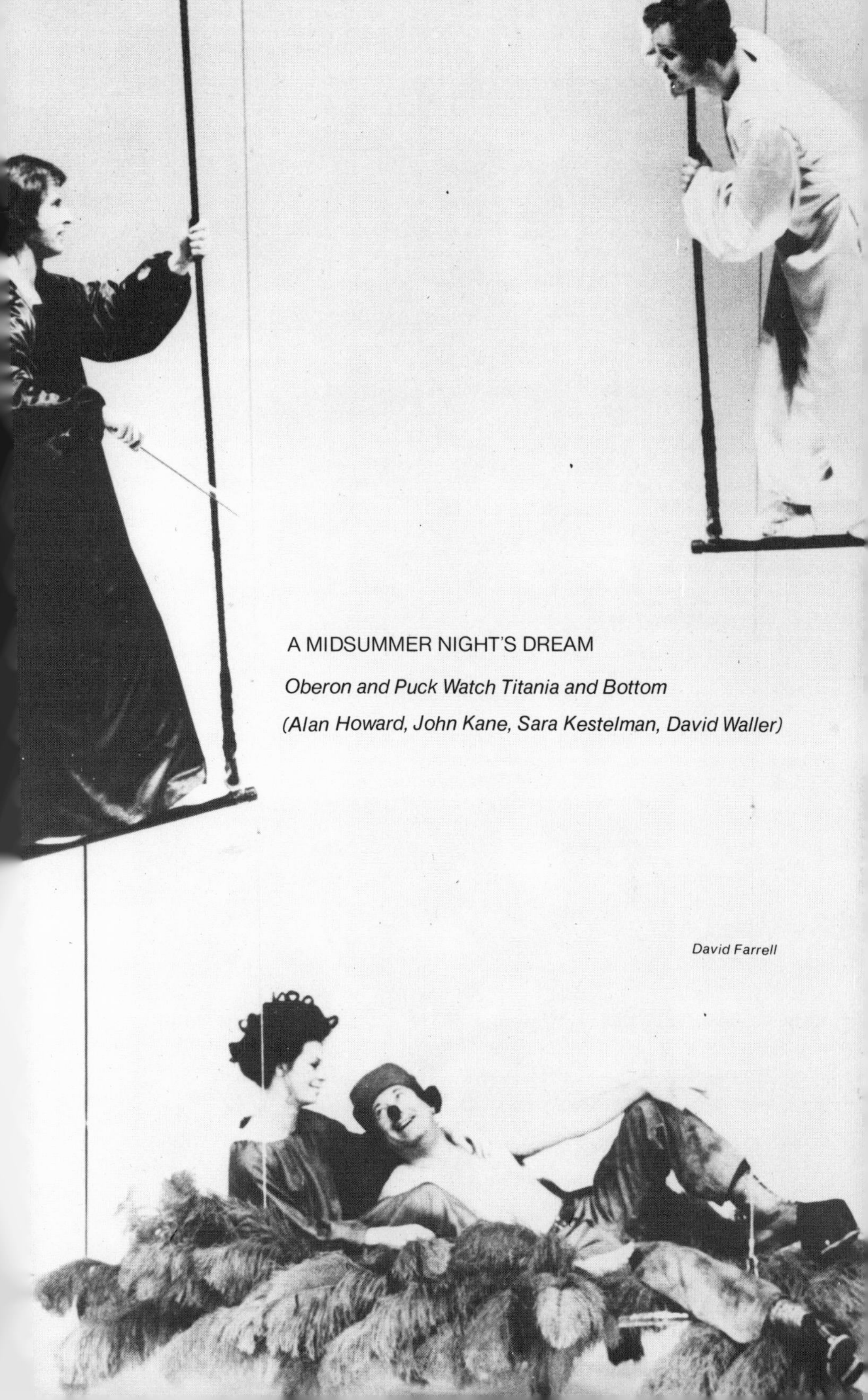

A MIDSUMMER NIGHT'S DREAM

Oberon and Puck Watch Titania and Bottom

(Alan Howard, John Kane, Sara Kestelman, David Waller)

David Farrell

The 'stage' on Top of the Mountain in Persepolis, Iran Nicolas Tikhomiro

SCENES FROM PETER BROOK'S ORGHAST *PART I*

Lou Zeldis and Katsuhiro Oida

Nicolas Tikhomiroff

ORGHAST *PART II*

Midnight in the Hills of Nasque Rostam, Iran

Nicolas Tikhomiroff

Nicolas Tikhomiroff

Dawn

ORGHAST *PART II*

Dusk

Nicolas Tikhomiroff

Nicolas Tikhomiroff

ORGHAST *PART II*

In the Ruins of an Old Fire Temple

David Hays

Peter Brook and his International Actors with the Theatre of the Deaf: A Workshop in Paris, 1972.

seven

The Phenomenon of Jerzy Grotowski

"Show Me Your Man and I Will Show You Your God."

Grotowski

In 1959, while Kaprow was experimenting with his happenings and the Living Theatre was still working in New York, in a provincial town in Poland just eighty miles from Auschwitz, eight unknown actors and a twenty-six-year-old director banded together to form a company destined to revolutionize theatre concepts in the Western world in a direction quite opposite from that of the Living Theatre. This "laboratory theatre" was intent not only on searching for answers to contemporary problems by confronting the past with the actors' own experiences, but on experimenting with a new aesthetic. More than any other experimental avant-garde theatre, their spectacular results threatened to smash the naturalism that directors from Stanislavsky to Lee Strasberg had for years inculcated in their actors.

Although the theatre was a collective, there was a leader. He was a visionary who believed that all psychological action on stage had to be linked to its biological and "mythic" roots, and he developed a technique to express his ideas. He rejected theatre as a synthesis of the arts and advocated, instead, a "poor" theatre—stripped of external trappings. His theatre would be so pristine and ritualistic that the actors would be holy and their act sacred. This man was Jerzy Grotowski.

To see the Grotowski theatre is to be transplanted into a black, brooding world of classical myth and contemporary degradation, executed with the delicacy of a poet. It is to be transplanted into a world of saints and sinners, idiots and wise men, heroes and cowards, sensualists and saviors—a world of Dostoevsky, Simone Weil, and T. S. Eliot, a world where Hebrew myths and Catholic parables challenge civilization, past and present. The theatre of Jerzy Grotowski is a microcosm of metaphysical man's search for self-definition and modern man's search for moral imperatives, and its concomitant paradoxical responses. It is a theatre of tragic suffering, of the uncovering of human complexities, and of the consequences all this implies. It is a theatre of negation—the renunciation of all artifice that impels the actors to reveal their own raw psyches as an emblem of man's agony. Formalized with exquisite skill in wails, chants, laments, and liturgies; in fits, beatings, and the fluttering of muscles; in spasms, leaps, and writhings; in images of crucifixions, crematoriums, and inquisitions, this agony is a metaphor for the actors' lives. It is they who define the Grotowski theatre; it is their scream we hear: a primitive, modern, Hebrew, Catholic, Polish, American howl. To see all this is to see the fusion of religious art and modern cruelty in a totally new form, and to apprehend the phenomenon of Grotowski.

The first appearance of the Grotowski troupe in an English-speaking country took place in the summer of 1968 at the Edinburgh Festival. The play was called *Akropolis*, a reworking of a Polish drama by the nineteenth-century neo-romantic, Stanislaw Wyspianski. In the original Wyspianski play, the action is set in the Crackow cathedral; in the Grotowski production, the settings have been changed to Auschwitz and the performance, like all of the Polish Lab plays, lasted only fifty-five minutes. Fifty people were allowed into a "theatre" that was actually a bare, workman-like room whose walls were painted black. In the center of the open space stood a rectangular raised platform, piled with scrap iron, a wheelbarrow, and a headless rag doll. The room was amazingly silent as the audience was led to its seats; wooden benches zigzagging around the "stage," almost impinged upon the process.

Aware that this was a special occasion, no one spoke or even whispered; the silence became unbearable. Suddenly the actors hobbled out. But were they really actors? One of the cast looked half-blind as he played a sentimental love song on a scratchy violin. Dressed in torn, worn-out sacks, heavy, oversized brown wooden clogs, and colorless skull caps that nullified their sex, the actors appeared to be scarecrows. Their gray faces (untouched by makeup) were death masks: eyes turned inward, smiles frozen, foreheads ossified—creatures from another land, tortured wrecks, dehumanized automatons: grim reminders of brutalization. All the same, they moved with exquisite control, their arms and legs dangling with the grace of a mobile sculpture. They spoke, chanted, whispered, sang, and intoned, creating an unrelenting rise and fall of sounds quite unlike anything heard before in the Western theatre.

One by one, they pick up their scrap iron to hang it on the vertical wires; working in unison, hammering, lifting, and hanging their pipes, they build their Acropolis turned crematorium. Chimney stoves and black pipes hanging from wires create oddly terrifying patterns, like emaciated dead bodies. As their fingers labor with the junk, we see them imagine that they are heroes from Greek mythology and Judeo-Christian legends. Intermittently they taunt and jeer at each other, sing slavic melodies, Latin liturgies, and Hebrew wailing songs. In the end they disappear down a trap door to the gas chamber. When the stage is bare, a voice calls out, "They are gone, and the coils of smoke hover in the air." The audience files out, horrified.

In *Akropolis*, as in all his productions, Grotowski expresses the predicament of a generation that witnessed and suffered cruelty first hand. Born in 1933 of Catholic parents, he lived under the

Nazis as a child and the shadow of the Russians as an adult. He was six years old when Hitler invaded Poland in September 1939, part of a generation in Poland that grew up under the onslaught of German brutality that was to climax in the slaughter of six million Jews (four million of whom came from Poland), the death of six million Poles, and the complete destruction of Warsaw. While Grotowski was a child, thousands of incidents of murder, rape, arson, execution, and savagery were taking place. When the Germans first entered Poland in 1939, they vowed to annihilate the Poles. They painted slogans on the Wehrmacht transportation column, warning that they would bring death. And death they brought. In a period of "the first eight weeks from September 1 to October 25 alone, over 700 instances of individual murder and 16,000 mass murders took place," tens of thousands died in merciless air bombardments, 80 per cent of the deaths were by execution, and all strata and all classes were subjected to mass deportations. The Germans wiped out whole villages and machine-gunned ordinary non-political peasants on the roads: villages and towns were burned down for no reason. "A total of 55 towns and 476 villages and 531 undefined and unfortified human settlements were burned."[1] These figures merely presaged what was to follow—the days of misery, starvation, torture, and death, Auschwitz and Treblinka. The *Black Book of Poland* and the *Black Book of Polish Jewry* are filled with thousands of horror stories that need no repetition here. This was the world—drenched with memories of the past, not only of Nazi brutality, but of Poland's bitter history—from which Grotowski and his actors emerged. To understand Grotowski, then, is to understand Poland; his work is inexorably linked with the history of his native land.

Poland, as Jan Kott, the critic and Polish theatre scholar, has noted, and Alfred Jarry before him, is "nowhere," or Poland is "everywhere"; it is a country that has been periodically invaded, partitioned, dismembered, oppressed, and brutalized. (And it is a country itself guilty of oppression: its past anti-Semitism is well known, as is its current anti-Semitism and political repression even under socialism).

In 1772, the western part of Poland was invaded and partitioned by the Germans; in 1793, the Russians took the eastern sector, the Austrians, the southern; in 1795, Poland ceased to be a nation. The country was occupied by three kingdoms: the Russians, the Prussians, and the Austrians. At the turn of the nineteenth century, Poland was no longer on the map. She had developed nonetheless a strong nationalist liberation movement, and at the height of European romanticism in 1830, encouraged by the furor of the mass revolutionary movements throughout Europe, the famous Polish Rising took place. It was the first of the revolutions—only to end in total defeat and exile, or the gallows for the patriots. The invaders, stronger and fiercer than ever, were determined to put an end to Polish resistance: it was forbidden even to speak the Polish language, and Polish culture was driven underground.

After the rebellion (Warsaw fell in 1831), many of the Polish intellectuals and artists went into exile; they settled in Paris and became part of the movement known as the Great Emigration. Their work banned in Poland, the émigrés were forced to write in symbols or allegory to avoid Russian censorship. But Polish nationalist ideals and heritage were kept alive through these forbidden poets; they "became the moral leaders of the nation."[2] And in that period of European Romanticism and revolution, these émigrés—destitute, alienated, and dying of loneliness—expressed Polish national aspirations and Polish romanticsm through a literature of personal suffering. They linked their pain with political oppression and their impassioned patriotism with Polish Catholicism: religion served as a rallying point for them, as well as for all classes and strata of the population. Gradually, religious mysticism merged with revolution, and Poland's suffering became an Idea; the country, a beloved sacrifice, and Messianism, a strong political movement. Expressions such as "Holy Poland" and terms such as "resurrection" became common vocabulary, and were widely used in the work of revolutionary writers. Poland became identified with Christ, and writers—such as Adam Mickiewicz (1798–1855) and Julius Slowacki (1809–1849)—became the embodiment of Polish ideas, Polish resistance, and Polish romanticism. Today Mickiewicz is considered to be Poland's national poet, and is revered by his countrymen both as a great writer and as a model of Polish suffering during the captivity. His greatest epic, *Forefathers' Eve*, which Grotowski produced as a young man, combines history and autobiography. It is a story of a young aristocrat who rejects his great wealth for revolution; it expresses the generation's social and political conflicts; it describes the myths, folklores, and legends of the Polish people in terms of Christ crucified: it dramatizes the great uprising in 1830 and its defeat the following year, and it "shows Mickiewicz's entire generation's intellectual and emotional coming-of-age."[3]

If Mickiewicz dramatized Poland as crucified, Julius Slowacki, influenced by Byron and Calderón, emphasized the individual crucified. In his mystic play, *Anhelli*, a youth is an "expatiatory victim for his country,"[4] while in another, *Kordian*, he portrays "the loneliness of the conspirator."[5] Notice the similarities in Grotowski's production of Slowacki's *The Constant Prince* and in his staging of Slowacki's *Kordian* against the background of an insane asylum, inferred by some to be a political protest. "Slowacki's contention, veiled in allegory, but clear to his contemporaries, was that the generation to which they belonged must die and be utterly forgotten before Poland's unhappy condition could be remedied. As Mickiewicz's idea was that the Poles must discipline themselves so as to live nobly for their country, Slowacki's was that they must discipline themselves so as to die nobly for it."[6]

Both Mickiewicz and Slowacki supported the cult of martyrdom, with its romantic death and ressurrection themes; they were mystics and visionaries who believed in spiritual transcendence. Their use of Aesopian language and religious symbolism was typical of writers living under oppression. But above all, they utilized romantic-religious ideas as a substitute for organized political activity, and thereafter religion and romanticism became the philosophical and aesthethic springboard to test political and metaphysical problems, as well as those of art and revolution, history and science, individual and national guilt, responsibility and personal sacrifice.[7] Virtually no subsequent Polish artist or intellectual has been totally unaffected by the romantic tradition, Grotowski notwithstanding.

The early Romantics established the basic characteristics that were to haunt Polish drama for the next hundred years. But at the middle and turn of the century artists were becoming involved with new forms and new philosophies, and their interests resulted, to a certain extent, in the weakening of Romantic beliefs, a development reflected in the work of dramatist Stanislaw Wyspianski (1869–1907), considered by the Poles as their first modern theatrical innovator—the Stanislavsky of Poland. Like Stanislavsky, he envisioned the theatre as a temple: unlike Stanislavsky, Wyspianski believed that dramatic literature should be abolished, and in keeping with the Symbolists in theatre, painting, and poetry, he "adopted the method of free association of ideas and of dramatizing visions plastically,"[8]—two tenets to which Grotowski and all the later twentieth-century avant-gardists adhered.

In addition, as a commentary on the modern world, Wyspianski intermingled Roman and Greek mythology with contemporary figures and, influenced by the Symbolists, he juxtaposed dream sequences with reality—exactly as Grotowski did in his updated version of *Akropolis*. Apparently aware of the naturalist movement as well, Wyspianski fused journalistic and documentary texts with his poetry.[9] He was especially interested in reviving ritual (thereby parallelling Mallarmé). His theatre was essentially romantic, however. It expressed the tragic destiny of man, and like his Romantic predecessors and progeny, his plays revealed a deep pessimism and an adoration of death. He differed from the Romantics in that he rejected the more naïve aspects of myth. In his play *The Wedding*, he deals with a belief that Poles had for centuries thought to be true: at the appropriate time, the ruling class and the peasants would unite, and all would be free. Testing the strength of this myth in the light of his own times, his play is a scathing attack on both classes as well as on the myth itself. Wyspianski expresses the same idea in *Akropolis*: there he contrasts ideal with real values—Christian humanism with Polish repression during the struggle for Poland's political revival—only to end the play on a dour and pessimistic note.

Further, Wyspianski's techniques foreshadow the future experimentalists' work with language. "His poetry," according to the Polish scholar Kazimierz Braun, "cannot be spoken or listened to in a normal way. His words can only be tested by shouting or whispering; they are made to be spoken in passion, to be acted . . . his dramas have an always changing rhythm; sometimes they involve the entire cast and sometimes they shrink to chamber-size dialogues . . . sometimes the poetry is built on movement or on conflicting dialogues, or on mime; then we get sudden bursts of music, dramatic sound, singing."[10]

Clearly Wyspianski and the early Polish Romantics have influenced Grotowski, if one judges by Grotowski's repertory of plays, their productions, and his world outlook. Not only has he directed Mickiewicz's *Forefathers' Eve,* both Slowacki's *Kordian* and his adaptation of Calderón's *The Constant Prince*, Wyspianski's *Akropolis*, but his productions deal either with existential questions as they relate to the past, or with a Polish romantic idealism linked to the past (and to religion). Indeed, the design of his work—complete with its crucifixes, flagellations, liturgies, and masses, infused with a bitterness and despair that conjure agonizing nightmares relieved only through death—is typical of romantic themes and of the entire "Polish Experience," a term used to denote the past suffering that seems indelibly stamped on Polish consciousness. In a country that, after centuries of oppression, finally established the Republic in 1918, was overrun by the Germans in 1939, established socialism in 1945, rose up against Stalinism in 1968, and revived anti-Semitism in 1969, is a country whose past cannot easily be forgotten. In fact, reminders are everywhere.

In Crackow, where Grotowski was educated and Wyspianski was born, to breathe is to experience tradition. Crackow is the site of Poland's ancient home of royalty and revolution, intellectual ferment and history, culture and education. Its famous university has been the source of education for Poland's professors, artists, and intellectuals, for centuries. Wherever one goes, one sees emblems of tradition—statues, pictures, churches, buildings—all stained with the blood of Polish martyrs from the uprisings of the 1830's to the occupation of the 1940's. Nor have memories of the concentration camps faded either: the socialist regime's attack on Jews and dissidents in 1968, its restrictions on free speech and travel, its capitulation to Russian domination, are grim reminders of past and present oppression.[11]

Little wonder that Grotowski is obsessed with the past. For him, the past is a means of working out his personal metaphysics, and for understanding his function in a country drenched in the "Polish Experience." However, Grotowski is not merely staging old masterpieces for their own sake—there would be nothing new in that—but, like Wyspianski, he is "confronting" the traditional content of the masterpiece, and testing its contemporary validity. In this attempt, he utilizes as devices religious symbols, allusions, and images to uncover the collective national unconscious. In the process, he seems to glorify Catholicism, despite his denials, for audiences assume that the emblems of the productions imply Grotowski's support of religion, and that the Catholic ambiance of his productions, when viewed as a whole, is due to Grotowski's philosophy. Grotowski's use of national symbols and romantic ideology, however, may also be interpreted as a springboard for a dialectical examination of the relationship between the past and the present, and between romantic ideals and contemporary brutality. Since the form often obscures the content, the dialectic, rather than illuminating, renders Grotowski's position imprecise. In such a country, this may be deliberate.

On the other hand, Grotowski often tilts the scale and reveals a certain partiality. The direction, in some pieces, is toward a nostalgic Catholicism. In *The Constant Prince* and *Apocalypsis cum Figuris*, for example, we sense Grotowski's feelings of loss and regret over the dead past; his response is child-like and deeply felt, in spite of his attempt at rationality. Living in a socialist but repressive society where Catholic religious feelings still run deep even among Marxist officials, Grotowski may be expressing what some people are feeling but cannot say publicly. His language, rooted exclusively in Polish associations of the past, may even be a form of political protest (although he vigorously denies this), and the religious aspect of his work a traditional means of opposing the regime. That Grotowski claims to challenge tradition only to use the emblems of tradition may seem contradictory, but it is not entirely out of keeping with the romantic heritage.

In view of the "Polish Experience," Grotowski's work cannot be openly political. His is the politics of creation. To create is to give credibility to man's indefatigable need for freedom, to create is an affirmation of life and a defiance of cruelty; to create is an act of love. And an act of love in Poland at such a time is a blow against oppression. In the tradition of romanticism, Grotowski offers up his art as sacred and his theatre as a symbolic recognition of the moral plight and suffering of the times. Let the theatre have a spiritual function; let the living actor forge a unique relationship with the audience. Let the actors (and the audience) see what they cannot ordinarily look at and experience what they ordinarily cannot feel; let each actor question the meaning of his life and create so as to give his life significance; let him confront his individual suffering and express it through his body and voice alone. Let him strive for "secular holiness," and let him totally reveal his "naked spirit" on stage as a means of unmasking social hypocrisy and of attaining transcendence and spiritual replenishment. Let him be so honest and revelatory that he vitiates his personal emptiness and counteracts the cruelty and oppression of the modern world. As did his revolutionary ancestors, Grotowski uses religious terminology: he speaks of theatre as Revelation leading to Grace, views the actors as "holy," the theatre as a temple, the performance as a confession, art as a "calling"—a unifying force, an act of freedom leading toward spiritual (and political) salvation. In this sense, Grotowski's theatre *is* religious while it is also therapeutic and covertly political.

Not only have Grotowski's aesthetics been influenced by the Romantics; they have been influenced as well by all the sophisticated theories of the world. Many of his principles are simple extensions of Catholic self-renunciation, which he has turned into a practical philosophy. Calling his theatre "poor," he has made poverty an artistic virtue, and he draws upon the Scriptures for support. Grotowski has said, "To be poor in the Biblical sense is to abandon all externals." To be poor in the theatrical sense is to reject traditional artifice. For artifice, even in art, is another means to hide the "naked" spirit.

Why use makeup, props, and costumes when actors can create masks with their own facial muscles; when a wheelbarrow can serve as a coffin, a bed, or a bench; when a colored cloth can be a wedding gown, a shroud, a king's robe? Why use music and lighting when an actor's voice, hands, or feet can be as harmonic or as contrapuntal as a string ensemble; when an actor moving around stationary white kleig lights can create his own shadows and nuances? Why limit actors to conventional words and ordinary movements when body impulses have their own rhythmic language, when an actor can chant as well as speak, sing, intone, and whisper like a fine symphonic orchestra? Why use traditional scenic design when settings should only be spatial arrangements to facilitate stronger communication between the actor and the audience? And why use new plays when national myths and old masterpieces can be interpreted in the light of contemporary experience? Accused of neglecting, distorting, abandoning the playwright (as were Meyerhold, Vakhtangov, and Wyspianski), Grotowski does reject dramatic literature as the basis for theatre, but paradoxically uses literature as a means of structuring a new piece. Grotowski and the company select from a text those passages they feel are analogous to their sensibilities; these they formalize and present as the production. The original text is virtually obliterated, to be sure, but the ideas embedded in the text remain and form a bridge, as Grotowski has said, "between our own individual roots and archetypal roots of the past."

Writing in *Teatr*, a Polish publication, Jan Kreczmar, actor and former head of the State Drama School in Warsaw, said:

> True that the poetic text [of Grotowski] usually gets lost in the rhythmic gallop of words, in shouts and whispers; the sense and logic are lost—but not the emotional content. In their place we get the sound and movement composition based on a surprising knowledge of the sensibility of human ears and eyes. By those means which are purely theatrical—rooted in acting and not literature—Grotowski and his actors communicate the ideas and thoughts of Calderón and Slowacki not any less accurately than if it were done by the most reverent handling of the text. . . .[12]

In claiming to utilize national-religious classics as a means of "uncovering the collective unconscious" (and here he borrows freely from Jung), Grotowski presents the classics in the context of myth and ritual theatre, albeit modernized. Grotowski, like other modernists imbued with an understanding of the religious aspects of myth and ritual, claimed that theatre had been part of religion through religion's incorporation of myth—"profaning or rather transcending" it. In this way, religion had given the spectator "a renewed awareness of his personal truth in the truth of the myth, and through fright and a sense of the sacred he came to catharsis."[13] In other words, theatre-in-religion awakened man to a sense of individual and universal truth through sacral enactment. But since the literal acting out of ancient myths is no longer effective, evoking and profaning the classical or cultural myth is a means of arousing the spectators' memories, their common roots or bonds, or their contemporary and timeless truths.

In the Polish Laboratory Theatre, this has meant a development of ritual not in its old sense, but nonetheless complete with rites, signs and "revelations." Despite Grotowski's denials, he seems headed toward a spiritual, if not a religious theatre; its undercurrents, if not traditionally Catholic, suggest at least an existential Catholicism. Writing in *The Theatre in Poland*, Ludwik Flaszen, the literary directory and co-founder of the Theatre, has said: "Experience has led us to the theatre of miracle plays. . . . How can one create a secular miracle play, a contradiction in terms? . . . It can be achieved through a profanation of myths and rites, through blasphemy. This kind of transgression brings back their basic background. . . ."[14] Concretely, "profanation" and "blasphemy" are expressed through what Grotowski calls the "dialectic of apotheosis and derision," that is, a montage of scenes juxtaposing classic, mythic, and traditional beliefs undercut by mockery, self-parody and nightmare. Grotowski's "dialectic" is similar to the "Priest-Jester" metaphor, an image discussed in Leszek Kolakowski's *Toward a Marxist Humanism.*[15] Kolakowski, the eminent Polish Marxist philosopher-playwright, a political exile since 1968, uses the "Priest-Jester" image to signify the Polish intellectual's ambivalence toward the social society, especially his conflict between Catholicism and communism. In the book, Kolakowski contradicts Adam Schaff, the Party's official philosopher, who contends that moral responsibility for the intellectual means supporting the principles of the Communist Party. Taking the opposite view, Kolakowski argues for intellectual skepticism and non-allegiances, and regards himself as "jester," synonomous with iconoclasm, rather than "priest," synonomous with catechism:

> In every era the jester's philosophy exposes as doubtful what seems most unshakable, reveals the contradictions in what appears obvious and incontrovertible, derides common sense and reads sense into the absurd. . . . Depending on time and place, the jester's thinking can range through all the extremes of thought, for what is sacred today was paradoxical yesterday, and absolutes on the equator are often blasphemies at the poles. . . . We declare ourselves in favor of the jester's philosophy, and thus vigilant against any absolute.[16]

Kolakowski contends that the "priest" is a symbol for the status quo, and the "jester" the mouthpiece for the contradictions contained within the status quo—each contributing to a dialectical process. Kolakowski has also utilized the "Priest-Jester" metaphor in his play, *Banishment from Paradise*. There he transplants the Adam and Eve story to a modern setting, to raise philosophical questions of free choice, absolute freedom, original sin, and the concept of paradise. He does not deny the Bible story, but challenges its sanctity.[17]

Grotowski has used similar methods. In *Akropolis* he displays a devastating skepticism. Characters elegize God, but hideous taunts punctuated by clanking tools and banging clogs undermine their pious speeches. Inmates dream they are heroes—Helen, Paris, Jacob, or Rachel—but as they reenact the myths, Helen becomes a male homosexual, and Jacob, asking for Rachel's hand, tramples his intended father-in-law to death. Later he imagines himself at his wedding, where his bride is a stove pipe covered with a piece of plastic for a veil. Further, the inmates are transformed into helpless, impotent wrecks, and not only wait to be gassed, but participate in their own brutalization: executioner and victim become identical. Jacob imagines that he wrestles with the angel; in reality he kills a fellow prisoner with a wheelbarrow. Prisoners think they see the Saviour, but they see only a headless rag doll. They recite hopeful prayers, but even as they do so, the Jewish Kaddish (prayer for the dead) is heard. In the final "apotheosis"—the cruelest derision of all—the leader of the tribe raises the headless doll like a crucifix, and the group, imagining their suffering is at an end, form a procession to follow the "cross." Reciting the litany, the Leader tempts them with the image of the Saviour, only to open the lid of the crematorium. Quickly he descends to the ovens, dragging the doll with him while the others, in an orgiastic trance, follow him to their deaths, reaching their "apotheosis" at last.

Grotowski's use of "apotheosis-derision" (or "Priest-Jester") results in complex reversals. On the one hand, in *Akropolis*, Wavel Castle, the setting of the original play, was once the home of Polish kings; on the other, the castle recalls the nineteenth-century Austrian invaders who were housed there. On still another level, *Akropolis* stands for the apex of Polish culture; conversely, Auschwitz represents its extermination. Finally, we are conscious of history reversing itself as we watch the present Polish regime revive the anti-Semitism and political exile of the past.

Akropolis is an explicit condemnation of brutality, but it casts aspersions on its victims as well; the inmates are unheroic; "ruined pieces of nature," ravaged by institutionalized and mechanized barbarism. Despite the Catholic symbols, signs, and references, the piece subtly attacks religion for its inability to mitigate suffering and castigates all of Western humanism and its notions of happiness. Dreams of the past, or of a better future, are mocked: the relationships between inmates are cruel and competitive, and in an atmosphere where to breathe is to deprive someone else of air, suffering is not redemptive; redemption is the gas chamber, a fate preferable to life in the camp. Nor do the characters—or Grotowski—polemicize about the triumph of man's spirit. Existence is bleak, bitter, ironic, and tragic. Man is what he does and what is done to him; history has shown what man is capable of.

Akropolis was a masterwork. The characters were expressionistic archetypes created from images, impulses, and essences; actors spoke in words that were rapid, almost incomprehensible in the way that words were elongated, strung together, breathed in, or sucked in. As in the original Wyspianski text, poetry alternated with prose; laughter, screams, and wails alternated with silence. The company took no bows, and there was no applause. All six actors remained in that "crematorium box" until the audience left. And "they suffer it—for what?" as Elizabeth Hardwick has observed; "For us, for themselves, as a witness?"[18] Perhaps as a penance for the suffering of others?

If *Akropolis* dramatizes the failure of humanism, Slowacki's *The Constant Prince*, based on the Calderón play (Grotowski's second offering in the New York engagement of October 1969), depicts traditional tragic heroism. Using the technique of "Priest-Jester" more ambiguously, Grotowski rearranged Slowacki's romantic belief in martyrdom. (Grotowski also conjures up reminders of his first theatrical mentor, Juliusz Osterwa, Poland's first modern theatre experimentalist, who created the Reduta, a theatre like that of Grotowski; in fact, Osterwa also produced *The Constant Prince*.) Then there are the images of Spain and the Inquisition, which provide a not-unlikely comparison, since Polish suffering finds much in common with Spanish suffering—the Catholic Poles, "liberated" by communism; the Catholic Spaniards, enslaved by facism. Thus the Calderón-Slowacki-Grotowski production is a cross-fertilization of repression.

The locale of *The Constant Prince*, seventeenth-century Spain, is designated in the Grotowski production by Goya capes, white shirts, red shrouds, and black boots. The audience, sitting on wooden benches, peers down upon the open playing space from behind raised walls, as though in a bullfight ring. There is very little plot: a half-naked man is stretched out on an "operating" table; two upright white kleig lights shine down on him. He is examined by three men and a woman. By their dress and manner they represent the status quo; one man wears a crown. Shortly, the half-naked man is castrated, and is then clothed to resemble those who "operated" on him. Another man is brought in—the Prince, wearing an open white shirt and red cape. He too is examined, tortured, debased, and humiliated, but he refuses to capitulate and eventually is put to death. At the end, he lies virtually naked, covered with a red shroud. This simple "plot" takes about 45–50 minutes to present, the length of a Catholic mass.

True to Slowacki's Romanticism, and in keeping with Slowacki's belief that redemption demands individual expiation, Grotowski's Prince represents tortured Poland, and the epitome of Catholic martydrom. The prince, inviting sainthood, masochistically submits to his suffering and death as a prerequisite for spiritual and political transfiguration. Through physical suffering, he attains beatitude, a triumph of the spirit over the flesh. Grotowski's attitude is ambiguous. Is he deriding or apotheosizing the Prince?

Perhaps he is thinking of Simone Weil, the French philosopher, who has been a considerable influence on him, and on Polish Catholic Communists in general.

Simone Weil was born Jewish, converted to Catholicism, and died a leftist. She thought that the perpetuation of the chain of evil could be broken by self-sacrifice. She led a painful, ascetic life, and her self-willed death has impressed intellectuals and artists everywhere. Gustav Thibon, her life-long friend, wrote: "She believed . . . that the creation of real genius required a high level of spirituality and that it was impossible to attain to perfect expression without having passed through severe inner purgation. . . . For her the only thing that counted was a style stripped bare of all adornment, the perfect expression of the naked truth of the soul."[19] Simone Weil lived the life of a secular saint: she literally starved herself to death during World War II as a sacrifice to those who died. The Constant Prince acts similarly.

Grotowski's Prince emulates the passion of Christ, and Ryszard Cieslak, the leading actor, becomes the perfect "naked soul," ready to submit to the perfect sacrifice. His body is an incarnation of the Miraculous; his public "confession," a display of suffering Beauty attaining ecstasy, and his work, a metaphor for Grotowski's acting principles and metaphysics. Conquering the body requires maximum dedication, fortitude, and commitment. The sacrifice of the body to the spirit results in grace. To achieve grace and "saintliness" in art, the actor must abandon his social mask, and disclose his Self: in the process he will find his "Man": "The actor does not act, imitate, or pretend. He is himself in a public act of confession. His inner processes are his own and not the work of a clever artist. In this theatre the aim is not the literal fact—no one bleeds or dies—but rather the literal *spiritual* act to which Grotowski's method leads the actor [emphasis added]."[20]

Hence, when Ryszard Cieslak says, "I will show you my man," and Grotowski says, "Show me your Man and I will show you your God,"[21] they mean that the actor will offer up his "confession" within the context of the play to reveal what he really is, his intellectual and biological Self—everything that custom, habit, and mores prevent him from doing in life. He will reenact his own trauma as in a ritual mass expressed through his own "body and blood." Cieslak's Prince, then, is an exposure of Cieslak's "naked soul." In religious terms, the performance is a means of his personal expiation; in artistic terms, it is an exposure carried to the limits through the voice and body; in psychological terms, it becomes the attainment of self-realization; in dramatic terms, it is a catharsis for the audience as well as the actor.

Cieslak's "unveiling" is accomplished by the display of personal images and associations, nuances and suggestions, sounds and body gestures so dense and tenuous that the performance is akin to poetry. The technique can in a sense be compared with T. S. Eliot's "objective correlative" principle—that is, an externalized situation, sign, or word corresponding to an inner state of emotion. Cieslak's body impulses and gestures are the objective correlatives: his almost-naked body, a "telegraphic" network conveying pain received, and his voice, a musical scale conveying pain released. Exposed on stage are his body impulses: every muscle trembles with fear, every action of the head, chest, arms, torso, and legs expresses the "movement" of pain—how it is anticipated, felt, and released in response to the exact moment and degree of endurance. Cieslak's voice records his suffering—in howls, laments, and moans, in hisses, shouts, and whispers; in sounds that echo Oedipus' grief, Lear's agony, the Jews in the ovens, the Blacks on the slave ships. As his screams rise to crescendo, the Prince demands more punishment, and actually beats himself to the accompaniment of his screams. According to some contemporary psychologists, this self-punishment may be a common traumatic reaction to massive brutality: the victim and the victimized become indistinguishable as both participate in the slaughter. But in Catholic terms, self-flagellation is a step toward grace. Cieslak's ravaged face as he submits to his suffering is translucent: his bewildered, haunted eyes focus on some mysterious place within him. His transcendence is obvious: at the end, he seems in a trance. The Polish critic Josef Kelera wrote: "A sort of psychic illumination emanates from the actor. . . . At any moment the actor will levitate. . . . He is in a state of grace. . . ."[22]

If *The Constant Prince* exemplifies the Polish Laboratory's controlled exposure of raw emotion in one individual, be it symbolic Man, Poland, or a tragic hero, then Grotowski's later piece, *Apocalypsis cum Figuris*, expresses the company's vision of Man in a more complex and shattering way. Departing to some extent from the metaphysical to include the psychological as well, the piece is structured on the group's improvisations and responses, rather than on any text; its iconography, however, is still Catholic. The work is like a wild and beautiful game depicting frustration and desire viewed in relation to a religious and repressive past in conflict with an irreligious and sensual present. It is a reminder of what theatre might have been at its very inception—an orgiastic ritual, complete with rites and sacraments, in celebration of primordial existence.

The actors in the play are revelers. They awaken from a sleep after a drunken binge, decide to play "fun and games," and choose to enact characters from the Bible. One casts himself as Simon Peter; the others variously as John, Lazarus, Judas, and Mary Magdalene. As a joke, the village Simpleton, who happens to be watching, is picked as Christ. The players change back and forth from the Biblical roles to themselves, acting out their subconscious associations of other worlds and other times. Passages quoted from the Gospels, Dostoevsky, T. S. Eliot, and Simone Weil, are contrasted with fragmented images that depict hope, exhaltation, depression, frustration, and rage.

The characters unleash their repressed sensuality and childish cruelty; they seem trapped between their perception of reality and their subjective emotions—between fact and fantasy, desire and action, guilt and sex. Conscious and unconscious feelings converge in swiftly changing body images and speech patterns until the sum total results in a dialectical supra-language expressing the vast range of man's psychological and existential complexities.

Apocalypsis cum Figuris, like all of the Grotowski pieces, was performed in a church in New York, and the number of spectators was limited to around forty. The audience entered the "theatre" quickly, first lining up outside and then being permitted to go in, one by one. The room was lit by one low kleig light, near which Grotowski himself sat, his black glasses and black suit perfectly in tune with the atmosphere. On the floor, asleep, lay the reveler-actors. Light shining through the stained glass church windows faintly illuminated the white-clad bodies on the floor to form a sculptured pattern against a predominantly black background. The audience sat in two rows at right angles to the playing space. There was a long moment of silence. Suddenly, an actress in a white mini and white boots rises from her sleep and throws a loaf of bread into the playing area. Bread, the central metaphor, the staff of life, symbol for the Host, is profaned by a young man, stripped to the waist and wearing white trousers: he masturbates into it. The bread is crumbled and scattered all over the floor, and eventually it is used, not only for eating, but to stone the Simpleton, to stuff down someone's throat in a moment of fury, to stuff down into someone's groin in a moment of orgy. Later it becomes the bread of Simone Weil's "from a cupboard you took bread which we shared." The conflict between the "heavenly and earthly bread" and mankind's demand for "miracle, mystery and authority" (as posed by the Grand Inquisitor in *The Brothers Karamazov*) emerges as the central issue in the play—and is, in fact, the framework for the questions that haunt the revelers. For example, the Simpleton continually searches for the miracle of the absolute and the mystery of Self. He tries desperately to find an indentity and seeks an answer through the others, but is continually rejected. Besides a Christ figure, the Simpleton is T. S. Eliot's spiritually impotent Gerontion and, as Cieslak plays him, Dostoevsky's "Idiot," untainted by evil, but capable of temptation. Tortured by his inner conflicts, excluded by the outside world, the Simpleton searches for the simplicity of love, but is confronted with the mystery of sex. As he makes love to Mary Magdalene, he is all ambivalence—

tender at first, but finally violent. His arms and legs contorted, his body at perpendicular right angles, he is grotesque—a magnificently conceived image of coitus interruptus, and of regret and recrimination that is a mockery of love and of the sexual mystique. The search continues: the Simpleton becomes Christ, bleeding from his wounds, but the group, like lascivious vampires, suck him dry, leaving him once again a Simpleton: bereft, excluded, and taunted. Then in a graphic confrontation, he is tempted by homosexuality and trembles there between desire and revulsion. Finally, after a frenzy of indecision, he scourges the revelers with his handkerchief, and thus dispenses not only with guilt, but with temptation and authority as well.

Simultaneously, the entire group enacts its sense of the tragic. Memories of loss engulf each character. Mary Magdalene speaks from the *Song of Songs*, but in an outburst of self-mockery, flaunts her drunken animality. The Simpleton, as he realizes his inability to respond to the past, speaks from "Ash Wednesday": he does not hope "to turn again." Like Gerontion, he is physically as well as spiritually impotent: his "house" has crumbled. John, speaking through the words of Simone Weil, is conscious of being unloved, and Simon Peter, speaking through the Grand Inquisitor, acknowledges his (and Dostoevsky's) sorrow over man's inability to conquer his contradictory nature, which prevents him from achieving freedom. In the end, in total darkness, when they all have played out the Last Supper, Simon Peter tells the Simpleton-Christ, in the Grand Inquistor's final words, to "go and come no more." We sense that the need for miracle and authority is dead. Christ will never come again. Perhaps in that utter darkness, mystery is the one thing still alive. But no one is left on the stage to play. We are utterly alone in the dark with our own responses.

Apocalypsis cum Figuris can be looked at from various angles. The play does not attempt to be explicit on the social or political level, yet the company implies its own attitudes toward love, lust, violence, and brutality. And though the problems of contemporary Poland might not be instantly apparent, the actors, through a fine blend of Polish folklore, recognizable national traits, and Catholic symbols, express their native milieu. Using the apotheosis-derision technique, Grotowski explores various themes: purity/impurity, excessiveness/simplicity, harmony/conflict, freedom/authority. Is the past a reality? Is Christ a figment of the collective imagination? Is belief in religion (since the rise of socialism) part of a dead illusion? Can harmony result from man's divided soul? Is Jesus no better than man? One is mindful that such questions are addressed to Polish Catholics, and that what Americans might perceive as an elegy for Christianity might be, for Poles, a blasphemy. The play implies a criticism of Christ's inability to reconcile human biological responses with his own preachings. For Grotowski's Christ figure—as simpleton, saint, and sinner—is not idealized; he suffers from much the same contradictions as Dostoevsky's Grand Inquisitor and, like the rest of humanity, cannot retain his spirituality. In the words of T. S. Eliot's "Gerontion," he bemoans his loss of power.

Apocalypsis seems to convey that Christianity is relevant only to a self-sacrificing saint (like Simone Weil), and for the rest, perhaps, something to aspire to. But the recognition is sprinkled with regret, and the realization that dead spiritual values have not been replaced by live ones is what evokes the players' cynicism and despair. True, the piece shows the conflict between religion and man's biological needs, but it never suggests a reconciliation. The matter is left open, even side-tracked—a deliberate ambiguity that raises questions but never resolves the problem, thus enabling Grotowski to be *both* priest and jester.

The central subject of the piece, however, indicates that Grotowski's view of human history takes no notice of changing social systems and the resultant change in human attitudes. Philosophically, Grotowski wonders about freedom and authority, sin and sex, history and man's character, innate brutality and innate benevolence, but these are, and have been, eternal questions. That Grotowski, for all his sophistication, chooses nineteenth-century subject matter may seem anachronistic, in view of twentieth-century problems. But apparently he has not broken with Polish romantic metaphysics. And yet Grotowski is not entirely impervious to the new.

In depicting uncontrolled drunks released from the confines of bourgeois, religious morality, he tries to investigate, as it were, unaccommodated modern man. But he supposes that unaccommodated man is irrational the moment he is left to his own devices. Drunken lusts, infantile jealousies, neurotic fantasies, and childish relationships underlie all his behavior. But even rebellious "irrational" man knows that there are limitations imposed on him; he also knows that total freedom condemns him to egomania, corruption, and demonic forces which, if accepted as normal, may lead to violence and murder. The same society that restricts man (and against which man rebels) can, in the name of freedom, also unleash in man anti-social behavior: hence man's dilemma. If he chooses freedom he is condemned, as Sartre has said, to responsibility and, paradoxically, to a limitation of that freedom. And so the question of what kind of "bread" will satisfy mankind remains; so does the concept of limitation as the source of tragic suffering. Recognizing these contradictions all too well, Grotowski sees both unaccommodated man and restricted man as lost, incapable of resolving his predicament. Nevertheless, in *Apocalysis*, Man tries: he pursues love but courts disaster, pursues friendship but needs solitude, craves affection but precipitates rejection, longs for freedom but is thwarted on all sides. Perhaps Grotowski views man as one who will always demand "Bread," not only biologically, but spiritually, while continuing to demand the restrictions as well.

Grotowski's interest in Dostoevsky is matched by his interest in Eliot, as evidenced by his choice of verse from Eliot's "Gerontion" and "Ash Wednesday" for the dialogue in *Apocalypsis*. And the choice is particularly relevant for the piece. In "Gerontion," Elizabeth Drew has pointed out, Eliot sees "civilization founded on money values and secular rationalism, with no religious communion or human sense of community, a nightmare world of isolation and instability, of restless nervous and intellectual activity, emotional stagnation and spiritual drought. Gerontion (the name means a little old man) is the shadowy symbol and spokesman of the sensitive intellectual in this world. Perhaps we are meant to compare him with the hero of Newman's *The Dream of Gerontius*, who looks forward with such full and serene joy and faith to the moment of dissolution and the acceptance of purgation."[23]

Grotowski has not only responded to Eliot's cry about the loss of God, but he shows a remarkable kinship to Eliot's aesthetics—to the poet's method of compressing central metaphors, his utilization of myths and history, and especially to Eliot's principle of the "objective correlative," his search to concretize an emotional state in his poetry. Aesthetically, Grotowski seeks the same: he has demanded a new kind of actor and a new training that will concretize an emotional state on the stage. To this end, he has worked out special theatrical techniques to support his goals, techniques which bring together and extend medieval Catholic ritual, twentieth-century Western theatrical ideas, and the theatrical traditions of venerable Asian cultures. In addition to his Polish ancestors, he has studied and drawn inspiration from world masters: Stanislavsky, Vakhtangov, and Meyerhold of Russia, the creators of Japanese No, the Indian Kathakali, and the Peking Opera.

As a young man, Grotowski worshipped Stanislavsky, but was critical of his theory of emotion memory, a technique which presumably enables actors, when working on a role, to reenact or recall their own life experiences in order to give a sense of fidelity to their acting. Grotowski believes that this technique of recall failed to recapture *specific* emotion, and that it has lead instead to hysteria and intellectualism. According to Grotowski, emotions lie dormant in the subconscious, waiting to be aroused, but only physical stimuli will uncover these feelings, as well as an organic understanding of psychic-physical relationships. Further, all emotion is linked to physical actions, Grotowski claims, and all physical action is linked to root impulses which, in turn, are linked to the collective unconscious. For Grotowski, the actors' concentration, then, must be on the root impulse. Although Stanislavsky began to work in this direction late in his life (having been influenced by the work of Pavlov), he did not thoroughly examine such actions as looking, talking, or touching in terms of uncovering their roots; instead he regarded these ordinary activities as basic physical actions in themselves. Neither did Stanislavsky examine muscular activity in connection with gestures. According to Grotowski, Stanislavsky saw no significance in a muscle expanding or contracting when an actor played with an object, and he drew no conclusions as to its possible psychological ramifications. Stanislavsky wanted only to find the point of physical tension and eliminate it and thus (Grotowski claims), Stanislavsky neglected the prospect that tension itself has an emotional source that can be theatrically viable.[24]

Grotowski studied the work of other masters as well. From Vakhtangov, he learned to blend naturalism and symbolism, a tendency he also found in Wyspianski. From Meyerhold, he adapted the concept of plasticity and developed the "cat" exercise in which the actor calls into play all his body motion by strenuously reenacting the activity of a cat—an exercise known and practiced in theatre groups around the world. On Meyerhold's model, he designed "corporeal" and "plastique" exercises, based on body impulses buttressed by interior images. And like Meyerhold, he believed in the supremacy of the body and in the possibilities of extending the theatrical experience through non-literary theatre.[25]

At the same time, Grotowski had a special interest in voice training; he studied the Peking Opera, whose actors, among other things, use a particular pitch and tone for each role, and work out special rhythms and tempos; their chanting and singing are freely interspersed with the spoken word, while the dramas themselves are not concerned with a literal story, but with its essences or climaxes. Grotowski's interest in voice matched his interest in ritual, which he expanded by studying the Japanese No and the Indian Kathakali. [Most of Grotowski's ritual work, of course, is derived from his Catholic upbringing.] In the No theatre, language, virtually unintelligible, is intoned or recited according to established rules, and every gesture and movement must be performed in accordance with traditional ritualistic patterns. In the Kathakali (a theatre on the southern coast of India, whose name literally means "acting out stories"), stories are epics that deal with violent death, the furies of the gods, and uncontrolled passions. Ritualized for hundreds of years (the form we see today was adopted in the eighteenth-century), the acting in Kathakali technique is composed of about 500 separate signs, a complete alphabet. Eugenio Barba, a disciple of Grotowski, writes: ". . . there are nine motions of the head, [in Kathakali] eleven casting a glance, six motions of the eyebrows, and four positions of the neck. The sixty-four motions of the limbs cover the movements of the feet, toes, heels, ankles, waist, hips. . . . The gestures of the hands and fingers have a narrative function and they are organized in a system of fixed figures called *mudras* ('signs' in Sanskrit). Those *mudras* are the alphabet of the acting 'language'. . . . There are sets of facial motions to express not only feelings and emotions, but traits of character of a more permanent nature, such as generosity, pride, curiosity, anxiety in the face of death."[26] In short, the Kathakali actor's hands tell the story, and his face expresses his attitude and emotional reactions to the story. This dualism enables the actor to be part of the tale and comment on it simultaneously—a kind of dialectic without language.

One of the most important aspects of the Kathakali is the way in which the actors work with their eyes. (In *The Constant Prince*, Cieslak's eyes always caused comment; his eyeballs dilated.) "Sometimes the face is absolutely immobile and the eyes alone do the acting. . . ." In one play, Barba reports: "a butterfly burns itself in a flame. The actor portrays this with his eyes alone." Of equal importance are the movements of the various parts of the body: "[They] are completely desynchronized. For example, the legs may be moving at an incredible speed while the hands sculpt the *mudras* with a deliberate and precise slowness."[27]

During their training the Kathakali actors work in complete silence; they endure painful exercises that result in the complete control of the actor's muscles; they follow a strict daily schedule of work, usually beginning at 4 A.M.; they are zealous, religious and live a monastic life. Particularly interesting is the Kathakali philosophy of theatre, parts of which Grotowski found meaningful. "The actor-priest offers his body to the gods," Barba writes, "like the Jugglers of Notre-Dame in the medieval legend offered his juggling to the Virgin Mary. . . . He offers his body with humility and supplication, quite willing to make any sacrifice for his art."[28]

Although Grotowski may know and make use of a tremendous range of theatrical and aesthetic theories, he has never embraced any theory unequivocally; he has always attempted to find the appropriate exercise to suit the individual actor. But if there is a general principle to which his actors adhere it is "exposure carried to outrageous excess." Actors are required to extend themselves beyond their normal limitations; they are asked to relinquish their stereotyped cultural mask to reach another level—the biological. During the process, they supposedly discover their physical impulses together with their unconscious, mythic, or archetypal roots which, in Grotowski's canon, are the basis for true creativity. An actor's task, therefore, is to re-create that which *precedes* the impulse and to formalize it before it is interrupted by thought so that spontaneous impulse coalesces with artistic form.[29]

The most important key to Grotowski's acting technique is *impulse*. And Grotowski has methodically and painstakingly researched its source. Taking up where Stanislavsky and Meyerhold left off, Grotowski asks certain questions: What is impulse? What leads to a particular gesture? What compels the actors to cry or howl, to speak softly or loudly, to move, to walk or to run? How can impulses be replenished, recorded, and repeated? For Grotowski, impulse is an externalization of feeling through the physiology of the individual. Impulse originates and exists in the nerve centers of the body. Impulse has its own dynamics, energy, sound, voice, and rhythm; it lies just beneath the skin, to be summoned by the proper stimuli. To learn the location and source of impulse requires an intimate knowledge and control of the body, achieved through what Grotowski calls the *via negativa*. Rather than enabling the actor to acquire skills, the negative way enables him to eradicate his blocks, the assumption being that "freeing," "annihilating," "burning," reducing the body to zero, to a *tabula rasa*, will eliminate repression and release pure impulses. Since the body is the center of the network of impulses, one reacts, speaks, and breathes with the body; indeed, every action in life is manifest through the body. Thus the actor must undergo a series of strenuous exercises (based on Meyerhold's biomechanics) to free the body so as to release the actor's impulse. If the actor becomes defenseless, then his honest feelings and integral Self will emerge. For Grotowski, this was a matter of giving oneself—in fact, giving oneself "totally, in one's deepest intimacy, with confidence, as when one gives oneself in love."[30]

Grotowski's training program is the equivalent of initiations into religious orders or cults. Following the Polish tradition, Grotowski interchanges sacred and secular words. The "novitiate" actor tears away his mask or veil (training), purges his sins through the exercises (and ultimately through the performance), is sanctified by approbation of Grotowski himself (the Father/Christ figure), and, finally, reaches an epiphany—in secular terms, a freedom tantamount to a successful psychoanalysis; in religious terms, a spiritual transcendence.

The success of this method depends upon the actor's ability to withstand the iron discipline and the unexpected fanatical dedication. Not only is the learning of new techniques required, but the actor must revamp his personality and way of life. He must be committed, fearless, and fervent in his belief in the possibilities of expressing his own body impulses, including the voice. Among the actor's imperatives (for Grotowski) is the construction of a personal "psychoanalytic language" that consists of sounds and gestures which are as unique to, and expressive of, the actor as is the self-contained language of words created by a great poet.[31] He must analyze "the hand's reflex during a psychic process and its successive development through shoulder, elbow, wrist and fingers—in order to decide how each phase can be expressed through a sign, an ideogram. . . ."[32]

The exercises are divided into two basic categories: the corporeals and the plastiques. The corporeals are a series of sharp acrobatic-like headstands, handstands, shoulderstands, and high jumps, done rapidly, continuously, and frenetically. The "cat," the basic corporeal exercise, is designed primarily for energy and the suppleness of the vertebrae. Actors get on all fours and stretch their bodies to resemble the cat in its various attitudes and positions. The plastiques are fast rotations back and forth of the joints: head, shoulders, elbows, wrists, hands, fingers, chest, hips, torsos; also exercises of joints going in opposite or contradictory directions—the head going one way, the shoulders another, for example. The exercises represent neither a formula nor a system; they are merely an approach, a way of leading one to find one's biological impulses.[33]

Anthony Abeson, a student of Grotowski, writes:

> [The exercises are designed to stress] our capacity for balance, plasticity, fluidity, and extension. Their purpose, however, was *not* that we develop physically, but that we learn, organically, rather than cerebrally, "essential things" about our bodies, such as resistances and points of balance. In addition, each exercise had to be done as the realization of a personal association, never as just an exercise, keeping the emphasis on expression and externalization. . . . The "stunt" or "result" aspect of the exercises was always avoided. We learned, for example, to explore our possibilities for balance not in the manner of the Flying Wallendas, but solely for our own knowledge. The gains derived from a headstand were not the visual ones with which, presumably, you could really wow them on the Ed Sullivan show, but stemmed from the step-by-step execution of the stand and from feeling, as you progressed upwards, the adjustments in the body as it adapted to the changes in its equilibrium. Once a point of balance became natural, we were always urged to find others. The exercises often went on for a very long time . . . and taxed our control and endurance rather than our strength. The exercises do not require superhuman force and can be done by anyone,

> regardless of age or sex. Our oldest member, a woman of ample age and proportions, had relatively little trouble. Nevertheless, certain exercises *were* difficult and sometimes frightening, at least when first encountered."[34]

Although Grotowski believes in the harmony of body and voice, he maintains that the one absolute rule is that "bodily activity comes first, and then vocal expression. . . . First you bang on the table and afterwards you shout!"[35] Grotowski is equally concerned with vocal expression, and he has adapted the Hatha Yoga breathing exercises for vocal use. Asserting that every actor's breathing is individual and based on the actor's physiology, Grotowski maintains that the power of the voice is linked with breathing (itself not a new concept), and that the "spectator not only hears the voice of the actor perfectly, but is also penetrated by it as if it were stereophonic . . . The actor must exploit his voice in order to produce sounds and intonations that the spectator is incapable of reproducing or imitating."[36] Exercises concentrate on the opening of the larynx, on inhaling and exhaling, on speech rhythms, on physiological resonators (a term used by Grotowski to designate the areas in the body where air can be drawn in, vibrated, and released). Resonators exist in the head, chest, nasal area, larynx, and belly, and voice can be amplified from these areas as well as from an infinite number of other places (spine, back of jaws, shoulders, etc.), of which most actors are unaware. Exercising the voice (in language and in sound) from various parts of the resonators is a complicated but original process. The hands thrust upward when speaking will in some actors automatically activate the upper or head resonator to push the voice upward toward the ceiling, while the downward motion of the hands in conjunction with the spoken voice may, in the same way, activate the lower resonators to directing the voice toward the ground.[37] The mouth voice, the occipital voice, the chest voice, and the belly voice can also, if properly controlled, produce the same directional effects and unique patternings as the careful calibration of sound and movement.[38]

Describing the vocal exercises during his 1969 work with Grotowski at Aix-en-Provence, where Grotowski has given yearly seminars, Abeson writes:

> The work was very strenuous, beginning with the singing of a song and continuing for a couple of hours or more. Each person was worked with in a different way, according to his vocal problems. He [Grotowski] allowed one girl, for example, to walk around the room aimlessly, singing a song over and over again for almost 10 minutes non-stop. He then asked her to raise her left hand to her collar-bone while continuing to walk and sing as before. Somehow, that simple gesture greatly changed her voice—it became softer and fuller. He then asked what personal associations that gesture held for her, and then let her continue, sometimes changing the position of her hands, sometimes asking more questions, in this way evolving a very personal type of psycho-physical approach with her. My own voice work, also based on singing, was equally personal and rewarding. I sang a couple of relatively simple songs, finishing with the Christmas carol, "Adeste Fideles." While singing, I was asked to direct my voice towards different parts of the room, listen to the various echoes as I did so. At the same time, I was moving almost continually, sometimes at my discretion, but more often in a very specific way, for example as Donald Duck. . . . At other times, I was meant merely to lie in certain positions saying one word over and over, for example, Dominum from the carol. After more than two hours of such work, I lay crumpled in a heap on the floor. My voice had begun to awaken in its entirety, and I could rest. . . .[39]

At the same seminar in Aix, Andre Gregory, the director, had a similar experience. He claimed that his voice was tight and rasping, and that he continually felt restricted. One day Grotowski asked him to assume the characteristic of some animal with which he, Gregory, could associate something personal or something extraordinary. Gregory assumed the position of a giraffe, and then "before I knew it," he said, "I was sounding like Yma Sumac."[40] Apparently the psychological image had triggered a release in his voice, enabling him to use it in any fashion. On a television program in which this writer interviewed Grotowski, he was asked how the actor Cieslak had attained his extraordinary vocal range. Grotowski replied: "It is because his nature has been unveiled. He is not divided between certain mental conceptions, that is to say, an intellectual 'me' and all the rest; he is a whole being. He is at the same time the spirit and the body, the sex and the intellect, the biology and the lucidity, and this 'and' is not this and that, it is all one. He is like a river of impulses, open, living, which directs itself toward other human beings, and that's how his voice is revealed."[41]

Although Grotowski is well known for his corporeal and plastique exercises, he has not excluded the use of texts during periods of training. While working with Peter Brook's actors at the Royal Shakespeare Company in 1967, Grotowski reportedly used a Hamlet soliloquy: "First, Grotowski instructed every member of the cast in turn to recite the text [*Hamlet*] with feeling, then—with detachment, then—as young people unable to grasp the full meaning and unable to see its depth, then—all actors together but every one in his own way and not in unison: each actor had to wait several seconds for his turn to join others in recitation. The aim was to arrive at a full concentration on the text, in spite of the misleading cacophony of well-known yet confused words. Then followed various exercises: gestures, movements of body and of facial muscles. The general effect was that of some black mass, and yet the sound logic of it was evident."[42]

Central to Grotowski's technique is its application to the individual. Since each person's body or voice reacts differently, exercises vary with each, even if the basic repertoire of exercises remains the same. Grotowski resists using the exercises as patterns or prescribed alphabets or rigid systems. The Grotowski actor does not *acquire* traits, stances, habits, nor does he concentrate solely on the plastiques or corporeals, which are merely suggestions or possibilities for extension, not ends in themselves. The actor does not have set exercises that he is required to follow, as does a dancer, for example. According to Grotowski, dancers are recognizable by their technical similarities, all having been trained and having mastered, regardless of individuation, a common alphabet. Although this is a matter of contention, Grotowski claims that all dance—modern or ballet—has a fixed formal alphabet in which form precedes content. Although great dancers have varied their alphabet, he maintains that a dance alphabet exists, and that this alphabet is the point of departure in dance—not the individual himself.[43] In the Grotowski method of training, everything is a result of the actor's research into his body and voice, which produce his living impulses, and it is those impulses that ultimately comprise the pattern of his performance.

During rehearsals, the actor's physical actions arising from impulses are scored and fixed; that is, a physical action becomes a "sign." A "sign" is an outward response to a pure impulse that preceeds that response, action, or sound. The finished performance is composed of such signs, and scored like music by the director. The score, then, is the extent of the exploration.

In the performance, if the physical and vocal gesture is given without the impulse, the essential meaning of the role will be missing. The score is a complete cycle of physical actions attached to impulses, which are linked up moment to moment so that the performance is tightly knit. Supposedly these signs, when added up, are easily discernable by the spectators. Grotowski has said:

> . . . the score, of course, is fixed, but it's not fixed in the sense of something that's absolutely fixed, but in the sense of having two banks—having two banks of a river. In other words, between this and that a human reaction which has its limits, its borders, but which each time is different. If a spectator can see a production three times, he thinks that it's absolutely the same thing, but if he's seen it ten times, he will then observe that each time it's something totally different. It's only the same—between the same banks.[44]

Inevitably, Grotowski's philosophical and aesthetic gestalt has influenced avant-garde theatre elsewhere in the West. He has given annual seminars in Denmark (which many Americans have attended), as well as workshops in London and New York, and has developed thereby a large following. Richard Schechner's Performance Group and some of La Mama's directors claim Grotowski as their mentor; Joseph Chaikin has also used some of his exercises. But Grotowski warns against slavish imitation. His method—a trial and error process—cannot be successful without one's own independent research. And those who use his name without understanding his intent are bound to fail, he feels. He has been particulary unimpressed by the phenomenon of American actors' searching for new gurus each decade to solve their artistic and personal problems, for he feels that Americans never develop a technique of their own to its ultimate end. Yet he is in constant touch with American actors and directors (he lectures frequently in America), and each year accepts some for training in Poland.

As leader of the "poor theatre," Grotowski is revered; his actors see him as father, brother, lover, genius, high priest. Once one is part of the holy movement, the respect is mutual. Though his methods might seem repressive by American standards, his disciples feel that his judgment is infallible; but outsiders find him secretive, detached, and fiercely disciplined.

The significance of Grotowski's art is not his exacting discipline, but his extraordinary creativity. He has evolved a modern theatre quite unlike any other. Rather than abolishing language, he has extended it; rather than exhorting the audience to act, he has involved them as silent witnesses; rather than fusing life with art, he has insisted on a formal technique. More important, his art—indeed, his personality—forced those lives that touched his to discover their own roots. Some decided to create poor theatres of their own; others rejected the holy life as incompatible with their temperament and times. Grotowski's art may not be for export at all. But those who experienced it recognized something very special—painful, perhaps, or astonishing, but a phenomenon which was to cast a powerful shadow over the entire avant-garde movement.

eight

The Open Theatre

"The connections are in our heads."

Joseph Chaikin

Happenings, the Living Theatre, and Grotowski's Polish Laboratory Theatre evolved the pattern for the sixties. Although each had its own set of principles and its own method of working, the trend became clear. Young people were forming groups, working in studios, and training in different ways—distinctly separate from those of establishment theatre. As was to be expected, faddists and fakers, sensing the vitality and originality of the experimentalists, jumped on the bandwagon and exploited the "new theatre" with superficial techniques and good public relations. Other, more serious groups produced only one or two pieces: experimentation was a long and arduous task, and there were few who withstood the trials. Even fewer were able to survive over any appreciable length of time, and to establish a repertory and a style of their own: the Open Theatre was one that did. Though it has undergone great change since its inception, and, though the company has now disbanded, the Open Theatre in 1973 was still trying to find a new direction for itself. Despite the outcome, the group, under the leadership of Joseph Chaikin, made an important and substantial contribution to the experimental movement.

During the early and mid-1960's, every morning a group of young people could be seen hurrying into a dilapidated old building on West Fourteenth Street. A creaky broken-down elevator took them to a messy loft five flights above the dirt and noise of the street. Upstairs it was quiet, relaxed, friendly. The group—actors in leotards, with long hair and bare feet—would be sipping their morning coffee, eating doughnuts out of a paper bag, or perusing the bulletin board cluttered with pictures of Che, Fidel, Malcolm. Then they would go onto mats and start their sound and body exercises. Everyone would slowly wake up.

In a corner stood a small man in jeans and a sweatshirt, drinking coffee from a container. He was the director, ready to go. He would walk around the room as the actors warmed up, touching their necks, legs, heads, whispering to them softly, and looking for areas of tension or for resonating sounds. He was Joseph Chaikin, one of the directors of the Open Theatre, to become famous for his work with *American Hurrah, The Serpent,* and *Terminal.* The actors to whom he spoke were then members of his company.

When the Becks and the Living Theatre left for Europe, some of the young people they had nurtured, like Joe Chaikin and Peter Feldman, stayed behind. Unable to uproot themselves, or unwilling to face the challenges and hardships that would confront the Becks in Europe, some of the ex–Living Theatre members formed their own groups and organized their own theatres—meeting together in lofts, cellars, studios, cafés. The concentration in New York was on group work, creative communities, theatre as politics; it was 1963, a year for experimental techniques, the same year that introduced Ellen Stewart's Café La Mama, Café Cino, the Barr-Albee experimental playwrights, and what was to become the Open Theatre. The winter of '63 saw a group of such people come together in a loft on Twenty-fourth Street: the critics Gordon Rogoff and Richard Gilman; the writers Megan Terry, María Irene Fornés, Jean-Claude van Itallie, Arthur Sainer, Michael Smith; the actors Peter Feldman, Joseph Chaikin, Barbara Vann, Jerry Ragni, and others. Several of them had been studying with Nola Chilton, who at that time was about to leave America for Israel. Members of her acting class, having grown accustomed to working together, decided to stay together and practice their art. They wanted to build a cooperative venture where all would be equal and no one would be leader. They all felt they were "beautiful failures"—unable to put up with the commercial theatre world. The group, because of its experimental nature, called itself the Open Theatre, to distinguish it from the closed theatre of Broadway. Joseph Chaikin was twenty-six at the time; he wanted to try his hand at directing. Chaikin's training had been extremely thorough. He had studied not only with Nola Chilton, but with Mira Rostova, Bill Hickey, and Peter Kass, all teachers of the Stanislavsky method. He had also appeared prominently in two Living Theatre productions: Brecht's *In the Jungle of Cities* and *Man Is Man* (performances which won him two Obies); he was an actor in demand.

Peter Feldman also had been prominent in the Living Theatre. He too had been a pupil of Nola Chilton, and an actor and stage manager with the Living. Both men discovered they had similar goals and interests. Not only were they dissatisfied with Julian Beck's concept of the theatre, but with the total theatrical scene: propaganda plays left them cold, and theatre as a business repelled them, as did the naturalistic style—which, for them, reflected programmed responses to their daily lives. "Method" acting, in their judgment, had become an approach that depended on personal mannerisms, an acting style which, coupled with the limitations of the text and its reliance on words, crippled the actor and trapped him into a set formula. Feldman and Chaikin found equally distasteful the lack of ensemble playing and reliance on the star system. No company other than the Living (and the old Group Theatre) had been able to build an ensemble company or a collective theatre, a goal of Chaikin and Feldman. But unlike the Becks, who also believed in theatre as a collective, they were not interested in focusing solely on political issues. They wanted to develop an acting style that would depict the individual's response to a depersonalized society. They envisioned theatre not as a revolutionary political weapon alone, but as an instrument of what Chaikin calls the actor's "personal crisis." Above all, they wanted the actors to be so technically proficient as to synthesize their political, personal, and social attitudes into art without resorting to bombastic dogmatism, cliché illustrations, or rhetoric.

Chaikin and Feldman began to experiment with acting techniques, relying on their training with Nola Chilton, whose influence, Feldman asserts, was decisive. She had been teaching actors to respond, with their body and voice, to inanimate objects and abstract sensations. In addition, some of the actors had studied with a director and teacher named Geraldine Lust, whose work with ritual theatre inspired the group to experiment with daily social rituals (which led to the Open Theatre's developing the "shared repetitive pattern"). But perhaps it was the influence of Viola Spolin (and her exercises in theatre games with the Second City company in Chicago) that was the turning point for the Open Theatre. Chaikin, having worked with Spolin in Chicago, introduced her improvisations—the "Mirror," "Inside-outside," "Conductor," and "Transformation" exercises—to which Chaikin and members of the theatre added their own variations. These became the mainstay of the Open Theatre's work.

As the group progressed, the actors, not wanting to be committed to a specific approach, refrained from self-definition and resisted formulating a unified aesthetic. Chaikin and Feldman, having organized workshops, were elected artistic directors. Members of the theatre remained equal, however; each paid a small fee for the maintenance of an informally organized studio. The purpose was exploratory: actors were admitted haphazardly; some merely drifted in, and either remained with one workshop or changed to another. Playwrights Jean-Claude van Itallie, Megan Terry, María Irene Fornés, and later, Sam Shepard, attended most of the sessions, and from their observations, they developed future plays. Gradually, Chaikin's workshop became the most advanced.

By the spring of 1965, the Open Theatre had enough money to

rent the Sheridan Square Playhouse in Greenich Village on Monday nights to show some of its experimental work. Over a period of several weeks, the company performed Eliot's *Sweeney Agonistes* and plays by van Itallie, Fornés, and Terry. Directors included Barbara Vann, Peter Feldman, and Joe Chaikin. Various pieces from workshop sessions usually rounded out the evenings. These Monday nights in the Village proved successful, and the group went on to other things.

Jean-Claude van Itallie had written a play called *Interview*, which was performed at the Martinique Theatre, and another short play, *Motel* (originally titled *America Hurrah*), which La Mama produced. These, along with a third of his plays, *TV*, subsequently were organized into the well-known version of *America Hurrah*. At the same time, Megan Terry wrote *Viet Rock*, a folk-rock collage about Vietnam which originated from her own Open Theatre workshop. With a cast of sixteen, it opened at La Mama in May 1966. Despite unenthusiastic reviews, it played at Yale, later reopened in New York (November 1966) to poor notices, and closed.

Almost simultaneously, the three plays that composed Jean-Claude van Itallie's *American Hurrah* opened (November 7, 1966) at the Pocket Theatre on Third Avenue: Jacques Levy (who conducted an Open Theatre workshop) directed *Motel* and *Interview*, while Chaikin directed *TV*. It was a tremendous success.

The members felt their commercial ventures with *America Hurrah* and *Viet Rock* had oriented the Open Theatre toward success and had divided the group's coherence. They decided that henceforth the company would commit itself only to experimental work. The turning point came when the Open Theatre won a Ford Foundation grant, which enabled it to work consistently on a project that turned into their production of *The Serpent*.

The Serpent changed the character of the Open Theatre. Formerly there had been many workshops, where actresses like Lee Worley, Joyce Aaron, and others had conducted their own experimental work. But when the company decided to concentrate on a full-length production, all the workshops were combined under Chaikin's direction, and their collective energies were channeled into preparing for the new piece. The Ford money made it possible to operate daily workshops, and for the first time, the theatre was able to hire special technical people: Kristin Linklater from New York University taught voice, and Joseph Schlichter taught sensitivity training based on principles of gestalt therapy. The group went into isolation for almost two years to crystalize and sharpen its technique and work out its philosophical perspectives.

As already mentioned, Chaikin and Feldman (and the rest of the company), disenchanted with the current acting styles, had united precisely to discover new directions in acting. They shared their generation's disgust with the manipulation of words by the politicians and the mass media. Also, having worked with the naturalistic play, they were no longer interested in duplicating naturalistic behavior on stage; they wanted to dramatize their own dreams and meditations in relation to their social conditioning. Soon they discovered that this objective could not be achieved within the playwright's prescribed text. So long as the theatre centered around the world of the playwright, the world of the actor could not be expressed. And it was the actor's creative force that determined the path of the Open Theatre. Slowly and pragmatically, the actors, together with Chaikin and Feldman, were gradually devising their own aesthetics: the content of their productions would be based on their "zones of feelings," their method of work, collaborative, and their form, a four-dimensional language of sound, gesture, rhythm, and silence.[1] Peter Feldman sums it up well:

> Our object was to make visible onstage those levels of reality which usually are not expressed in situations: the elusive, irrational, fragile, mysterious or monstrous lives within our lives; the elements of personality which lie behind the roles we assume as our identity . . . [Our object was] to confront elements of dream, myth, fantasy, ritual as well as social and moral problems . . . to express the fragmentation and multiplicity of experience, and the inconsistency of internal and external "truth" about character or events . . . to break down the actor's reliance upon rational

> choices, mundane social realism and watered-down Freud, and to release his unconscious through non-rational, spontaneous action celebrating the actor's own perceptions about modern life.[2]

Mainly under Chaikin's leadership and with training derived from the voice and body teachers, the company developed a fine technique, as was later acknowledged by most critics. But perhaps the unique development in their work was their commitment to collaboration. In an article about the ensemble in *Newsweek* (May 26, 1969), Chaikin was quoted as follows: "There are two main values in working on a piece in this collaborative way. One is the discovery of finding deep common references. It takes time to reach these; the cliché references all need to come out first. And the second value is the astonishing power there is in the performance of an actor who is actually playing out an image which he himself introduced."

Thus, in the Open Theatre, the director was not the usual "genius" who single-handedly infused the actors with inspiration. In the Open Theatre, the actor's contribution was equal to that of the director. Without the actors, collaboration was, in fact, impossible. Once the group decided upon a theme to work on, the actors and director analyzed the work in all its ramifications, not only by lengthy daily discussions, but in concrete artistic terms. Through improvised responses and attitudes, executed in sound and gesture rather than in words, they created the play as they went along, and established form and content simultaneously, the one a natural outgrowth of the other. In this manner, they evolved their fragmented images, their devastating social and political stereotypes, their implicit meanings through mere gesture, and their instant non-verbal communication, all of which were attempts to relate form to social and political content. From the beginning, the Open Theatre members had seen themselves as outside the establishment, indeed in opposition to it, though they never really called for radical change. Their art had been personal and expressive; they sought to convey dissociated sensibilities and to challenge the meaningless verbiage of contemporary life. Their collaborative effort was not only a way of making theatre, but of sensitizing themselves in a mechanized and repressive society and of reinforcing the theory that collaboration can surpass individualistic creativity. In the Open Theatre, an actor discovers who he really is, said Joyce Aaron: "the play becomes the actor's language, only his, and the play defines him and helps him to be in touch with his true nature."[3]

The world the Open Theatre wanted to express is comprised of the actors' meditations on certain subjects. Most of their perceptions were generally non-intellectual, comtemplative, extraordinarily fragmented, and politically unsophisticated. Their work was a search for self-definition rather than a finished statement. Given the fact that they always had been dissatisfied with the establishment, and in their early productions openly critical of the status quo, their later works had been relatively circumspect, and only tangentially political. True, they had always tried to synthesize their creative impulses with their social and political awareness, but it was their artistic development that appeared to have gained ascendancy, and was their real mark of distinction.

Some critics have compared Chaikin and the Open Theatre to Grotowski and the Polish Laboratory Theatre because each sees theatre in terms of the actor and each worked with sound and body. The Polish Lab's philosophy and theatrical style, however, are fully defined; the Open Theatre's were ambivalent and diffused. Grotowski's images are rooted in romantic-Catholic Poland; Chaikin's, in American life. Grotowski stresses a formal, disciplined precision in training and in performance; Chaikin believes in intuition and instinctive experiences. The Polish Lab works with vigorous physical energy, tempestuous paroxysms, biological root impulses; the Open Theatre, with Yoga meditation and relaxation. Chaikin's actors concentrated on dreams and reveries and drew upon social problems for inspiration. The Polish Lab is metaphysical, non-topical, immersed in finding the universals, the essences, the paradoxes of human nature; it is bathed in unrelenting agony.

The Open Theatre, were also aware of pain, nonetheless expressed joy, humanity, and a certain placidity.

A major difference between the Polish Laboratory Theatre and the Open Theatre is their method of work. In the Open Theatre and in its workshops, Chaikin strove for an atmosphere of friendly relaxation; he organized the work around group dynamics, so that he was intimately involved and personally concerned with each member of the group. He was unauthoritative, uncommanding, and almost always open to suggestion (in fact, Roberta Sklar of the Open Theatre was credited as being assistant director of *The Serpent* and *Terminal*). On the surface, the group members appeared to be emotionally dependent upon one another for sustenance as well as for artistic replenishment, and therefore, the Open Theatre gave one the impression, however erroneous, that it was a family. In short, the group's atmosphere was quite unlike the strict, formal, rigidly disciplined one of Grotowski's Polish Laboratory Theatre. Further, the social worlds of the Open Theatre and that of Grotowski are totally different. Living in the New York City of the 1960's and '70's elicited a style that Grotowski's group can scarcely comprehend. When asked, for example, why the Open Theatre began its day with Yoga meditation rather than with vigorous exercises in the Grotowski manner, Joyce Aaron said: "I walk only three blocks to the studio every morning, but in those three blocks I face the world: garbage in the streets, drunks in the hallways, noise, dirt, pollution. I need the quiet of the studio. I need to lie down on the floor and connect with my own center. I must divorce myself from the turmoil of the outside world before I can concentrate on art."[4]

The Open Theatre created its own mode of behavior and its own responses to the outside world. As was the Living Theatre, the Open Theatre had been influenced by youth culture, yoga ritual, sensitivity training techniques, gestalt psychology, and the writings of R. D. Laing. But its members had adapted each idea to their personal needs. In general, they rejected all authoritarian patterns, but, unlike the Living Theatre, they had not subscribed to an over-all ideological position; their politics, determined by personal choices of the members, ranged from the non-political to draft counseling and supporting the Black Panthers.

The Serpent, their first full-length production, most successfully demonstrated their philosophy and their form. Based on the Book of Genesis, *Serpent* examines such problems as freedom and authority, choice and its consequences, sex and love, violence and war. Created in an atmosphere of warmth and good feeling, at a time when the whole group had a unified and healthy sense of purpose, *Serpent* is an expression of the vitality, wit, and energy that had characterized the Open Theatre. Although the final script was structured by Jean-Claude van Itallie, the completed text incorporated the collaborative principle. Van Itallie worked with the company daily, he watched their improvisations, he knew the actors' problems, and he shared their sensibilities. What he did was to give form to their consciousness.

The Serpent, then, grew almost entirely out of the actors' perceptions, responses, images, and the patterns that affected their lives. What was Paradise like? How did Cain kill Abel? What is relevant in Biblical myths? But the play was intended, as van Itallie has said, "to call up dreams, not answer or describe moral questions." By its choice of subject matter, however, the work implies a search for moral imperatives. For, out of contemplation of questions of choice and authority, freedom and fear, sexuality and love, violence and guilt—and especially dreams of a lost paradise—the Open Theatre pointed out the extent to which the human condition remains familiar and unchanged. The work is seldom explicit; it invites our associations and stimulates our sensibilities. It is a stunning example of evocative theatre.

The piece begins as we become aware of the actors: they sit among us in the aisles. Faint sounds are heard all over the auditorium—a bell, a soft whistle, a dainty scratching noise, a tiny tinkling reminiscent of the Chinese theatre. Suddenly we are aware of human breathing: "HA, Ha, He He, Hi, HI"—the actors have spoken their first words, a breath and a vowel. As if in a ceremonial ritual, they march up from the aisles to the stage, all the while slapping their chests, legs, and thighs, creating vigorous contrapuntal arrangements of sound and gesture, which they intermingle with:[5]

> First Woman of the Chorus: I no longer live in the beginning.
> Second Woman: I've lost the beginning.
> Third Woman: I'm in the middle, knowing.
> Third and Fourth Women: Neither the end nor the beginning.
> First Woman: I'm in the middle.
> Second Woman: Coming from the beginning.
> Third and Fourth Women: And going toward the end.[6]

Time forward, time backward, time remembered in our collective unconscious, and time caught forever through a camera lens are leading motifs expressing our fragmentation—an existential fact of life. The first sequence deals with the assassinations of John F. Kennedy and Martin Luther King, one of the most moving and technically brilliant moments of the piece; it is enacted as if in a rehearsal, or as a rerun of the Zapruder film of the Kennedy killing.

On center stage are two couples on their knees, who give the appearance of riding in an open car. They are President Kennedy and Jacqueline Kennedy, Governor Connally and Mrs. Connally. Behind them is a chorus-crowd, to the side, an "assassin-Director"; he calls the "shots." Pointing his rifle toward the moving automobile, he "kills" the President over and over again as he "shoots" his twelve frames. After the initial counting, he calls out the numbers at random until the frames are precisely ritualized: each number corresponds to an exact and almost infinitesimal moment in the incident. For example:

> 1: All four wave.
> 2: President is shot in the neck.
> 3: Governor is shot in the shoulder.
> 4: President is shot in the head. Governor's wife pulls her husband down and covers him with her body.
> 5: President falls against his wife.

6: President's wife begins to register something is wrong. She looks at her husband.
7: She puts her hands on his head.
8: She lifts her knee to put his head on it.
9: She looks into the front seat.
10: She begins to realize horror.
11: She starts to get up.
12: She begins to crawl out the back of the open car, and to reach out her hand.[7]

The effect is to imprint forever on the human consciousness not only the magnitude of the horror, but the impact of the media image. Meanwhile, in the background, Martin Luther King delivers excerpts from his famous "I have a dream" speech; he too is shot. Throughout, the crowd, shifting from one position on stage to another, plaintively explains:

I was not involved.
I am a small person.
I hold no opinion.
I stay alive.

I mind my own affairs.
I am a little man.
I lead a private life.
I stay alive.

I'm no assassin.
I'm no president.
I don't know who did the killing.
I stay alive.[8]

The chorus chants its lines to the rhythm of a drum. The lines, divided among four sections of the group, are broken down into the vowels and consonant sounds of the most important words, and although the literal meaning is obilterated, the chant is powerfully effective. The chorus' external vocal rhythms blend with the internal meaning, and the feeling behind the sounds is patently clear.

As in a film, the scene instantly shifts. We are in the Garden of Eden; everyone breathes the same "communal first breath." The atmosphere is pastoral, non-sensual, benign. Although conventional as the concept of the Creation is, the visual configurations are original. In the Temptation of Eve, five men, holding apples in each hand, arrange themselves in a body pyramid—one on top of the other—so that we see five pairs of arms and legs extended like branches of a tree. Apples appear to be in the actors' crotches and armpits; five tongues lasciviously hang out of five mouths, hissing, slithering, and wagging; five pairs of arms, legs, and torsos are undulating, insinuating, seducing. The swaying bodies, the drooping tongues, and the ten apples unify the Serpent and the tree. Eve, already aroused, is anxious, inquisitive, repelled, titillated. The apples meanwhile seem to hang like exposed testicles, suggesting desire, orgy, orgasm. Finally Eve eats. It is as if she has been penetrated and fulfilled. Adam virtually chokes on his first bite. Unable either to swallow it or spit it out, he is horrified as bits of the apple stick in his throat. Yet the fatal choice has been made. Now the snakes throw dozens of gorgeous red apples on the floor and greedily the actors munch and gobble their forbidden fruit, offering some to the audience. Soon the hilarity and satire of this is undercut by God's curses. One actor delivers the curse as he lifts up the actor he is cursing. Then the cursed one is dropped and lies spent, as if in the Inferno, while another is lifted, mouths his own curse, goes limp, and falls to the ground. This is repeated until the curses become louder and louder and the noise becomes unbearable. Throughout this part of the action, the sweating faces of the actors are intensely pained; they appear not only doomed by the Deity, but by their own self-destructiveness.

The piece reaches a climax with the murder of Abel. "And it occurred to Cain to kill his brother. But it did not occur to Cain that killing his brother would cause his brother's death," is the theme. The actors, on benches, begin by breathing in unison; "they are breathing Abel's breath." Cain, a picture of horrifying beauty, stands alone on stage. He seems strangely without premeditation or viciousness. The murder is done quietly, meticulously, ritualistically; Cain doesn't know what killing is, or what will actually kill his brother. Nothing is said: no voices are heard, only the steady, intense breathing. Each bone in Abel's body is "broken" methodically and painstakingly; suddenly all breathing stops. A senseless, obsessive, archetypal killing has taken place, recalling the assassinations of Kennedy and King.

The "begat" scene,—the discovery of sex, birth, and death—ends the play. Actors lie prone on the floor, they."discover" each other by touching one another's eyes, hair, and bodies, and quite by accident discover the purpose of the genitals. Quite by accident, too, they put the genitals to use in a hilarious mass fornication while the "begatting" is enumerated by an actress intoning from the Bible. Then, as the group reaches a mass orgiastic cry, the men turn into children and the women into mothers, until all meld into images of old age. While the life cycle is completed, the play ends, and the actors, mocking American sentimentalism, nonchalantly begin singing, "We are sailing along on Moonlight Bay . . ." Walking down into the audience, they continue to sing while offering the red shiny apples.

The discipline and technique of the company (as they appeared in *The Serpent*) was superb. Acting with "typical" American spontaneity, the company was admired all over the United States and Europe for its loose improvisational techniques and its refusal to be explicit. Even in performance, the actors tried to rediscover each other, and always left themselves open for surprises, an attitude that spurred their creativity and encouraged freshness. The techniques and the infectious spirit of the group were exhilarating, and encouraged spectators to feel part of the theatrical experience. However, the Open Theatre had its weaknesses.

The Serpent was an experiment in using myth to find the relationship of the past to the present. The actors were on a "trip," groping backward and forward in time, in an effort to define themselves and American culture. The piece was structured like an abstract film collage, juxtaposing contemporary assassinations with the murder of Abel, contemporary sexual mores with the innocence of sexual discovery, and contemporary alienation with Paradisiacal harmony. Aesthetically beautiful, the work never elicited associations beyond the easily recognizable and often banal daily conditions of life, which when expressed artistically, were lyrical and touching but not profound. As a result, the Open Theatre's effort to deal with existential man was considerably diluted. What emerged was the next-door neighbor: Eve resembled Jane Smith; Adam, Joe Smith; and the chorus of women, New York Jewish-hippie-bohemian-Village artists. The actors' continual projection of themselves and their personal backgrounds inhibited any larger intellectual concept. Despite the sweep of the theme, no attempt was made to develop a sense of objectivity or of epic; the actors relied mainly on their own sensibilities. Their aesthetic goal in this case inhibited a deeper probing into the unconscious mythic, or historical behavior patterns that shape those sensibilities. And so the open quality of the performers, based on idiosyncratic behavior and private perceptions, became dominant and produced a self-perpetuating paradox: openness alone resulted in an amorphous piece, its substance light, its tone personal—its content vague. And though Chaikin claims that all "the connections are in our heads," it is this kind of remark that tends to avoid the issue.

All the same, the production of *The Serpent* proved to be a qualitative development of Open Theatre style. The techniques in many scenes were outgrowths of sound and body exercises which, worked out through the years, were sophisticated and original. The piece showed more fluidity than, say, the work of the Living Theatre. The actors' movements were economical and gentle, less cluttered than those of the Living, though not as compelling but surely not as abrasive. Film technique was apparent in that an actor was able to shift at a rapid pace from one particular time, place, situation, and character to another, and as in a rapid movie scene, continuity was established, then swiftly broken, resulting in a fragmented, changing reality. Especially inventive was the theatre's work with repeated sound and ritualized movement. Sounds, like improvised "jaming" in jazz, were combined with words—very few words. When the technique was used properly, the result was an impressively large, harmonized proliferation—a symphony of sound and gesture. When this kind of jamming reached a fine point, various repeated patterns of sound emerged, called "emblems." These were explored and further distilled, and the result, in *Serpent*, was tantamount to a Greek chorus. *The Serpent* reflected the Open Theatre's success in evolving a distinct expressive form which, in its next major work, *Terminal*, it developed to an even greater extent.

Terminal was the Open Theatre's effort to produce a *totally* collaborative work. Composed entirely from the actors' own images, with words written by Susan Yankowitz, the piece was based on the group's meditation on death—on the actors' personal responses to the idea of their own mortality. First performed in the studio (and later in the Washington Square Methodist Church in Greenwich Village), *Terminal's* only scenery was four white slabs. The company was dressed in off-white jersey leotards resembling hospital gowns. At the sides of the stage were little boxes or chairs on which actors sat when not performing. The announcement of scenes, and the playing of harmonica and tambourine music, also take place from these areas. When the performance begins, the church is extraordinarily dark; on stage an actor "announces" the "celebration" by blowing on a bugle that sounds like a ram's horn. Now a procession of actors comes down the aisles playing on two-penny instruments; the song recalls Elizabethan strolling players and an American country dance, and the red canopy that actors carry symbolizes the traditional Jewish wedding altar. Once on stage, the living chant that they have "come among the dying to call upon the dead," and later the living enact their own state of dying.

As the living call upon the dead, they arrange themselves in constantly shifting spatial relationships, creating a vocal composition based on the repetition of the verbal motif: "We come among the dying to call upon the dead." Spoken, chanted, intoned, whispered, interrupted, broken down to bits and pieces, the simple verbal line emerges as a symphony. As the sound rises to full intensity and the actors' bodies, kinetically arranged, form an asymmetrical design, one is reminded of the technical purity of a Klee or a Mondrian. Soon the living (or the dying) perform a primitive ritual dance "on the graves of the dead." Holding small candle-like sticks which, banged together, create rhythmic variations, the actors move like bags of bones. The banging on the "graves," accompanied by a distant drumming, reaches a fever pitch of sound: the awakening of the dead is also akin to machine-gunning the living.

In the next section, the dying enact their bodily functions mechanically: breathing, running, eating, eliminating; then they are given last rites. Silently, a man and woman stand in the center of the stage. She: "This is the last chance to use your eyes," and she hands him a black patch. He covers one eye. She: "This is the last chance to use your voice," and she hands him another black patch. Silence. He covers his mouth. She: "This is the last chance to use your legs." Silence. The scene is over in no more than one minute—a minute of the most penetrating and chilling uses of silence. Then a montage of finely etched images (expressed through the actors' faces and bodies) "float" onto the stage, expand, contract, collapse, and sometimes converge slowly and gracefully as the "dead now come through to the dying." Groups suddenly arrange themselves into configurations, startling the audience by creating a flash of light followed by an equally sudden instant of darkness. The dying see themselves in the actual state of dying, avoiding death but experiencing it through the dead; they see themselves as they were in the past, recollecting daily violence, dead dreams, and false myths; they see themselves killed, embalmed, judged. Witnesses to the death of their parents, three women remember their mothers and fathers. One actress wonders about the routinized killing of her father's energy; another "sees" her mother but can't believe she is dying: a third "sees" her father on his back, re-creates his dying moments, even his death rattle. A few montages later, the dying act out their guilt: they "see" blood on the streets and, acquiescing reluctantly to the system, begin to carry their "slabs" on their backs. Remembering the captivity of the Jews as well as their own personal alienation, they bellow out agonizing Hebrew wails. Finally they crawl on their bellies to be judged by Gabriel who, standing on a ladder, shouts through a bull horn: "You saw, you saw, you can't say you didn't . . . the judgment of your life is your life." The group remain on their bellies. Then, as if to stand apart and release themselves (and the audience) from the scene's chilling implications and effects, the actors repeat the opening harmonic chant. Carrying the same red canopy, they begin to play on their two-penny instruments; suddenly they stop, pause, then play and stop again. They peer out at the audience sardonically, and the piece is ended. What are they saying? Nobody knows for sure.

In *Terminal*, the directors Joe Chaikin and Roberta Sklar[9] made a superb effort to capture that ineffable state between waking and dreaming, when one can see the beauty in the horror, the extraordinary in the mundane, and even the celebration in dying; as such, the result was an exquisite piece of craftsmanship, a stunning testimony to their poetic sensibilities. Yet the over-all effect was coldly clinical, for the passionate realities of living, and hence of dying, were never fully captured. Again, as in *The Serpent*, there were no original philosophical statements; instead, we were presented with an imaginatively designed vision. The actors seemed to have been enclosed in gorgeous marble: their forms, bare and precise, and their bodies lean, supple, shiny. Stripped to a minimal show of emotion, as well as to fine abstractions of sounds and movement, *Terminal* forfeited feeling for form. What was left was not a mosaic, or a tapestry, but a line drawing which finds its parallel in the static patterns of a formal court dance. For example, a motif emerges at the beginning, and in a few scenes the motif is reiterated and explained. A second one follows, with yet another elaboration. Each theme is repeated and expanded, but not resolved. Although the repetition ritualizes the piece, it also revealed an emptiness and diffusion that helped to disengage rather than involve the spectator. The drama never reached a climax—each moment was self-contained. There were brilliant scenes—Shami Chaikin's Hassidic chant, Paul Zimet's witch doctor's death dance, Ron Faber's resistance to being embalmed—but emotion was unnecessarily reined in, and there was a curious absence of love. In addition, the lack of the sort of humor usually associated with Open Theatre work rendered the production somewhat sterile. After a while, the unrelieved horror became diminished and, ultimately, unmoving.[10]

Some critics felt that *Terminal* is a metaphor for a dying society; if so, the metaphor didn't work. There were allusions to American complicity in violence, but as a whole piece *Terminal* is the Open Theatre's least socially conscious work. It was not only the tone of despair that divorced it from the radical sensibilities of its time, but whatever social dilemmas were depicted, they were neither focused nor clearly delineated, and seemed oddly unrelated to contemporary problems. In fact, the piece reflected such a hopeless picture of existence that it came as no surprise when the Open Theatre chose to offer Samuel Beckett's *Endgame* as its third play in the 1970 repertory, a production which was neither illuminating nor very satisfying. All the same, the repertory the Open Theatre presented that year, proved to be one of its most successful. On June 14, 1970, after a decade of working with many of the same members, and after playing their last performance of *The Serpent*, Chaikin and the Open Theatre decided that it was time to reorganize.

For several years there had been undercurrents of discontent. The Open Theatre had become closely identified with Chaikin, whose productions received consistent critical acclaim. Peter Feldman had directed various peices, but had never participated as fully as Chaikin in the development of the group: either by design or accident, Feldman's work was not included in the repertory on a regular basis. It was felt that Chaikin's creativity had earned him the right to become the company's undisputed head. Chaikin always had considered the actors his equals, and collaborated with them in creating the pieces, an attitude that gave actors the feeling that the theatre was theirs as well as his. But over the years, the company had grown dependent upon him; no other director remained with them, nor appeared to have his talent.

The Open Theatre had never lived a communal life. It was an artistic collective and, presumably, the group determined policy. Contrary to its public image, however, the group had its factions and tensions, even if they were always minimized once the work began. But during the 1969 tour in Europe, the grumblings which heretofore had been kept in check had erupted and threatened to break up the company.

Chaikin was well known by 1969, but he had avoided commercial outlets for the company. The widely acclaimed *Serpent* did not play in a regular theatre for a long run until 1970. Audiences saw it in the company's studio loft, where they sat on mattresses or on the hard floor. Chaikin refused to establish the company in an off-off Broadway house that could guarantee income and security; he felt the group would be subjecting itself to the instant-hit or instant-failure syndrome, in which life depends upon box office, tickets, fees, and money. Unwilling to accommodate himself to these conditions, Chaikin and the company traveled abroad each year and played in commercial houses in Europe. He replied to the criticism about this apparent contradiction by insisting that he had never felt the personal antagonism toward European commercialism that he did toward its American counterpart, and that European engagements were thus less distasteful. Chaikin also maintained that audiences in New York were the culturally conditioned, middle-class cognoscenti, while the Open Theatre's European tours seemed to attract a more varied audience.

When the Open Theatre returned from its 1969 European tour, having performed the repertory in Paris, Berlin, and Amsterdam, the group had already been undergoing a sharp self-appraisal.

Under discussion was its relevance to the current American political scene, the desirability—or undersirability—of playing in the New York area, the kinds of audiences to be sought, and the nature of the productions, as well as the actors' relationships to one another.

Chaikin maintained that he needed to work with a smaller company, not only for artistic, but for practical and political reasons. The experience in Europe during the 1969–70 tour reaffirmed his belief. When they had played Europe in the fall of 1969, the group was threatened by the French anarchists, who wanted to shut them down despite the presence of an audience of two thousand persons. Jeering, heckling, and generally obstructing the performance, the radicals shouted for the Open Theatre to go home or to play free in the streets, but to stop playing for "bourgeois audiences in bourgeois houses." Sympathetic to the demands, the company nevertheless gave its performances, but met with the radicals afterward for some long discussions. Having always been associated with radical causes, the Open Theatre had dedicated its performances in Europe to the Black Panthers. But political action took place only on an individual level; members of the company never agreed collectively to use their work as a vehicle for political expression. Now, after the 1969 tour, some wanted the theatre to continue as it had in the past; others thought that the group's focus was unclear, its target undefined; still others wanted to radicalize the theatre. Chaikin, formerly ambivalent, was prepared to reorient the company toward a more leftist political position. He felt that whatever separation existed between the personal, the political, and the artistic should be unified, but he wanted to steer clear of agit-prop or guerrilla theatre. He hoped to play in hospitals, prisons, colleges, high schools, and factories, so that the actors, experiencing the actual social situation in America, could translate their perceptions into artistic terms.

In addition, Chaikin faced another dilemma. To perform nightly the same work to any and all comers (even though it meant money) seemed to him a waste; it would limit the group's experimental work. Besides, he wanted to choose the "context of each performance, to make each one a creative act . . . to choose our compromises very carefully . . . to play free in the streets under certain circumstances, to charge money under others." He was looking, he claimed, for a "delicate balance between our radical commitments and the realities of living in America."[11] In order to balance the various difficulties, Chaikin envisioned a compact, compatible group. The tour in Europe, with its wrangling discussions and complicated personality problems, had led him to believe that personal hangups and divergent views were indigenous to a large company, and obviously detrimental to its work. And so the company was trimmed down; some of the older members left of their own volition, and a few stayed on. Under Chaikin's direction, those few produced two new works, *Mutations* and (in the spring of 1973) *Nightwalk*. At the end of the 1973 season, this small group, the last of the Open Theatre, was finally dissolved.

One of the Open Theatre's glaring weaknesses was in its inability to develop a unified and defined philosophy, a world view that might have deepened its work. Content to rely on a vague, romantic counterculture life style and liberal/radical principles, while at the same time envisioning themselves as revolutionary idealists, the members of the group were unable to coherently articulate their beliefs. They obviously despised the establishment, with its commercial audiences yet their desire to play only to college audiences and the radical fringe excluded them from the mainstream of American life and dimished their effectiveness. The company was caught in the usual paradox: to play for diverse audiences meant to enter the business arena; to play for select audiences meant to encourage elitism. Even if the Open Theatre had gone totally commercial, American life being what it is, the company could not have survived unless it showed a profit, and like the Living Theatre, it would have been digging its grave. Painfully aware of these ramifications, but refusing to bow to the realities, the Open Theatre sought a middle road—it chose to be bound by rather narrow, romantic concepts, and to depend upon its own life style and sensibilities to feed its work. And this was not enough.

The actors were mostly unaffiliated rebels who regarded art as a means of expressing *themselves*, not as a means of furthering a radical principle *through* art. In this sense, they inherited the romantic tradition. While working as part of a collective, some were as subjective as actors anywhere, and "acted out" their problems through the cross-currents of the group. Personal expression became a national slogan among the counterculture. Why should the Open Theatre have remained unaffected? They too accepted aspects of anarchism and individualism. That they were far less at home with these beliefs than the Living Theatre is indisputable. But their work and outlook were nonetheless influenced by the subjectivism that had become part of the culture they lived in. Hence the members of the Open Theatre could not resolve the question of what kind of artists they wanted to be, what kinds of audiences they wanted to reach, and what kind of theatre they wanted to play. Since they were not clear about their goals, and since they had no real tradition to build on, they joined, sometimes half-heartedly and often innocently, the American romantic quest for a purity that didn't exist, and for a theatre based on their own individuality.

Nevertheless this individuality was always original. The Open Theatre, despite its shortcomings, was the only group to have worked consistently to achieve a distinctive and cohesive style, a tribute to the artistry of Joe Chaikin. Chaikin painstakingly and meticulously developed a technique that was uniquely his own. Admittedly, his canvas was small, his view sometimes narrow, but the tone and texture of his work were authentic—based on his own genuine poetic sensibilities and commitment to his own vision. In the end the work of the Open Theatre remains haunting. Evocative, gentle, sad and funny, even depressing at times, the work was always fresh and always beautiful. And this is by no means a small achievement.

nine

The Environmentalists and Some Others

Totally opposite from the lyricism of Joseph Chaikin, but an equally important voice in the American avant-garde theatre movement, is Richard Schechner, who, in 1968, organized a company called the Performance Group. As editor of the prestigious *Drama Review* and Professor of Drama at Tulane and later at New York University, Schechner had been a propagandist for every "new theatre," in America and abroad; indeed, without *TDR* (*Tulane Drama Review*, before it became *The Drama Review*), "new theatre" information would have been scarce. But Schechner was not only an editor and an academician. Long before he assumed his duties at *TDR*, he had directed several successful productions for the Free Southern Theatre, so it was not surprising when he eventually resigned from *TDR* to devote himself entirely to his newly organized company.

The Performance Group rented a garage on Wooster Street in New York, reconstructed it into an environmental theatre, and in the fall of 1968 produced its first major success, *Dionysus in 69*, loosely based on Euripides' *The Bacchae*. At the time of its inception, the Performance Group consisted of thirteen actors, students from New York University who, presumably, had common goals and could work together to achieve them. When choosing the Greek play as a start, they decided to use the Grotowski method of "confronting" the text, rather than adhering to the drama's literal line.

Schechner had been particularly influenced by Jerzy Grotowski, who had come to New York University in the fall of 1966 to give a four-week seminar. Except for that period, he had never studied with Grotowski, although it often has been assumed that Schechner was his disciple. True, their attitudes to texts were similar in that both believed that new approaches to sound, space, and movement were essential for the development of new theatre, but Schechner's aesthetics and finished production—in fact, the whole tone of his work—are totally different from those of Grotowski.

Early in his career, having been influenced by happenings, John Cage, Marshall McLuhan, the Living Theatre, and later, by anthropological studies of primitive ritual, Schechner warned against the evils of the proscenium arch, which he claimed separated people from one another. He believed that the division of space between the audience and the performers was artificial. Once rules of space are broken down, he maintained, the audience will be participants as well as observers, and each event would then determine its own space—a basic principle of environmental theatre. Further, Schechner claimed that environmental and ritual theatre would be a means of bringing people close together, in contrast to the proscenium theatre, in which people are isolated by the enforced seating arrangement. In environmental theatre, there are virtually no boundaries between actors and audience. The audience may sit or stand anywhere—on tables, chairs, boxes, benches, or the floor; the "setting" *includes* the audience as part of its pattern, and the audience becomes part of the action. In other words, the environmental theatre abolishes theatre "architecture;" space is designated to fit a specific play, event, or spectacle, for environmentalists believe that spatial relations determine audience responses.

Schechner wanted to apply his observations that the principles of environmental theatre were related to primitive ritual, as far as the breakdown of space was concerned: for example, rituals could be held in the streets of a town, in a square, or spread all over the village. Villagers could participate in the event like actors; a ritual could last for days or hours. With this pattern in mind—where "the show" constantly moves from place to place, in temples, streets, squares, and the audience may stand, move or sit—Schechner envisioned a ritual-based theatre in a contemporary environmental setting.

True, the Living Theatre's *Paradise Now* and Grotowski's productions also used environmental and ritual techniques, but Schechner's concept of ritual was different. It is illustrated in the following description of his reactions to an environmental street happening in 1967 which, he writes, "combined film, still images, taped and live sound":

> I was in the street [East Seventh Street, New York City] that night. It was an impressive scene. Older people sitting on the stoops were commenting to each other in the way families do when they watch home movies. . . . Kids were dancing to the music of several local bands and enjoying the films; two large projectors were mounted on an equipment truck in the middle of the street, and more than a dozen projectors were working from inside apartments, throwing images through windows and onto outdoor surfaces. . . .
>
> Watching, participating myself, I thought immediately of *nonliterate theatre* [emphasis added]. *The Seventh Street Environment* had neither the tradition nor the communal craftsmanship of the Orokolo cycle play; but it had the same qualities of celebration, casualness, and necessity. Having participated but once, I wondered if these people would ever forget. Even more important, would they insist on doing it again? Probably not. . . .
>
> The space of Seventh Street breathed with the images and sounds living in it; the habits of summer open windows and street life were lifted out of their routine and transformed. The environment of the street didn't change, but its possibilities were explored. A found space was found interesting; found people were found alive. Technology was used to celebrate, not exploit, the lives of those who had too frequently and too relentlessly been exploited. . . .
>
> The *Environment* was significant art not because it gave all

> those "poor people" a chance to see themselves as they saw themselves; it was significant because celebration, casualness, non-professionalism, ritual, necessity and environment confronted one another. The multiplicity and simultaneity of the images, the haphazard coordination of film, sound, apartment and street life made real that special kind of time cluster and edgeless space that is the basis of a newly rediscovered art. An artless art without professional performers; one in which the makers and the watchers were all participating; an art of spatial insideness. An art that cannot be "reviewed" or "criticized." In other words, an event.[1]

The "event" described in *The Seventh Street Environmental* is central to Schechner's concept of a new theatre. An event may or may not be a formal play; it can be a party, a celebration, a ritual; it may take place in streets, subways, or converted garages; the actors may be amateurs or professionals, but its principle characteristic is that it take place in a natural or designed *environment.* Clearly this is totally different from a situation in which a management rents a theatre, advertises, charges money, and clings only to the proscenium stage.

For Schechner, events, environmentals and primitive rituals are intimately related, a belief that caused a good deal of controversy. He believes that an exciting new kind of theatre is to be achieved by combining a ritual with a real event, which he calls an "actual." "Actuals" can be rock festivals, T-groups, the saying of the Mass, the celebration of Rosh Hashanah, street parties, and football games, and could all be considered theatre. So could the tribal combat of the Australian Tiwi's, for they "all combine ritual ceremonies with the actual event."[2]

Schechner's ideas are not without precedent. The Iranian director Parviz Sayyad, writing about an Islamic religious ritual, has pointed out: "[The Ta'zieh ritual has] two main modes of execution." The first mode is "scattered"; the second, "centralized." In the "scattered" and original version of the ritual, the performance is played out in the village, the music is simple, and neither the "reciters" nor the director is professional. "The directors of the Ta'zieh, or members of his family are often to be seen moving about among the performers. . . . The spectator feels a complete harmony between himself and the performers. For him, the player is himself a spectator who has gone out onto the stage and will once again become a spectator after performing his role. The performer is not aware that he is 'performing.' Playing his role appears to him as a religious duty, like saying his daily prayers."[3]

In the second mode of playing this ritual, the performance is "centralized." This means that the space and place of performance is decided upon by professional people, professional "reciters" are used, productions are formalized and embellished, and no extraneous material is allowed. The performers are not part of a village, and thus the harmony established by villagers (in the first type of performance) is absent. "For the foreign spectator, only the wailing and crying of the audience brings to mind the ritual origins of the performance. . . ." The differences between the two modes of performing, Sayyad maintains, is that "in the 'scattered' form the performance tends more towards ritual, while in the 'centralized' form, it tends more towards theatre."[4]

Apparently, Sayyad makes a distinction between theatre and ritual, a distinction that Schechner does not acknowledge. For support, Schechner draws on the work of Margaret Mead, who maintains that Western patterns of art have created a schism between art and ritual, between art and community, and between artists and audience. Mead argues that to sit in rows of chairs to see a play or hear a concert, or to see sculpture and paintings in a gallery separates the spectator's body and emotions from those of the artist and his art. She claims that the passive role of spectator divorces the public from the artist and tends to encourage elitism in the arts. In contrast, the artist who is integrated into the community, where his special talents are recognized but are no longer separate and apart, the spectator and the artist directly revitalize each other.

Schechner's goal is precisely to integrate the actor, his art, and the spectator into one event that re-creates the immediacy of ritual. To this end he has worked out a performance theory: First, the entire process involves comingling a written text and ritual acts with real events which comprise the actors' inner associations and responses to the text. The responses are then combined with the actors' exchanges with the audience and his fellow players. The involvements, associations, and exchanges are all scored and become the working text. A "ritual contest" (initiation rites) for the performers as well as the audience must take place before both can participate. The work is to be performed in a space specifically designed for the event.[5]

With these principles in mind, *Dionysus in 69* was conceived. Euripides' *Bacchae*, the text of which incorporates myth, ritual, rites, and celebration, was an excellent choice for testing Schechner's theories. On one level he was able to use the formal text, loosely interwoven with "actuals" which comprised the actors' personal associations and their interaction with the audience. He also merged the formal text with contemporary rituals, such as Yoga meditations, game-playing, encounter techniques, and the trappings of youth culture. The production resulted in a double structure; it was both "scattered" and "centralized," illusionary and actual, ancient and modern. Its most contemporary feature was the environmental, consisting of a maze of wooden towers and scaffoldings—designed by Michael Kirby and Jerry Rojo—upon which the audience climbed and sat. On the steps of the ladders, planks, and flat surfaces of the structure were multi-colored square cuttings neatly stitched together like a patchwork quilt. The platforms, towers, and scaffoldings, with their varied heights and dimensions, created a symmetrical pattern, and an intriguing vantage point; people loved to climb to the highest spot, from which they could see both the specific action and the entire setting. The scaffold environmental, enabling the audience to see everything simultaneously, gave them a sense of being part of the performance, and as in the *Seventh Street Environmental*, the ambiance was like a party or a celebration—the difference being that the audience were strangers to one another, a contradiction to be discussed later. Since there was no formal setting, and it was not easy to climb the scaffolding, some members of the audience were uncomfortable. For others, the jeans, slacks, and casual clothing best suited to this kind of space (a decided departure from the bourgeois theatre) was a relief; it made the theatrical event natural, less status-ridden. Instead of the stiff self-importance of an opening night on Broadway, the atmosphere in the garage was free, informal, carnival-like; it heightened anticipation.

The audience stood in line outside the building until, one by one, they were allowed into a semi-lit theatre-garage. People groped to find a "seat," and as members of the audience climbed the planks, they could see that actors were already doing headstands, head-rolls, and high jumps, and chanting fragmented sounds and phrases. The actors performed all over the room; some were in the open space in the center, others ran up and down the highest planks, hid in corners under the scaffolding, or leapt from plank to plank. They delivered their speeches from many parts of the room and as they jumped about acrobatically, their voices sounded increasingly resonant, richer, deeper, fuller. "Good evening, sir, may I take you to your seats?" was the one single line repeated over and over again, to remind one that there were indeed no seats at all. Upon finding one's place on the scaffolding, one realized that the performance had already begun; the "Bacchantes" were running all over the place chanting lines and whispering into the ears of those seated. Suddenly an actor walked out into the open space—totally naked.

The tall, scrawny, mustached, long-haired, actor in horn-rimmed granny glasses, speaking unmistakable New Yorkese, declares that he, William Finley (and he *is* William Finley), is the God Dionysus, and that he is here "to establish my rites and ritual . . . and to be born, if you'll excuse me." With that, a ritual begins: it is an imitation of the Indian Asmat ritual birth. Four totally naked women, legs extended, stand between the legs of five totally naked men who lie face downward—a mass of undulating flesh. Groaning, moaning, and screaming as though at one and the same time having an orgasm and giving birth, the women push Dionysus through their legs. He struggles on the top of the men's nude behinds, and at the crotches of the nude women. Suddenly he emerges. He declares himself to be the God Dionysus, only to quickly affirm that he is Finley the actor. Then he invites the audience to participate in a "celebration, a ritual, an ordeal, an ecstasy," commemorating his "nativity." The actors take up flutes, tambourines, temple bells, and congo drums, and some of the audience strips down and joins in, while others merely watch as a ritualized orgy begins. Incidentally Schechner claims:

> Of the more than 1300 lines in Arrowsmith's translation of *The Bacchae*, we use nearly 600, some more than once. We also use sixteen lines from Elizabeth Wycoff's translation of *Antigone* and six lines from David Grene's translation of *Hippolytus*. The rest of our text we made ourselves—some of it written at home, some worked out in workshops. The textual montage, the arrangements and variations, developed organically during rehearsals and throughout the run. The performers wrote their own dialogue. I wanted as much personal expression as possible in a play that deals so effectively with the liberation of personal energy. There is a formal pattern to the text's construction, however. It is not improvised. . . . The first person to play a role establishes its over-all textual shape. Therefore, Finley and [the actor Bill] Shephard had a great deal to do with the words of Dionysus and Pentheus. The greatest textual liberties were taken for the role of Dionysus. In other parts we did as much with displacement, montage, and split emphasis of the Euripides/Arrowsmith text as we did with direct rewriting or new writing. But in every case the creative energies of individual Group members were put to work.[6]

In any case, in the Performance Group's version of the text, Pentheus, King of Thebes, has been spying on the Dionysian revelers; he appears on the top tower and demands that the rituals be stopped. A victim of a revulsion-attraction syndrome, Pentheus is determined to confront Dionysus. But Dionysus (or Finley) asserts his godliness and challenges Pentheus. As an act of submission, Dionysus insists that Pentheus perform fellatio upon him. Meanwhile, the ceremonial orgy takes place. There are attempts at wild dancing, petting, and carefully simulated sexuality with the audience. This kind of activity produced a certain amount of expectancy among the spectators, but few went beyond the simulation point—an obvious contradiction to the living event theory. Colloquial dialogue, and scenes based on contemporary motifs, are interspersed with the Euripides text, and several levels of reality are projected. Actors are characters in the play and deliver the textual lines, but they also address one another by their own names, and depart from the text to allude to contemporary issues that presumably parallel or underscore those in the narrative. As characters in the play and as themselves, they challenge the audience to participate in the Dionysian sexual encounters and confrontations. On some evenings, a few men in the audience had become what the group considered excessive in their sexual responses, and had to be discouraged by the company. In scenes where Pentheus is mocked and isolated to indicate his humiliation and ostracization, the actors play contemporary children's games. In this manner they aim to fill out the Euripides text with emblems and games that are recognizable symbols of pop culture.

After the group orgy has been played out and Pentheus has performed the fellatio off stage (down a hatch leading to a "jail"), he is condemned to die. In preparation for the murder, the naked Bacchantes organize a ritual bloodbath. The women, having dipped their hands in red paint, caress the nude body of Pentheus one moment, and claw him to death the next, thus completing the cycle of birth and death. Dionysus, who has been watching impassively all along, warns the audience not to defy him. With Pentheus dead, the actors break the "illusion," wash the "blood" off their bodies, and get dressed in public view. Dionysus-Finley, already clothed, ascends one of the highest towers to announce his candidacy for President, and barrages the spectators with *Dionysus in 69* buttons. The audience files out, leaving the actors scrubbing the "blood" of the floors, as though to vitiate the event.

Schechner's desire to create "actuals" is a desire to make theatre efficacious, a wish he shares with all experimentalists. One assumes this means involving actors and spectators in communal and ritual acts to elicit new perceptions and new feelings. Schechner's aim is, then, the same as the Living Theatre's in *Paradise Now*, and in fact Schechner's production raises the same questions. To what extent can an audience with no deep religious or political affiliation in common be part of rituals and/or "actuals"? Does audience participation actually alter feelings and perceptions? To what extent is participation simply an acting-out process, and an exhibitionistic ego-trip? What specific aesthetic aspects in ritual can serve as models for contemporary theatre? Finally, will mixing real events and ritual action be a breakdown of all form?

When the actors in *Dionysus* created their physical configurations based on specific primitive rites, the result was arresting and visually powerful. But whenever they used colloquial equivalences—for example, the actors' interjecting their own language as a response to the outlines of the Euripides tale—the result was weak. So was the use of "actuals." The performers interrupted the action of the Euripides-based text and departed from their assigned roles in order to give their biographies, to free-associate, play games, address the audience, improvise, and interact with each other. This, one assumes, was done to express themselves and the text simultaneously. But the mixture created a sense of confusion; the result was a hodge-podge that offered neither a sense of social nor aesthetic significance. Here is some of the dialogue:

> DIONYSUS: . . . You're acting as if you don't know what you're doing. . . . You don't know who you are.
> PENTHEUS: I am Pentheus. Son of Echion and Agave. And King of Thebes. . . .
> DIONYSUS: Pentheus? Son of Echion and Agave and King of Thebes? Bullshit. You're Bill Shephard. You're in the Group. You're no god, but you are in the Group. Pentheus? Echion? You're coo-coo. Take him away. . . .

Or another version (when other actors play):

> McDERMOTT AS DIONYSUS TO BILL SHEPHARD: Pentheus? Son of Echion and Agave and King of Thebes? Bullshit. You were a little man with a big dream. And now you're a big man in trouble. That's who you are.
> DIONYSUS TO RICHARD DIA: Pentheus, son of Echion and Agave and King of Thebes? Bullshit. You're Richard Dia. You were born in New York City. Your father makes mandolins. You're a nice guy. Sometimes we have coffee together. You're in the Group. You're no god, but you're in the Group. When you get like this, you're impossible. Will someone please take him away?[7]

Patently this escape to ordinary Pirandelloism is unoriginal; moreover, the language is unimaginative. It matters very little what an actor's name is, where he was born, why he chose his profession, or what he dreamed the previous evening (some of the gratuitous details actors supplied), except to the actor himself and perhaps to the actors in the audience. It *would* matter if the actor dramatized this information into a meaningful aesthetic experience. Even then, it would depend on an audience's common sensibility—class, race, and status—as to how involved they could become with this sort of performance. In *Dionysus in 69*, actors revealed personal details as if they were stunning metaphors or remarkable insights. The result was a banality that mitigated the ritual goal.

Attempts at ritual seem less successful when actors and audience share no common ground. In actual fact, ritual has always had a moral, religious, practical, or psychological significance, and has never existed for its own sake. Rites were a need. Spring meant a rebirth of the crops and food, a relief from the darkness of the winter; thus rites often accompanied the change of season. Rites helped primitive people to overcome the mysteries of the universe; their dances and ceremonies were offerings to the mysterious elements, in exchange for survival. Even the wearing of masks had a purpose: the wearer believed he was united "with the mighty power."[8]

Dionysus in 69 had no moral or religious purpose, and its psychological content was diffuse. To "celebrate" the birth of Dionysus had no significant meaning for American audiences, especially as the celebration was depicted in this production. Dionysus, god of ecstasy, is a pathological killer despite his initial hippie-like stance, which, at the onset, suggested that it was he who might be the hero. But as the play goes on, Dionysus orders Pentheus brutally murdered. As the victim, Pentheus arouses one's sympathies despite his conservatism, and thus the audience's loyalties are divided and confused. Without specific, clear-cut allegiances, most people find it virtually impossible to become part of the ritual celebratory acts: the need to believe in the moral value of the ritual is mandatory to real participation.

Schechner's explication of the birth ritual (below) is informative, but his intellectualizing after the fact of performance—and to a public whose frame of reference may be totally different from his own—defeats his purpose. He presumes that explanations change perceptions, and that everyone's sensibilities are similar. This tends to make his thinking and his work doctrinaire, a common enough fault of the experimental theatre. He writes:

> 1) The birth ritual is a birthing not only of Dionysus but of each of us through him. 2) Undressing before the birth ritual is a sacred and surgical preparation. At once potent and sterile. It is a way of clearing the way. 3) The fetal meditation, in the squat, is a way of clearing and purifying the mind. The associative opening ceremonies are a foretaste of the actualization of the performance. The mediation is the beginning of "this night's performance." We rise, one at a time, as each finds either peace or balance. 4) We leave the fetal position to birth ourselves. 5) The ecstasy is an ordeal/celebration. It is the "all-night dance." The mats are the sacred place. To leave the mats is to leave that place and negotiate with the profane world. Leaving takes courage and incorporates the knowledge that life must be lived and that life is not pure. The audience may participate, clothed, off the mats. But they must not come on the mats unless they are as we are. The use of musical instruments is optional. The perfect ceremony

> uses no instruments. But, as we know, most ceremonies are not perfect—props are part of the human condition.
>
> The second phase of the nudity—the death ritual and body pile—is more clearly defined. It is the second half of the birth ritual. It is the result of profanation and at the same time a sacred act. To die is natural—to kill is both obscene and sacred. For birth, the audience is invited or at least permitted to participate. For death, the audience is challenged.[9]

Whether the audience felt challenged is a moot point, but it was ill-prepared for the ritual rules. Since the rules were kept secret by circumstances of the piece, some members of the audience felt participation an imposition. Even the zealous young people, eager to join in, could not really justify their participation. Some people seemed embarrassed and self-conscious, especially when the actors attempted to involve them in a simulated sexual or physical act: strangers touching one another—a cliché perpetuated by the merchandisers of instant joy—is simply too superficial an act to have any ritual or even psychological significance. One may as well be touching the skin of a dog or cat. Why people cannot touch each other naturally is not the point here, but that, in the context of a public performance, one is not prepared for this kind of activity, and perceives it as ersatz therapy, vulgarized into pop culture.

Some members of the audience, however, did participate in sexual "play." They were induced to make love to Pentheus, or to the Dionysian women. This raised another problem: were they to be restricted, controlled, or just be "themselves?" If a spectator makes love to Pentheus, who is she: herself, or a reveler of Thebes? If she be the latter, should she be rehearsed? If the former, her responses may be extreme. Perhaps spontaneity in this case might lead to anti-social behavior, a rape, or an act of violence—not an illogical consequence in such an atmosphere. What prevents the real event from becoming *too* real? (All of these questions already had been raised by the Living Theatre experience.) If, on the other hand, the actor playing Pentheus is interacting with a member of the audience in a love scene, who is he: himself, or the persona in the play? How should he respond; as the actor, or as the character? If he mingles his own responses with that of the character, one set of characteristics may be diametrically opposed to the other, and an attempt at reconciliation may prove ludicrous. If there is artistic validity to participation, on what level should an audience participate, and on what level does it enhance the audience's and the performers' experiences?

In the case of the *Dionysus in 69*, the roles of the actors and audience remained unclear, not only because the ritualistic aspects were not accepted, but because the audience's involvement centered around sexuality, and that tended to complicate the problem of participation still further. Egotism and sexual exhibitionism ran high, and some participants, eager to exploit the sexual situation, limited true experimentalism and even invalidated it. Nor did nudity help. The company discovered that nudity could be another form of pretense, that to be nude was not the equivalent of freedom or real nakedness. Perfectly aware of this, one actress in the Performance Group said:

> As I stood before a man in the audience, naked and covered with blood . . . he grabbed me. . . . As the moment came for me to return to a central scene, I was unwilling simply to walk away from him, feeling that if I did I would reduce him to a prop and negate the interactions I had with him during the evening . . . as I led him to the center, he broke away, dipped his hands into the bloodbath, and then began swiping at me. He was going to kill me with my own pretension. I felt constrained to continue with my lines and eventually he went away and sat down.[10]

Schechner himself, sensing the failure of audience participation, wrote: "With increasing frequency, audiences gawked, talked or wanted to make out with the performers. Sometimes this was pleasant, but on more than one occasion a nasty situation unfolded in the darkened room. The performers refused to continue with the caress. One girl put it very bluntly: 'I didn't join the group to fuck some old man under the tower.'"[11]

In addition, the ideological weakness of the play contributed to the confusion. The tone of the production seemed to celebrate the long-haired bacchants, as though hippie-ism were a virtue in itself. In presenting a dialectic between Euripides' *Bacchae* and the contemporary American scene, the Performance Group was unable to sustain its Dionysian vision. On the one hand, in this production, the Dionysian cult represents freedom, joy, ecstasy, sexual liberation, and self-realization—aspects of the revolution the company apparently supports. As staged, Pentheus represents law and order, repression, restraint, and the mores of the establishment—aspects of reaction to be rejected. But the Dionysian "radicals" brutally murder Pentheus. He becomes a sympathetic victim, and his problems seem more compelling than those of Dionysus; Pentheus' inner discomfort and self-doubt are more vividly dramatized, while Dionysus seems smug, arrogant, self-satisfied—and dangerous. Schechner claims that he intended to "explore the politics of ecstasy," but his aim became submerged by the moral ambiguity of the work. Nonetheless, Schechner himself seemed aware of the moral tension between revolution and freedom:

> There are many young people who believe that an unrepressive society, a sexualized society, is Utopia. Nudity, free sexual expression, communal rather than family units, "inner space," and sensory overload are becoming political issues. The discothéques—the Palm Gardens, the Fillmore, the Electric Circus—are places of public assembly and direct political action. A new way of living is being demonstrated. But this same ecstasy, we know, can be unleashed in the Red Guards or horrifically channeled toward the Nuremberg rallies and Auschwitz. There, too, at the vast extermination camps, an ecstasy was acted out. The hidden fear I have about the new expression is that its forms come perilously close to ecstatic fascism.
>
> Liberty can be swiftly transformed into its opposite, and not only by those who have a stake in reactionary government. Ritualized experience without the built-in control of a strong social system—an Asmat society or an Orokolo society—can

> pump itself up to destructive fury. So I must end with an indelicate question. Are we ready for the liberty we have grasped? Can we cope with Dionysus's dance and not end up—as Agave did—with our sons' heads on our dancing sticks?[12]

But the work remained ambivalent, its tone and focus shifting from position to position. Further, technical innovations, seemingly embraced for their own sake, cluttered the production and obscured the relationship of form to content—one of the ongoing problems of the avant-garde.

If Schechner was not entirely successful, certainly he and his designers, Michael Kirby and Jerry Rojo, can be credited with creating the first popular environmental settings in New York. A number of productions were influenced by the work of the Performance Group and by the concepts expressed in Schechner's article "Six Axioms for an Experimental Theatre"[13] (for example Luca Raconi's adaptation of Ariosto's *Orlando Furioso*).[14] To date, one of the most important influences can be measured by Andre Gregory's production of *Alice in Wonderland* designed by Eugene Lee. The play was performed in a room that allowed only a hundred spectators, who entered through a "hole" in the wall. There, in a shabby, half-darkened space, hung an old parachute which seemed, ominously, to threaten the audience. In the center of the playing area were simple tables, chairs, and other paraphernalia that looked dirty, tacky, old, and shopworn. The audience sat on wooden crates, stools, folding chairs, and low benches. Added to the anxiety of the atmosphere were raggedy costumes (designed by Franne Lee) that consisted of patchwork quilts, torn shirts, scarves, calico and gingham dresses, absurd pajamas, and odd pieces of colored cloth that might have been collected from "grandmother's" attic, or from a rummage sale. The only props were umbrellas, newspapers, croquet mallets, and a ping-pong ball.

This time the environmental was overshadowed by the acting.

The director, Andre Gregory, had studied with Grotowski (among others), and applied the Grotowski exercises—the plastiques and the corporeals—to produce a very American *Alice*. The production, only partly successful in portraying its version of the savagery of Alice's dream, lacked substance and depth, and the actors' mastery of their bodies was its most interesting aspect. Gregory expected the actors to "take chances," and, unlike naturalistic actors, who are virtually "dead from the head and larynx down," to approach their "inner psychology through the body." He wanted them to use words and body movement in order to "find their instinctual link to gesture that would release their animal energy."[15] And so their fast and fluid animal characterizations, mad game-playing, and imaginative acrobatic movements achieved an invigorating agility. But ingenious as the movements were, the line of the play seemed to be missing, along with Gregory's point of view. Still, his work with incorporating Grotowski techniques made a substantial contribution to the development of a new kind of American acting.

Meantime, other experimentalists were taking different directions—John Vaccaro's and Charles Ludlam's concept of a Theatre of the Ridiculous, for example. The two are no longer partners, but their work stems from similar attitudes. Influenced by the Dadaists (and, to a certain extent, by the Surrealists), they are entirely nihilistic, for to have an ethos, as Stefan Brecht has pointed out, would be to dignify life, and this would be contrary to their aims.[16] Viewing the world as ridiculous, Vaccaro and Ludlam express their sensibilities—especially their fantasy lives—through savage humor and grotesque nightmare. The content of their plays is composed of fantasies that are primarily based on homosexuality, transvestism, Hollywood stardom, and bitter and excoriating parodies on the "straight" world. Anti-intellectual in the extreme, the Ridiculous present a scabrous *demimonde*, complete with scatological obcenities and smutty humor. The actors, mostly openly homosexuals, play caricatures of themselves, interchange male–female roles and act out their "doubles" while ridiculing the contemporary bourgeois culture.

The plays are sometimes linear, but most of the time nothing makes sense, and deliberately so—the plot, dialogue, and characters are designed to be ridiculous. The performances are not individualized; actors are types—freaky, creepy, funky—who are on stage, it seems, to express their infantile fantasies or glamorous conceptions of themselves as "actors." Although the work may be intended to lampoon puritanism, it is so overladen with erotica that any comment on subjects other than sex is tangential. On the other hand, there is a certain kind of mad hilarity to it all.

In *Bluebeard*, for example, Ludlam plays a zany scientist who wants to invent a third sex; the piece satirizes comic strips, pop personalities, Hollywood movies, and famous dramatic literature. In Vaccaro's work, he expresses the underground world of subways and nightclubs, and in his plays, one is apt to encounter beggars, madmen, derelicts, drunks, and cripples—the blind, diseased faces of humanity. Or one might find burlesque comics, strippers, drag queens, transvestites, and ventriloquists who fornicate with their dummies. Dirty jokes, allusions to buggery, fellatio, and every variety of sexuality complete the picture—all of which is usually set against loud mesmerizing rock music. Metallic makeup adds to the garishness of Vaccaro's productions; sequins, faded scarves, enormous codpieces, fright wigs, dusty ostrich feathers and tacky furs. The actors sometimes resemble Jean Harlow, Greta Garbo, Joan Crawford, Clara Bow, Shirley Temple, or even Frankenstein and Dracula—the entire camp fantasmagoria of Hollywood.

Representing the theatre of the Self carried to the extreme, the Theatre of the Ridiculous is a theatre of exaggeration; it is obsessed not only with erotica, but with a Hollywood romanticism that attracted, betrayed, and finally captured whole generations. Carried to its ultimate, this *demimonde* is like a Fellini circus, a Satyricon where everything is possible and nothing is forbidden—the complete indulgence of ego.

Whereas the Theatre of the Ridiculous supports an aesthetic of the "ugly" for its own sake, Robert S. Wilson (and his Byrd Hoffman School of Byrds) has developed an aesthetic of the Beautiful—also for its own sake. Wilson, a twenty-nine-year-old native of Texas with a degree in art and architecture, began working in his spare time with brain-damaged children who, he discovered, responded to dance and movement therapy. Dance had always interested Wilson, and as a result of his work with the children, he stopped painting and devoted himself full-time to dance and theatre; in a very short time he produced three full-length pieces: *The King of Spain; The Life and Times of Sigmund Freud; Deafman Glance; KA MOUNTAIN AND GUARDenia TERRACE.*

When Wilson presented *Deafman Glance*, a three-hour spectacle in which not a word is spoken, in Paris in 1971, Louis Aragon was so moved that he wrote an open letter to the dead André Breton, with whom he had had no contact for the past 40 years: ". . . [the production] is a miracle. . . . I never saw anything more beautiful in the world. . . . Never never has any play come anywhere near this one, because it is at once life awake and the life of closed eyes, the confusion between everyday life and the life of each night; reality mingles with dream—all that's inexplicable in the life of a deaf man . . . it is not surrealism at all . . . but it is what we, who fathered surrealism, what we dreamed it might become after us, beyond us. . . ."[17]

In the contemporary fashion of characterizing theatrical styles, Wilson's work has been called the Theatre of Silence (also the Theatre of Crisis). Much of it is wordless, and in some of his later workshop pieces, where words are uttered, the effect is that of silence nonetheless. The pieces (conceived by Wilson himself and embellished by the company) also have no plots, no dialogue, no character development. What they do have is a striking appeal to the visual sense, so that it is not so much that there is nothing to hear, but that there is so much to see.

What one sees in Wilson's plays are giant painterly collages moving in space: people, puppets, masked figures, papier-maché animals, real animals, plants, architectural structures, and objects and activities of all sorts are juxtaposed on stage simultaneously, in very slow motion. The effect is less of a theatrical event than a surreal trip into the world of art and the semi-conscious, blurred world of marihuana or hashish.

Though kaleidoscopic, Wilson's presentations are not random: they are carefully planned. With an unfailing eye for color, space, and architectural planes, Wilson directs a huge canvas of sometimes eighty actors (and live animals) deftly and smoothly, leaving nothing to improvisation: the dozens of exits and entrances, the complicated and beautiful spatial arrangements and elaborate lighting schemes, the trapdoors, flying furniture, opulant costumes and makeup, and a variety of theatrical tricks are all synthesized to create a cohesive pattern. Images are designed to evoke emblematical figures from the worlds of myth, fantasy, religion, and literature, mounted so that each moment is reminiscent of a famous painting, a piece of sculpture, an ancient frieze.

Deafman Glance, for example, is a three-hour collage-epic composed entirely of silent sensory apparitions. Inspired by Raymond Andrews, a deaf boy whom Wilson befriended, and who is also an actor in the piece, the work, on one level, depicts the boy's fantasy world, evoked through the ever-shifting imagery. On another, it is an allegorical expression of Wilson's attitudes toward religion, myth, memory, and folklore as perceived through his conscious-unconscious life. It begins with a macabre ritual. A black woman in a black Victorian gown, wearing one black glove, stands against a white blackdrop on a proscenium stage. In slow, slow motion, she stabs her two children to death, while the third, Raymond, looks on. Traumatized, the boy floats, as it were, into a non-verbal world from which he then watches the stunning display of his (and Wilson's) visions. The setting represented the history of the ages: The Last Supper's long table stands before a primitive hut surrounded by tropical trees, with an Egyptian pyramid in the background and a fishing bank, evoking the American South, in the foreground. The colors, costumes, makeup, and masks are blended to produce the tone and texture of great paintings: Rousseau's lush greens, Giorgione's lusty rusts and browns, Watteau's delicate blues and whites, Memling's grays and Lautrec's reds.

As dozens of images parade by, fantasy mixes with reality, comedy with romance, and ordinary activities with bizarre ones. A giant frog plays host to two red-wigged ladies and a W. C. Fields–fat man; a boy sits fishing all night long; a naked pregnant woman walks slowly around the stage; an eight-foot Bugs Bunny and a menacing Dracula dance on; in a corner, a boy washes an old man's feet; throughout, a man blithely builds a wooden bin, while at the sidelines stands a white-haired fairy princess with a blue bird on her sleeve. Parasoled ladies from the world of Henry James and young Isadora Duncan girls in white dresses gracefully float about; a lineup of Black mammies do a jig; a woman slowly leads a live goat, and a papier-maché ox lights up after swallowing the sun. Then there are moons that rise, stars that fall, volcanoes that erupt, fish that crawl, trees that grow taller, and animals that grow smaller. Finally, there is the apolcalypse: the characters sink into the ground, into their graves, and smoke rises, filling the theatre with a gray mist. A gang of apes emerges, eating apples. A requiem is heard; the apes kneel, and one plays silently on a harp. Two white-wigged eighteenth-century figures appear—Marie Antoinette and George Washington—and stand in all their whiteness against the blackness of the apes, while in the distance a phonograph plays "The Loveliest Night of the Year." Slowly, slowly, the apes munch their apples, which quietly rise out of their hands to the heavens as the stars quietly fall to the ground. The music plays on, and the curtain drops.

All this is done in the slow, sometimes imperceptible motion that is characteristic of Wilson's productions. The actors use tiny, graceful, gliding steps, giving the impression of weightlessness, even otherworldliness. At one time they seem to be space-walking, at another, they are solid and stationary. They can sit or stand as quietly as a still life, immobile as mummies. Their bodies are always balanced, symmetrical, and natural; their faces, sometimes as serene as the Buddha, suggest an intriguing, though impenetrable inner life. Each actor is moving in relation to cosmic rather than theatrical time, so that a person may take the whole evening to walk across the stage, or a half-hour to drink a glass of water. This may be excruciatingly boring, but it can also be hypnotically soothing.

Wilson's experiments with time are not entirely new. The Living Theatre's *Frankenstein* and *Mysteries,* Chaikin's *The Serpent* and *Terminal*, and indeed the Oriental theatre and dance are well-known for their work with time and ritualized movements. Peter Schumann's Bread and Puppet Theatre has been experimenting with time and movement relations for more than ten years; so have various avant-garde dancers. But Wilson's power lies in his ability to combine "timeless movement" with wordlessness, and to direct a stunning *mise-en-scène* as though each movement were a painting.

Wilson has not gone without being criticized for the interminable quality of his tempo and for his obscurantist point of view. Some critics have complained that the slow motion is a detriment to communication, and that its significance would be lost on the average American theatre-goer, who would find it merely tedious. When questioned about the pace, Wilson, a lanky, shy man who is reluctant to speak of his work, said that the movements were designed to emit "body signals," small, detailed motions that indicate changes in emotion. "Slow motion is a release from the rapidity of the outside world. When one is released from its tension, then perceptions and responses can be on many different levels. A lot actually happens inside one's self in slow motion that we are not aware of. . . . My aim is to make actors aware of every tiny movement in the body and its exact relationship to the space in which they move. The slower *they* move, the more you *see* things."[18]

But there is more to it than that. An important object of Wilson's theatre seems to be therapy for the actors, on an Oriental model.

Influenced by both Isadora Duncan and Zen Buddhism, Wilson strives for freedom from inhibition and from repressions by the application of unchoreographed free movement and the Zen life. Not surprising, then, that his actors are non-professionals who regard the work as an expression of their personal beliefs and an outlet for personal problems. Most of the performers are ordinary, mid-Western untheatrical types; some are middle-aged; one is an ex-waitress from Iowa; another, a housewife from New Jersey; in one piece Wilson's grandmother appeared. Many want to belong to a family, and were attracted by Wilson's spirituality. One member, Ann Wilson (no relation), claims that "the company is connected by religion in the fullest sense of the word."[19]

To be sure, the tone of the pieces is religious; they especially reflect the Zen search for serenity and exaltation. The slow movements, performed with a strange tranquility and a quality which seems to demonstrate the absence of ego, are reminiscent of Zen-inspired No drama. The actors' undulating Buddhas, their ability to suspend an arm, a hand, a leg, in space for long periods of time, their composure and contemplative sitting, are borrowed from Zen principles. Their seemingly banal activities on stage are also related to Zen. An actress may drink tea, arrange stones on the ground (a Zen ritual), or hold a child to her bosom all evening—hardly theatrical moments in Western terms—with a ritual pride and reverence that transform these simple acts into poetic ones, and illustrate the Zen principle that simplicity is not only beautiful, but all the more beautiful when experienced in its innumerable details. Wilson also expresses here an interest in process—what goes through a person's body, when he drinks, moves, sits. The focus is on the act itself—raising a hand, for example—rather than the effect of the act. These mundane activities are as much a part of Wilson's productions as fantasy or mythological imagery; thus, the actors play double roles on stage: they perform these tasks as themselves in the world of Zen, and when they need to enact imaginary roles, they use the principles of Zen-oriented art.

This duality is most evident in Wilson's later piece, *Overture,* an introduction to a larger work, *KA MOUNTAIN AND GUARDenia TERRACE, a story about a family and some people changing. Overture* was shown to the public at Wilson's refurbished New York SoHo studio for one week in April 1972. It is six hours long, and divided into two parts, the first beginning at sunrise, 6 A.M., the second at sunset, 6 P.M.. The studio was open all day so that, Wilson said, "anyone could come in off the street, see a play, and eat a meal."[20] Lunch was served at a long table in the communal kitchen, each day representing a different cuisine—Persian, Indian, Spanish. One could read in the top-floor library [furnished with pillows, low tables, and oriental rugs], the walls covered with books on Oriental art and religion, and decorated with drawings and photographs.

Overture has the quality of a religious ritual. In the anteroom stood a small altar decorated with leaves, tiny statuettes, and colored stones. Hand-painted paneled Japanese-like screens of flowers, birds, animals, and calligraphy (all made by the company) were arranged against the walls, and pillows served as seats. The atmosphere was misty, suffused by incense. In front of the audience stood a wooden, truncated pyramidal structure covered with a beige scrim on which was painted a huge dinosaur skeleton. From the top of the pyramid hung a turtle and an egg; inside was a three-dimensional drawing under glass of the architect Paolo Soleri's concept of ideal cities. The piece itself follows no obvious logic. One remembers only fragmentary images: tiny flames that suddenly ignite into small fires, like miniature burning bushes; a Rodin-like sculpture of a thinker, alone on the stage; a Chagall-like fiddler on the table; a girl arranging stones and twigs; a Black woman in a white gown pouring water out of a pitcher; two children wearing sailor hats. Intermittently, a voice intones: "To the West is America, to the East is China; the fish are out of the water, the wounded stag is on the hill." A portly, middle-aged woman speaks in a steady monotone, painfully remembering her youth in Iowa City; she recalls the parades, the circus, and the town creek. The noted dance critic Edwin Denby reads from John

Ashbery's poetry. There is Buddhist praying, Zen incantation, silent meditating, and slow whirling-dervish movements. Then one hears proliferated sentences, phrases, puns, riddles, and weird, lonely, dislocated sounds—owls screeching, children whimpering, animals crying, deaf mutes howling. The whole piece is both an evocation of personal anguish and a depiction of a family trying to find spiritual relief through religion, memory, and art.

In France in the Spring of 1972, Wilson continued to develop *Overture* at the Abbaye de Royaumont, a twelfth-century monastery where he and his company were housed, while preparing the piece for presentation at the Shiraz Festival in Iran in August of that year. Working diligently and quietly among the old stones and spires, the actors seemed to resemble the monks who once inhabited the ancient monastery: their daily regimen included exercise, chapel praying, meetings, and workshops, and then a totally silent supper. At the end of their stay, a portion of *KA MOUNTAIN* was shown to an invited audience. In these segments, Wilson tried to integrate language into his highly visual sensibility. One new section was a simply staged playlet with dialogue that combined the real and the fictional. Presented in an ordinary room at the Abbaye, it depicted the courtroom trial of Sue Sheehy (one of the actresses) for the murder of her mother. The setting—only tables, chairs, benches—was like a stark drawing, all black, gray and white, all straight lines and no curves. White lights added an eeriness to the ambiguity and mystery of the work, in which witnesses take the stand and are asked questions and answer impassively. The verdict is never known, the murder never solved. Suddenly, as the end approaches, all the actors group themselves together, as if they were in an ancient frieze on a Persian wall; a tall thin girl in a long mauve dress makes a perfect gesture of indescribable agony, while a hideous giggle is heard in the background. Then someone whispers, "*c'est fini.*"

Walking out of the Abbaye, one felt that it too had become part of the play; its long halls were candlelit, and all along the walls were the actors in their white garments, like ossified ghosts in *tableau vivants.* Some just sat and read as though they were encased in glass; several stood immobile, with great bushes of green leaves on their heads; others were grouped like statues from the Elgin marbles. The monastery was dark and silent, but for the Bach playing in the background. The night outside was dead black.

What Artaud hoped for—poetry in space—Wilson has attempted. Yet he lacks the abrasive, electrifying elements associated with Artaud's concept of Cruelty: the vigorous sexuality and the political and social outrage. Wilson's blandness is typical of the Zen approach, which implies awareness without tension, meditation without ego drive, and subliminal, controlled emotion. Wilson's and his company's search for inner peace, for relief from loneliness, death, and despair, is soothing, not stimulating. His work lacks vibrancy, conflict, and a sense of urgency. Yet his imagination is exciting. Utilizing past and present experimental techniques, Wilson, like the Surrealists, creates grotesque and fantastical images; unlike them, he is very American, even folksy (Zen Buddhism notwithstanding). Like the happenings, his productions have relied upon the power of the plastic arts; unlike the happenings, the plasticity has been formalized into a cohesive, harmonious *mise-en-scène.* Like the avant-garde dancers, he has questioned the essence of time, movement, and space: he is finding answers in the Oriental belief that free movement is predicated on the metaphysical union of body, psyche, and spirit. And because Wilson has become a true mystic, he has tried to integrate his artistic talent with his principles in an effort to create a ceremonial, religious theatre. But for all his genuine feeling and extraordinary talent, his theatre is designed for an esoteric elite in search of purity in art, and, as such, it has a very limited appeal.

Although his work is significant, it brings us right back to the silence created by Beckett and Ionesco. In fact, when Ionesco saw *Deafman Glance* in Belgrade, he was moved to comment:

> Beckett has succeeded in creating a few minutes of silence on the stage, while Robert Wilson was able to bring about silence that

> lasted for hours! He has surpassed Beckett in this: Wilson being richer and more complex with his silence on the stage. This silence is a silence that can speak. However, what is interesting about both Beckett and Wilson is the fact they they are above politics. They are interested in the existential—not social—destiny of man. In this, Wilson has gone farther than Beckett, for in his play, "Deafman Glance," despite silence, he conjures up the whole tragedy of man and his history. Wilson speaks of the metaphysical defeat of man. The whole of existence has been condensed here into four hours which bring us to an apocalyptic end. . . .[21]

What Ionesco finds Wilson's greatest asset—the "tragedy of man and his history" unconfined by political and social dimensions—diffuses the strength of Wilson's evocation and renders his art stylized and decorative for its own sake in a way that Beckett's never is. Nonetheless, whatever Wilson's images may lack in intellectual force and emotional ability to encompass a particularized world view of man's estate, the audience does respond to the beauty of the images themselves, which, in essence, have no country, no religion, and no philosophy.

While some groups inevitably have reached a plateau, and others have disappeared, Peter Schumann's Bread and Puppet Theatre continues to flourish. Totally outside the establishment, in fact, virtually unknown in the commercial theatre world, Peter Schumann is unaware of fads and fashions, and remains confident that his theatre of puppets can be exemplary. When you see the Bread and Puppet Theatre, be it in a street, a gym, a church, or an auditorium, you are handed a loaf of bread. You break off a piece, and hand the rest to your neighbor, who, in turn, breaks off his piece, and passes on the loaf. When everyone has tasted bread, the puppet play begins. By beginning in this way, the audience has participated in an instantly recognizable religious ritual: eating bread—communion—is sharing the staff of life.

Bread has been used over the centuries as a symbol of one of man's basic needs. The association of bread and theatre (and particularly of bread and puppets) is, for Peter Schumann, creator and founder of the Bread and Puppet Theatre, a way of expressing homage to an equally important means of sustenance. Schumann, his wife and family, and all the theatre's puppeteers are artistically and spiritually committed to their theatre, not only as a livelihood, for they have been consistently poor, but as a way of life. For the last ten years, this way of life has been strongly linked with baking bread and creating puppets:

> The power of bread is obvious. People are hungry. The job of bread-baking involves baking the loaves well for chewing and digestion and making them available to everybody.
>
> Puppeteers and artists never know for sure what they are good for and what their job does for other people. We want to join the breadbakers, make good bread and give it out for free.
>
> The world in which we live seems to consist mainly of politics or the organizations of man. War and hunger have to be abolished; water, air and soil have to be brought back to life. . . . War is made up by the mind, and poverty and hunger exist through our inefficiencies. Our mind is hungry, and Jesus says: man does not live from bread alone, but from puppet shows as well. . . . What is the purpose of a puppet show? To make the world plain, I guess, to speak simple language that everybody can understand. To seize the listener, to persuade him to the new world. To spark the movement of the listeners.[22]

The Bread and Puppet Theatre considers itself radical enough to "spark the movements of its listeners," but its radicalism does not consist of a complete commitment to New Left activism (although the company has played for political causes and left-wing demonstrations). Instead, its strength (or weakness) is rooted in a nineteenth-century Romanticism that envisions man as divine, sacred, and good, needing only the simplest means—bread—and the most elemental environment—"water, soil and air"—to lead a meaningful life. Man is prevented from achieving his destiny because he makes war, collects material objects, and depends upon superficial accouterments for satisfaction, unaware that all meaning depends on one's inner life. Only bread, dreams, and love are essentials. Only the uncluttered, simple life committed to the highest principles, is meaningful. The members of the Bread and Puppet Theatre are like a tribe of primitive Christians, living in a world in which love, suffering, and compassion are fundamental precepts, a world that denies the psychological and the intellectual, a world that finds man caught between social evils and his desire to be transcendent. Thus, with its deep sense of personal morality and religiosity, the Bread and Puppet Theatre "tries to merge its daily life with its theatrical style . . . it tries to raise the performer's lives to the purity and ecstasy of the actions in which they participate."[23]

Except for their strong feelings about the Vietnam war, Schumann's pieces do not deal with the contemporary aspects of such problems as love and sexuality. His main sources of inspiration are the Bible, fables, folklore, parables, and children's literature. The tone of his pieces parallels lieder; they are simple and direct, touched with exquisite poetry. The decor is like that of folk art. The settings require no more than a table, chair or bed. The backdrops are hand-painted; the instruments, from a penny arcade; the costumes, from rummage sales. Only the puppets are magnificently grand.

Perhaps Schumann's most famous puppets are the "Gray Ladies," often the central figures in his plays. Over ten and fifteen feet tall, they represent eternal womanhood, the archetypal mother figure, the suffering women of Vietnam. They are entirely gray: gray Oriental faces that expose their pain; huge gray hands that move slowly and with remarkable power; gray angular heads, necks, and torsos that appear to float through space, and long gray cloth covering their bodies, and draped over cocked ears which seem to be listening to a secret prayer.

One particular piece, *The Gray Lady Cantata* (in the version performed at the Public Theatre in April 1971), begins with a prologue. Peter Schumann, wearing his raggedy jeans and worker's shoes, his beard and hair disheveled as usual, sits below the stage and plays scratchily on a violin. Accompanying him on penny instruments are a group of masked actors, right out of George Grosz. An eerie bell signals the start of the show. Two masked figures pull the curtain open. On stage, against a simple gray backdrop of tiny hand-painted flowers, sits the Gray Lady at home. Her sorrowful face, huge hands, and the graceful folds of her robe instantaneously capture the essence of all those who suffer in silence. Upstage, behind a long table, her neighbors sit drinking beer and laughing; their masks convey their vacuousness. Suddenly the neighbors are all magically whisked away; cups, saucers, beer cans, and tables "fly" off the stage. Now the Gray Lady is alone with her son, waiting, listening to the moments of life around her, perhaps to the movements of live within her. Her head moves ever so slightly toward her son, who also sits and waits. Each movement is slow, deliberate, like a ritual Japanese dance pattern; even the movement of a finger conveys the special plasticity of puppet life. But the puppets never seem to be automatons. They convey a strange inner life and, as they move, seem totally human. The son (in a mask) puts on his coat; it is a soldier's jacket. Behind him is a huge, fat, red-faced male puppet wearing black wings—the angel of death. The son embraces his mother. He goes out. The angel follows. The woman sits immobile; only her hands flutter momentarily; the folds of her garments now remind us of a sculptured *Pietà*. Slowly, a huge pear-shaped crystaline tear appears in the corner of one of her eyes. Slowly, slowly, the tear rolls down her face; as the electric light catches it, it is like a falling star in slow motion. And the falling of the tear which takes only a second in real time, becomes in theatrical time, a long sacred moment, underscoring the pity, the beauty, and the wonder of a falling teardrop.

In the second scene, the Lady sits alone. A little black bird appears at the window. She follows it into the fields. Now she is joined by peasants, working in the fields. An airplane made of black papier-maché appears overhead; the peasants are killed and the Gray Lady is wounded. She crawls on her knees back to her house. There her sister puts her to bed, and she dies. "But it isn't so bad," says Peter Schumann, "because the gentleman-angel is there and asks her for a dance, and the whole world makes music for them. And that's the end."

This childlike story, with its folklorish quality typical of Schumann's brand of simplicity, does not disguise the sophistication of his art. The puppets are like sculpture moving through a hushed atmosphere punctuated by odd sounds: a tolling bell, a faint rustle, an occasional word or two: "We are not using sound as decoration anymore but as integral to the actions," says Schumann:

> Sound sparks off action just like a word, and sound can be perfectly descriptive. . . .
>
> As for speech, or the word, we would like to discover it, to find out what a word means and not just let language blubber along. In conventional theatre language blubbers along with very little meaning or very little understanding of what it does to our minds or ears. . . .
>
> The word has to be discovered; it is not given to us as we use it now, with our neighbors. . . . It's very important to find honest language. It's our ultimate goal . . . our pieces do use some words, but they're stripped down, confined, specific, careful, and concentrated.[24]

The slow gesture and movements of the puppets are all carefully worked out: they magnify a specific moment in time as well as a moment in a day. And these movements are enacted as though they are mysterious, miraculous, and marvelous. Concentrating thus on silence and movements enables the puppets themselves to be the message: they obviate the need for literalness and individuation of character. Representing archetypes, they are part of the Bread and Puppet vocabulary and language, and in some plays, certain puppets function as emblems and symbols. The Gray Lady is Vietnam, but she is also wisdom and suffering, pain and compassion, strength and inarticulated beauty. Behind her half-closed eyes, her vision is turned inward toward the sacredness of life. Her face, the bruised face of humanity, is ostensibly simple, almost benign. Yet she is activated by her beliefs and buttressed by her ability to be in touch with her real feelings. Not motivated by political or social theories, her strength and existence rest on mysterious and ineffable feelings of love, which finally are the source of her power. Had Peter Schumann tried to write dialogue to convey the inner life of the Gray Lady, he might have had to resort to poetic metaphor lest the character become banal and sentimental. But the puppets are the metaphors. Like great poetry, painting, and sculpture, they are denotative and connotative, exacting and ambiguous, childlike and complex: they evoke the purity of the early Christian believers.

Like the bread they bake, the puppeteers believe that their art should be handmade. This releases them from advertising, lighting, costuming, and the rest of the problems associated with commercial productions (even their programs are drawn by hand), and represents a repudiation of art as business, or art as a finished, manufactured commodity, merchandised especially for the bourgeoisie and the cultural establishment. Thus the company's costumes are sewed and patched; lights are bare electric bulbs, props are papier-maché, and sounds are sometimes taped from the streets. Utilizing poverty as a philosophical as well as an aesthetic credo, the puppeteers believe money corrupts and weakens artistic creativity. For Schumann, creativity does not require capital, nor does it demand art perfected by machinery, technology, advertising. Bread and art go together—both should be organic, handmade, simple, rough, and soul-satisfying.

Although many critics have found Schumann's philosophy and style less than revolutionary, the Bread and Puppet Theatre expresses its own kind of radicalism. Totally independent of the artistic elite, Schumann goes his own way; he continuously reminds us of the brutality of war and the emptiness of capitalism. Nonetheless, he does not impose these reminders through displays of hostility and violence. Instead, the over-all tone of the theatre is undidactic, tender, immensely sorrowful. To a certain extent, Schumann is haunted by Christian mysticism, as expressed in one of his best works, *The Cry of the People for Meat*, a medieval mystery play with modern overtones that traces man's evil to the loss of Paradise. The story of man's fate from the Greeks through Genesis to the Crucifixion, this work perfectly combines Peter Schumann's philosophy and aesthetics.

Before the play begins, Schumann summons the audience by beating on drums and announcing that the group will enact the Bible. A fantastically large Mother Earth—a twenty-foot puppet attached to poles—is carried in. Her half-open mouth reveals irregular teeth; her eyes seem to be terrified, as if focused on some atrocity; her hands, claw-like, are out of proportion to the rest of her body; her hair is clipped, like a man's; her bosom is huge. She wears an ordinary housedress with an apron.

Then another huge puppet, fifteen feet high, appears. He is Uranos, a lascivious-looking Father, a vulgar Uncle Sam with an unlighted cigar held between fat fingers, a typical red-necked honky. He wears a crown, and his open mouth reveals a set of jagged, shark-like teeth. With his fixed smile, and his stereotyped, empty gestures, he is an evil deity as well as the father of modern imperialism.

The two gods do a lusty dance, kiss with a large smack, and Mother goes behind a screen to give birth. A puppet, nine feet tall, rises from hundreds of pieces of stripped newspapers on the floor, and Cronus, the son, is born. In an instant, he kills his father, taking the crown to become the king. The battle is described by newscasters over a microphone, as though patricide were a thrilling sports event.

Suddenly actors appear, wearing masks of predatory animals—a mass of sharks' teeth, ugly snouts, misshaped bodies, wriggling snakes, distorted beards, blind eyes, a profusion of fangs. Two humans rise from the group, slowly and unobtrusively. They are Adam and Eve. Schumann, playing God and carrying a searchlight, mounts the stage and breathes life into Adam's nostrils, but Eve comes to life without help.

Cronus expels them from Paradise; Eve gives birth to Cain, who wears a sign over his eyes: "Everything that moves shall be meat for you." Cain appears, looking like a unicorn, his mark imprinted on his forehead. Carrying two swords, he tames the beasts who, as they become subservient to his will, turn into subjugated man. Thus the killing of animals is equated with man's lust for oppression, murder, and war. The company then enacts the Bible from Adam to Noah. A key scene is the herding, killing, and sacrificing of the animals, which again underscores man's cruelty.

The ceremonial aspects of the piece come to life in the story of Joseph, in which Schumann uses dozens of different puppets, small and funny, and large and splendid, representing kings, prophets, and partriarchs. Later, Schumann uses his famous Gray Lady puppets: one appears as the Virgin, only to be struck down by Cronus. In another sequence, we see Mary arriving at Bethlehem, greated by another set of Gray Ladies. One carries a naked doll, and we hear her, apparently speaking as a Vietnamese woman, lamenting the death of her husband. Now the scene shifts, and a soldier tries to bang down an door, presumably to round up the Gray Ladies, while an airplane (of black papier-maché, held up by strings) suddenly appears on the horizon. The plane strikes; the Gray Ladies are shot. Slowly, slowly, they sink to the ground and die—only their hands are seen rising above their bodies, as if praying.

The next part of the work deals with the life and death of Jesus. Before the Last Supper and the inevitable end, Schumann, presumably in the role of a modern Jesus, gives the traditional blessings, while the company acts them out. For example, Schumann calls out: "Blessed are the poor for they shall inherit the earth," and a red flag appears on two poles. Then: "Blessed are those who hunger and thirst after righteousness," and the actor is decorated with bags of fruit, stings of beads, and wreaths of flowers.

In the final scene, the table is laid with the theatre's freshly baked bread, part of which the actors distribute among the audience. Jesus and the twelve disciples enter. The faces of the puppets, with the exception of Jesus, are deadened; their heads are larger than their bodies; their noses are bulbous and swollen; their chins are extended; their jowls are protruding; they neither see nor smile. Suddenly, in the midst of the eating and chanting, a plane appears; the chanting becomes louder; the plane comes closer; there are horrendous screams; the table is knocked over. Jesus is "crucified" by the bomb.[25]

The content of *The Cry of the People for Meat* reveals Schumann's strong religious convictions, despite his use of radical political emblems. His belief in the Paradise myth appears to be part of his ethos. According to this piece, killing is based on elemental and primordial drives, not on cultural struggles or class differences. Schumann's version of the beast killings implies that he prefers the vegetarian life, not on the grounds of good health, but because all life is sacred. (How does Schumann justify self-defense, or the Vietnamese active resistance against their invaders?) Repudiating science and technology, his work exemplifies man's desire for simplicity—not a new point of view, to be sure, but an example of Schumann's similarity to those Romantics who deplored the rise of industrialism and saw it as an invitation to abandon the cities and return to the land. And, also like some of them, Schumann uses the folk spirit and childlike dreams to symbolize a lost paradise. His is a world that acknowledges no sexual problems or psychological aberrations, a vision that sees man deprived of a paradise by a subversive capitalism as well as by his own wicked hand.

The value of Schumann's art, like that of much of the counterculture, does not lie in the content of his work, but rather in its form. Not only has he furthered the aesthetics of sound and gesture, but he has combined all this with sculpture, painting, mime, dance, and ritual. And although the work is often an expression of outrage and disgust, Schumann is essentially compassionate. Pity, love, and lyricism underline all the work—very rare qualities indeed in a violent society.

ten

The Achievement of Peter Brook: From Commercialism to the Avant-Garde

Of all the experimentalists discussed in this volume, Peter Brook is the only one to have emerged from a successful career in the commercial theatre. Although at this writing he is connected with an ensemble company, he is also the only one who achieved prominence without the help of either a performing group or a set theory, yet he has been consistently challenging. He continues to produce theatre that is both popular and elite, modern and classical, literary and non-literary.

Brook's reputation as a theatrical genius is well earned. For whatever he has directed—his startling *Titus Andronicus* in 1955, his somber *King Lear*, his reworking of the texts of *Oedipus* and *The Tempest*, his cruel *Marat/Sade*, his unorthodox *Midsummer Night's Dream*, his experimental *Orghast*—he has always been in the forefront of theatrical innovation. He has been criticized often for being too eclectic, but it is precisely his avoidance of dogma that has afforded him the opportunity for artistic expansion. It is more than a supposition to say that the achievement of Peter Brook is rooted not only in his creative fertility, but in his being British, in his Shakesperian training and, paradoxically, in his experience in the commercial theatre—even in his being born into a bourgeois family.

As the son of a Russian-Jewish intellectual who became a wealthy businessman in England, Brook's early talent for drama, music, and painting was not allowed to wither. A child prodigy, he was educated at Westminster Gresham's School and later at Oxford, where he developed his gift for languages (he speaks Russian, French, German, Spanish, and Italian). His determination to be a film director gave way when, at the age of twenty (in 1945), he was offered a West End production, he became committed to the theatre. By the time he was twenty-four, he had already directed at Stratford (*Love's Labor Lost*) and in London (*The Brothers Karamozov* and Sartre's *No Exit*). At twenty-six, he was appointed director of Covent Garden Opera, where for two years he grappled with the clichéd acting-singing styles of the divas. Finally fed up, he then was to direct every conceivable kind of production in Paris, London, and New York: *A Winter's Tale* with John Gielgud; Miller's *A View From the Bridge*; Williams' *Cat on a Hot Tin Roof*; Eliot's *Family Reunion*; Genet's *The Balcony*; Anouilh's *Ring Round the Moon*; and about thirty other plays. In between he tried film, television, and opera. For relaxation, he studied theatre in Russia, Mexico, Germany, and America.

By the sixties Brook's reputation in the London theatre was so well established that he could have spent the rest of his life simply repeating himself—and holidaying in Majorca. But the restless Brook surprised the West End establishment when he accepted an offer in 1962 to join the newly-organized Royal Shakespeare Company. The RSC offered him the freedom to work on Shakespeare as well as to experiment with Brechtian and Cruelty techniques, his growing interest at the time. In addition, he was to be part of a production company whose creative energies would reflect the new sensibilities then developing in England.

Brook's urge for experimentation coincided with the fortuitous radical changes that were then taking place in the English theatre—in particular within the Royal Shakespeare Company, which was still in the process of reorganizing itself and searching for new directions. The long-brewing renaissance that was to modernize English drama had already begun with the emergence of the Angry Young Men in 1956. In Oxford and Cambridge, in the red-brick universities, in the working-class districts of Yorkshire, and in London's East End, young writers, directors, and actors looked back in anger and forward with enthusiasm to dismantling what the establishment had reverently worshipped for generations (false gentility, hypocritical façades, trivial drawing-room plots, irrelevant sentimentality), a goal they shared with the Absurdists and existentialists. The young artists who were banded together to overthrow tradition finally affected the staid and prestigious Shakespeare Memorial Theatre Company in Stratford-on-Avon, then suffering from diminishing audiences and lack of artistic concept.

When in 1960 the Board of Governors of the Shakespeare Memorial Company (renamed the Royal Shakespeare Company) appointed as director a young and erudite iconoclast, Cambridge-educated Peter Hall, he invited Brook and Michael Saint-Denis to be co-directors. Together, they immediately announced their intention to "modernize" Shakespeare. It meant exploring new methods of producing Shakespeare so that the work would have immediate impact on modern audiences. Intent on finding an equation between Shakespeare and their own generation, Brook and Hall were interested in "examining fundamentals," in evaluating "those forces that activate us above or below political commitment or social anxiety."[1]

Audiences in the English-speaking world had come to assume

that Shakespeare was always best when produced in the "typically English way." This usually meant a pictorial and genteel Shakespeare, one that "everyone" could understand. But actually that depended on worn-out traditions based on a peculiar English stodginess popular with the Victorians and Edwardians, and carried over into the 1930's and '40's. Individual English stars still performed Shakespeare, sometimes superbly, but the productions in Stratford had remained banal and simplistic, rehashed mountings of the past. Hall's and Brook's approach reflected the work of Absurdists like Beckett and Pinter, who, they felt, bore a direct relationship to modern conceptions of Shakespeare. Thus they formed a company in London (in addition to the one in Stratford), where they would do "modern" experimental plays which they hoped would invigorate their interpretation of Shakespeare, and which, in turn, would affect their interpretations of the moderns.

At the time that Brook, Hall, and their colleagues were working at revitalizing Shakespeare and the modern theatre in England, Bertolt Brecht's and Samuel Beckett's plays, then considered avant-garde, were popular on the Continent. Brook was fascinated by the Berliner Ensemble productions as well as by Beckett's Absurdist philosophy, and it was no secret that Beckett's *Endgame* influenced Brook's *Lear.* Brook was especially struck by the work of the Polish scholar Jan Kott, whose *Shakespeare Our Contemporary* insists that Shakespeare was dark, savage, and cruel, that power, politics, and murder were crucial to the morality of Elizabethan times, that treachery, greed, and violence are elemental, and that *Lear* was not only the story of the tragic hero's fall, but the story of "the fall of the world."[2]

Kott interprets Lear as a study in "philosophical cruelty."[3] In *Lear,* he maintains, morality clashes with daily practice, so that Lear's actions cannot be explained by rational examination, but by understanding philosophical aspects of the absurdist world: In *King Lear* ". . . orders of established values disintegrate. All that remains at the end of this gigantic pantomime is the earth—empty and bleeding. On this earth, through which a tempest has passed leaving only stones, the King, the Fool, the Blind Man and the Madman carry on their distracted dialogues."[4] This world, Kott asserts, is also the world of *Endgame*. It is as parabolic as *Lear*. Beckett, sensing the truth behind *Lear*, "eliminated all action, everything external and repeated it [the theme of *Lear*] in its skeleton form. . . .[5] In both Shakespearian and Beckettian *Endgames* it is the modern world that fell; the Renaissance world, and ours. Accounts have been settled in a very similar way."[6]

Just as Jan Kott (and Beckett) contributed to Brook's intellectual concept of *Lear*, Brechtian techniques stimulated his theatrical concept of *Lear*. A Brechtian production is focused on a central metaphor, which is expressed in terms of a concrete object. A throne, a rope, a wagon, a screen, a stool, a bench—anything that will suggest the social ambiance and embody the metaphor of the play—can become a point of concentration. The actor is detached from his role in a way that leaves him free to comment on the action, and his cool, intelligent approach is designed to interest the audience in large essentials rather than in the immediate moment. The actor's aim is to blend the characters' past and present to render existential as well as historical realities, and allow a distance between emotion and reason. The tone of a Brechtian production (and similarly, that of Brook's *Lear*) is economical, bold, virile, and faithful to social and political realities—expressed not only through visual metaphors, but through the texture of the sets and costumes, the sounds and lights, and the open, curtainless stage.

The sets and costumes of *Lear*, which Brook himself designed, were particularly Brechtian. Using a completely lighted stage to dispel any possible romantic illusion, Brook designed a severe set against which he hung abstract objects that resembled abstract sculpture. A granite throne, quite unadorned, is mounted on a platform in center stage; behind it stands a huge oblong chunk of corroded metal. To one side hang massive metal sheets, counterpoised by a long, wooden, worm-eaten table on which sit pewter mugs. Downstage a rough bench and two high-backed chairs complete the setting. Lear's daughters wear brown leather tunics over long plain dresses reminiscent of the Berliner Ensemble's costumes in *Coriolanus*. The men are dressed in leather cloaks and capes; Lear himself wears a gown that is made of leather and nailhead-studded gray burlap. The massive set looms as the central metaphor. Everything is stark, solid, ominous. For the storm, three rectangular, vibrating, rusty bronze sheets sound the thunder as they descend like mysterious objects from the heavens. Later, when both in rags, the blind Gloucester and the mad Lear meet, the stage is bare.

At the onset, Lear's council chambers suggest a primitive kingdom; his throne, the color and texture of stone, a hard, brooding, immovable object, an appropriate artifact for an obsessive, power-driven tyrant. The rough, unadorned setting, the noticeable absence of velvets, silks, and gold—all opposed to traditional staging—are deliberately designed to emphasize a no-man's land (or perhaps an every-man's land), a barbaric age which, despite its dark bleakness, expresses a penetrating cold beauty, original and modern in tone, theatrical and shocking in effect. From the very beginning, we are witness to an inexorable and devastating ritual—the deposition of the old king. With the lights on full strength—the better to catch the growing insanity of Lear and the excruciating moment when Gloucester is blinded—we experience the fierce relentlessness of Brook's direction. In his interpretation, the universe *is* indifferent, and man is alone, alienated, absurd.

The acting reached neither the heights nor the depths; Paul Scoffield as Lear did not strive for the emotional transcendence usually associated with the recognition scenes. But in the end, with his white crew-cut hair, short beard, and white gown, he resembled a late sculpture of Michelangelo—rough, unpolished, but overwhelming, "a ruined piece of nature."

Lear was one of Brook's great achievements—widely acclaimed all over the world. Still some critics insisted that Brook's direction distorted Shakespeare and imitated Brecht. Actually, in the bare, open stage, the episodic quality of the acts, the sparse furnishings,

Brecht had borrowed from the Elizabethans (as well as from the Chinese); thus, paradoxically, the *Lear* was a testimony to Brook's fearless application of "new" aesthetics, which, in fact, could be traced to their source in Elizabethean times.

Although Brook's next project had nothing to do with Brecht or Beckett, the terrible savagery expressed in the *Lear* production had accelerated his interest in cruelty. In 1964, supported by special funds from the RSC, he began experiments in Theatre of Cruelty concepts, from which were to develop his most famous production, *Marat/Sade.* The Theatre of Cruelty experiments coincided with the beginning of Brook's break with the proscenium theatre. Though he was a product of West End commercialism, he recognized that the conventional theatre (which he later called "deadly") showed signs of decay, and he intensified his search for new form. Sound and movement, fragmented montages, happenings, and especially Artaud, stimulated him. Always aware of the most recent developments of the times, he spent months investigating, improvising, and experimenting. At the end of three months, Brook and Charles Marowitz, his co-director at the time, presented an evening of Cruelty consisting of sound and movement nonsense sketches, a dramatization of a short story by Alain Robbe-Grillet, two collages created by Brook (one, entitled *The Public Bath*, was later used in *Marat/Sade*) some scenes from Genet's *The Screens*, Marowitz's collage-*Hamlet* (a play of disconnected, newly arranged lines and scenes from the original Shakespeare text), and John Arden's *Ars Longa, Vita Brevis.*[7] Though the performance itself was not very successful, it was Brook's first attempt at non-verbal theatre, and represented a qualitative change in his work. Moreover, it led to the amazing inventiveness in his next production, the *Marat/Sade.*

When Peter Weiss, then a little-known German playwright living in Sweden, sent Brook his new play, *The Persecution and Assassination of Marat as Performed by the Inmates of the Asylum of Charenton under the Direction of the Marquis de Sade*, it proved to be the turning point for Weiss and Brook. Finally, here was a play whose text was a fusion of Brechtian intellect and Artaudian sensibility, a text that included music and movement, song and language, naturalism and surrealism, Pirandelloism and ritualism; a total play, and a play-within-a-play. Here was a play to bridge the gap between Brook's commercial past and his experimental present, a play that depicted a world beyond the absurdity of Beckett and the techniques of Brecht, a play rooted in history and pathology, which enabled both Weiss and Brook to deal with the concept of theatre as therapy.

Since the play's framework is de Sade's play-within-the-play enacted in a lunatic asylum, Weiss was free to expand in any number of directions: there is the drama of the murder of Marat by Charlotte Corday; the French Revolution, and the future of all revolutions; the political dialectic between Marat/Sade and the inmates, whose mental diseases parallel the historical characters they are enacting. All of these interact with a double audience: the spectators (the director of the asylum, his wife, and daughter) watching de Sade's play, and the real spectators watching the Weiss play. The lunatics are the link; their role-playing and real roles not only mirror a sane/insane world, but their existences are symptomatic of Cruelty—of madness and murder, repression and revolution, politics and psychosis.

The historical level of the play is embodied by the two leading characters: Sade, a disillusioned revolutionist, predicts the downfall of the French Revolution and all revolutions, (because man is motivated by pleasure, and not by political passions). Marat claims that the bourgeoisie betrays all revolutions, that terror and force are inevitable in a revolution because the bourgeoisie will never peacefully relinquish its property or its power.

The psychological play deals with the inmates' illnesses and obsessions, which parallel those of the characters they are portraying. Marat is enacted by a paranoid who imagines that everyone is ready to assassinate him, corresponding in reality to Marat's well-grounded fear of a plot against his life. Charlotte Corday, Marat's murderer, is enacted by a patient suffering from sleeping sickness; the nuns, her guards, reflect Corday's real past insofar as she was educated in a convent and views her mission as that of a zealous martyr. Her lover, Duperret, in semen-stained pants and with erect penis, suffers from satyriasis; more interested in copulating than in sermonizing, he takes every opportunity to attempt the former.

An outline of the plots fails to describe the richness of the production. The inmates' specially created makeup to emphasize their physical deformities, their mimed tableaus, the numerous montages, sounds, and expressionistic movements, the use of color, the duality of the action—all testify to Brook's intentions: to fuse the Brechtian overtones with the Artaudian cruelty explicitly indicated in the text: "With Artaud," Brook said (in a January 1966 *New York Times* interview), "it's a complete involvement of the spectator by performances of such intensity that all his intellectual barriers are smashed. In Brecht, it's the exact opposite . . . pouring cold water all the time on emotional involvement so that the audience's critical faculties can come into play." Obviously this fusion of the cerebral (Brecht) with the sensory (Artaud), always a delicate amalgam, created controversy, but Brook's direction was the most spectacular in decades, and no critic, however carping, could dismiss it. Critics were "shocked," "stunned," "exhilarated," "thrilled," "provoked" and "spellbound." Still, a few complained: on the one hand, Brook's directorial virtuosity overshadowed the play; on the other, Brook's virtuosity "saved" the play; the question of which was more compelling, the direction or the writing, became a central issue. While questioning the director's relationship to the playwright is valid, it tended to distract from Brook's (and Weiss's) momumental achievement and to focus on an academic matter. The real issue is not whether Brook uses Brechtian and Artaudian techniques, or whether he overstepped his role as director (as if this could be measured), but that Brook added his own aesthetic techniques *in visual, concrete metaphors*, and that these metaphors grew not only out of Artaudian theory, but out of the Weiss text. In the end, this is what is creative and daring about Brook's work. He refuses merely to illustrate or stage the text; he evokes what is beyond the text.

For Brook there is no contradiction between the theatrical image, as represented by Artaud, and the poetic abstract image—the word—as represented by Brecht. If the characters of Brueghel, Hogarth, and Goya—so varying and contradictory—were to be dramatized in one play, their words, movements, and psychology would represent a fascinating problem of harmonizing contraries. So Brook is attracted to those plays and techniques that express human contradictions, and is challenged by the prospect of synthesizing opposites. But he questions whether modern playwrights can ever equal the richness and complexity of Shakespearian verse, for example. Brook had always complained about the improbability of finding material as stimulating as that of Shakespeare. In Weiss, he apparently found the challenge he was looking for.

Was Brook actually successful in his attempts? One has only to recall the giggling, drooling, scabby spastics of *Marat/Sade*—their electrified hair, bulging eyes, misshapen heads, and disjointed bodies, dressed in cardboard gray hospital garb, looking like mummies swathed in old bandages. As they entered on stage, one sucked her thumb, another rocked her "child," a third peered out menacingly at the audience; one by one the paranoiacs, schizophrenics, catatonics, manic depressives, came out on stage to enact their play. Surrounding them are their guards, nuns in black habits and beefy men in coarse butcher aprons. To the side, in the boxes, sit the loony musicians who will play the bitter, eerie, German Expressionist, Brechtian–Weill-like music (written by Richard Peaslee) to serve as an ironic underpinning to the action of the play. This will be matched by a bizarre, surrealist quartet of rouged and lipsticked singers in clown-like outfits, who, like zany freaks, sing the not-so-zany songs, while the other lunatics mime the words. The madmen will be the executioners for the revolution, spilling red, white, and blue buckets of blood—for the people, for Marat, and for the aristocrats. Using every bit of space, including the pit, which serves as a giant basket for the guillotined "heads," Sally Jacobs designed the bathhouse on a bare stage. On one side, in an iron tub, sits the naked Marat, suffering from an incurable skin disease. Draped in wet bandages, he is forever scratching, writing, talking, waiting to be murdered. To the other side on a Louis XIV chair sits Sade, aloof, weary, infinitely sad. In a box to the side of the stage sits Coulmier, the bourgeois director of the institution, with his wife and daughter, pompus, smug, and hideous. Every inch of the stage has been used—boxes, pits, aisles. The lights are on full strength.

The "assembly" drifts on to the tolling of bells and the traditional stamping of the Herald's stick signifying the beginning of the play—a ritual mass will be enacted whose ending we already know. Now the lunatics forget the lines, stammer, stumble, act out their own illnesses as well as that of those they play, and, as they enact the murder of Marat, carefully controlled by Sade, they raise essential philosophical questions.

The actors work on many levels: they are always the inmates, with the attendant manifestations of their madness; simultaneously, they are actors in Sade's play. Corday almost sleeps while speaking—smiles apologetically, is on the verge of hysteria, but is in love with her knife. Accompanied by the grisly nuns, she goes "three times to kill Marat," and holds her knife as she would a penis. She whips Sade with her long hair, while the inmates in the background make the savage cracking sound of the whip and Sade, on his knees, bare chest exposed, cries out in short, orgasmic gasps. At the same time, Corday finds it difficult to resist her lover, whose one obsession is to satisfy his constantly erect penis. While they discuss the Revolution, Corday passively allows him to molest her, he all the while stroking her vagina as well as his own genitals.

The rest of the lunatics, with the exception of Marat and Sade, integrate their individual madnesses with their acting "roles." As "actors," they pantomime the beggars, shopkeepers, and urchins; the deaf men, blind men, priests, and aristocrats who represent the class struggle. Later they are alternately Marat's parents, a grotesque cortege of citizens of France during mass trials, the judges, witnesses, and executioners during the Terror. As the play progresses, the inmates, growing restless, are put down by the male nurses, and when Sade's play gets too radical, Coulmier threatens to punish them, insisting on his right of censorship.

The play-within-the-play weaves backward and forward in time, and events are repeated, as in a ritual. Finally, illusion and reality become indistinguishable; the inmates have come to believe in their own acting. In a savage but phantasmagoric nightmare, the lunatics, whose fury had been rising, shout for freedom and liberty; they take over the asylum, turn over the furniture, and attempt to rape the nuns and kill the guards. But the guards, encouraged by Coulmier, wield their clubs and sticks; a fierce battle breaks out: a real revolution is on. Now the inmates march down to the apron of the stage, menacing the audience. Suddenly a whistle is heard; everybody stops short; a stage manager runs up on the stage to control the company; the audience is saved. Relieved that it is really only the end of the play, the audience applauds the actors. But the actors (or inmates) parody the applause. A steady, rhythmic, ironic clapping breaks out. Standing there at the edge of the apron, virtually impinging upon the spectators, smirking sardonically, even viciously, the inmates continue to clap. Some of the audience, sensing the actors' mockery, leave quickly; some sit and wonder about the identity of the sane and the insane, and about the meaning of revolution. Sade looks on, triumphant.

The philosophical ramifications of madmen enacting the revolution are explicit enough in Weiss's text, and need no further discussion here. But for Brook as well as for the audience, insanity as a theatrical device was entirely provoking. An insane asylum has been a common enough metaphor; as used by Brook and Weiss it opened up great possibilities. Brook and the actors were given a chance to exercise their imaginations freely and still remain within the context of a prescribed text. Anything could be justified and believable, and everything could be interchanged.

Hair could be a whip; a knife, a penis; a bathtub, a hearse. The montages could move instantaneously and jaggedly, not as super-imposed theatrical devices, but because the inmates' inner rhythms dictated it. Odd voices, exaggerated sounds, unconventional speech patterns, or peculiar movements could be justified; the inner and outer mind of the inmate could be separated, merged, pushed to its extreme. In fact, various acting techniques which often have been compared to certain symptoms of madness, could be tested to the limits in Brook's production. Naturalism was appropriately used to depict the specific physical characteristics of various forms of madness; surrealism, for the Herald and the Quartet of clowns and Marat's dream sequence; expressionistic German carbaret for the songs and music; ritual for the trials and killings; the Brechtian "alienation" for the dialectic between Sade and Marat. Further, Brook's and Weiss's over-all conception served as an ironic Artaudian metaphor. Artaud claimed that theatre as therapy could "cure" audiences by "cruelty" techniques. Sade (the play-within-the-play) and Weiss and Brook (through their production) implied the same. Whereas Sade failed with the lunatics, Weiss and Brook succeeded with the audience: critics, scholars, and the public argued about the *Marat/Sade* for months.

The *Marat/Sade* was a qualitative step that signfied the demarcation between Brook's past and present. Experimentalism had yielded up splendid fruits, but Brook's appetite did not diminish; on the contrary, he committed himself to the "new theatre" and would not be deterred. True, he had found a sympathetic home with the Royal Shakespeare Company, but he was restricted by English censorship of the time, and by English actors whose training encouraged beautiful diction and carriage but discouraged spontaneous and uninhibited expression. Determined to continue his experiments, Brook decided to work with international artists rather than depend solely on his compatriots. He recruited Joseph Chaikin and Jerzy Grotowski to come to London for a collaborative production, *US*, an anti-war piece composed of a mélange of improvisations elicited from the actors' responses to the Vietnam war.

US (later called *Tell Me Lies*) had no formal script. Utilizing newspaper articles, collages, and improvisations, Brook and his colleagues worked to combine politics and art, the first time Brook actually worked on political themes. "It was a collective search," writes Albert Hunt, a member of the company, "by a group of people who wanted to say something true and honest and useful about a subject we all felt was very important—the Vietnam war."[8]

US received mixed notices. Irving Wardle of the *London Times* wrote that it was derivative of every kind of theatre imaginable; the *Christian Science Monitor* critic said it was "bad taste amounting to obscenity," and the *Guardian* critic claimed it reminded him of a "Holy Week liturgy, or a confessional," but that it was "a moving tribute to the principles of Christianity"; the critic from *The Listener* wrote that the experience of *US* "developed into one of the major experiences of my life," and Jean-Paul Sartre wrote that it was a turning point in a new kind of theatre.[9] And it was.

Brook, already immersed in the non-verbal, was convinced that he could bring language alive by using it in the context of myth, ritual and celebration. And so when Kenneth Tynan, the literary manager of the National Theatre, suggested that Brook direct Seneca's *Oedipus*, long considered untheatrical, Brook accepted. For him, it was to be an experiment in ritual.

In this production, based on the translation by the British poet Ted Hughes, Brook worked with Irene Worth, John Gielgud, Colin Blakely, and some younger actors from the National Theatre Company who tried to find non-stereotyped means of expressing language. They worked on new breathing methods, listened to religious recordings or primitive tribes, and tried to adapt aspects of primitivism to suit their roles. Actors delivered lines in rapid, sucked-in breaths, conjuring up images of drowning, suffocating, or choking, an effect that added an intense horror to long speeches which otherwise would have been bland. Instead of relying on the power of delivering the word as clearly and realistically as possible, the actors used breathing, intoning, and incanting as well as the denotative word. The ritualistic aspect of the production was plainly evident. Brook designed his own sets and costumes. On stage sat a huge, golden, revolving, box-like cube, which, when opened, revealed a raised playing area; when it was closed it reflected a psychedelic light that "blinded" the audience. The rest of the stage was enveloped in gold metal sheets. Actors appeared on stage carrying little gold stools to sit on. Creon, Oedipus, and the chorus were dressed in ordinary brown slacks and brown turtleneck sweaters; Jocasta, in a simple black gown. Their movements were without flourish; precise, majestic and formal, like a ceremonial. As the audience enters the theatre, the cube is revolving, and some members of the chorus, on stage, have begun drumming on the stools. The sounds recall a primitive ceremony, religious, ominous, and purposeful. Other members of the chorus are leaning against the pillars, hanging, as it were, from the balcony, or standing in various parts of the orchestra: they chant, incant, scream, and hiss out their lines. Using the aisles as well as the stage, they enact the tragedy all around the audience, trapping them in the ritual. There is no intermission, and again, the lights are on throughout.

The last moments of the play are particularly stunning; Jocasta's death is in itself a startling symbolic moment; she inserts Oedipus' "phallic" sword into her vagina. Then a huge object, covered with a gold velvet cloth, is wheeled onto the empty stage. Accompanied by ceremonial drumming that becomes louder and louder, the object is finally unclothed to reveal a gigantic fifteen-foot upright golden phallus. Then to the tune of "Yes, We Have No Bananas," the masked and silver-clothed chorus, followed by a white Dixieland jazz band, dance around the phallus and descend into the auditorium, recalling the celebration of the phallic rites, which, Brook claimed, were observed by the ancient Romans after the performance of a tragedy.

The ending incurred some of the critics' distaste. Martin Esslin, writing in the *New York Times*, noted that the audience response was not one of solemnity but of "disconcerted giggles." He felt that Brook's choice of the diety Priapus (the Greek god of fertility) to emblemize the play was made "just because *his* image [Priapus'] is the only one that still has an immediate meaning to us. . . . but it is the wrong meaning, and produces, as the audience reaction at the first night showed, the wrong reaction."[10]

The fifteen-foot phallus remained the center of controversy and tended to overshadow the most essential aspect of the production: Brook's work with sound. Here is a description, written by Charles Marowitz:

> . . . what Peter Brook has done is to treat the Senecan text like a richly textured piece of music with solos, choral responses, parallel harmonies, and counterpoints. The sound components of the words have been carefully organized to create the maximum degree of tonal variety. Actors hiss, throb, vibrate, and intone throughout the evening. In some cases, they whisper the words with other actors, acclaiming, producing a kind of human echo-chamber effect. Frequently harsh-sibilant sounds whizz around the auditorium, from one group to another, creating an exciting stereophonic effect. Individual speeches are constantly invaded by group-sounds, frequently mickey-mousing narrative descriptions, occasionally providing a subtle counterpoint to speech. There is a certain physical excitement in the sounds themselves, and the incessant drumming and droning makes frontal assaults on an audience which traditionally expects the auditorium to be a sanctuary for the drama.[11]

Marowitz's negative criticism, however, was that Brook's innovations were undigested, and superimposed upon the production for the sole purpose of showing the director's prowess, not for expressing the content of the play.

For others, the play came to life, although whether its theme was illuminated is subject to speculation. Some critics felt that Brook tried to synthesize movement, sound, and classical words with the structure of the play, and that this necessarily negates the play's content. This argument, raised also by *Marat/Sade* critics, often is based on a recognition of Brook's virtuosity that is accompanied by a longing for him to succumb to more conventional solutions. Brook's desire to experiment with a masterpiece is similar to Grotowski's: he wants to convey not only a more meaningful experience to the audience, but to uncover the play's hidden aspects in terms of its modern equivalency. Just as many film directors no longer depend on actors, writers, or story lines, but on themselves as the *auteur*, so Brook's method is the message. Why should the *auteur* concept be accepted in films and rejected in theatre? That some critics deplore a director's creative innovations signifies that they believe theatre is still solely identified with the writer and that the director's role is simply to "stage" the play and move the actors about. Is the playwright sacrosanct? Perhaps his role, as well as that of the director, should be redefined.

These are some of the questions that may have prompted Brook's next project, in 1968. Under the auspices of the *Théâtre des Nations,* Jean-Louis Barrault invited Brook and the Royal Shakespeare Company to organize a company of international artists—actors, directors, and scenic designers (including Joe Chaikin, Victor Garcia, and Geoffrey Reeves)—to examine and experiment with some fundamental questions in form: "What is theatre? What is a play? What is the relationship of the actor to audience? What are the conditions which serve all of them best?[12] As a frame of reference for this research, Brook decided to work on ideas from Shakespeare's *The Tempest.* The play appealed to him because he believed that buried deep in the text were underlying symbolic themes that could be found to produce something other than the sentimental and pallid versions that were usually presented. Among other things, he wanted to "see whether *The Tempest* could help the actors find the power and violence that *is* in the play; whether they could find new ways of performing all other elements which were normally staged in a very artificial way . . . and whether the actors could extend their range of work by using a play that demanded this extension."[13]

Brook hoped that by bringing together foreign artists he could achieve a synthesis of style relevant to our times. Equally important, he wanted a testing ground for the techniques he had been exploring. What resulted was not a literal interpretation of Shakespeare's play, but a working out of abstractions, essences, and contradictions embedded in the text. The plot was shattered, condensed, deverbalized; time was discontinuous, shifting. Action merged into collage, though some moments were framed and, as in a film, dissolved and faded out. Whenever Shakespeare's words were spoken, they were intoned and chanted. Brook tried to strip the play of preconceived language patterns connected with classical interpretations of Shakespeare. In addition, he was interested in finding the relationship of the audience to actors in a new kind of space and what responses and experiences are possible when all conventions are dispensed with.

To this end, *The Tempest* was performed in the Roundhouse in London, formerly a nineteenth-century station house for end-of-the-line trains, now a circular building with an enormous round dome. Inside, the "theatre" looks like a huge gymnasium—no stage, and enormously high ceilings from which hung a circus-like white canvas tent. A number of low Japanese-type wooden platforms of various dimensions jutted out into the open space. Stationed right, left, and diagonally are several giant mobile pipe scaffoldings with wooden planks, on which actors and spectators sit. At various moments, these scaffoldings, complete with members of the audience, were "rolled" or "flown" into the open playing area. Otherwise, the audience sits on three sides, on boxes, benches, stools, and folding chairs; five musicians (on drums and other percussion instruments) sit parallel to the platforms. The lights remain on—at full strength, and very white. Spectators can sit anywhere, and many choose the scaffolding, especially the highest planks. Before the performance, people mill around the arena: actors and audience are indistinguishable. But soon the actors warm up: they vocalize, dance, play ball, do handstands, turn cartwheels.

The actors wear work clothes. Ariel, played by the Japanese No actor Katsuhiro Oida, is dressed in his native kimono; Prospero, the English actor Ian Hogg, wears a white karate suit. Both are thereby set apart from the other members of the company. A group appears in the center of the open space: they arrange themselves in pairs, stand perfectly still for a moment, and then a ritual begins: it is the "mirror" exercise. Actors in pairs respond to one another kinetically. This is combined with a low hum that grows louder and louder, and, as the audience becomes quieter and quieter, we know the play is about to begin. Suddenly the actors "break the mirror," and run onto the platform.

The actors face the audience and display their "masks" (made with their facial muscles) and correlative physicalizations. They accompany these with animal sounds, grunts, moans, howls, whispers, intonations, and gibberish—attempts to find a correspondence between the facial, the physical, and the vocal. The "masks" are those of the people aboard the ship, just prior to the tempest; they are meant to convey social strata as well as archetypes. (According to one actor, the masks were derived from a study of the seven deadly sins. Later, someone suggested the actors study the seven deadly virtues so that they could assume a mask-on-top-of-a-mask, as people do in life. The difficulty of creating contradictory masks produced a good deal of distortion, so that no mask was really clearly distinctive.) While part of the group plays the passengers, others play the ship itself; the remaining enact the altercation between Prospero and his brother. Meanwhile, Ariel has been invoking the storm: he uses the sleeves of his kimono as wings with which he calls forth the spirits; his speech (a combination of Japanese words and non-verbal sounds) and powerful No foot movements call up the wind, rain, and thunder. As the storm increases, the shipwrecked crew moans: "Lost, all is lost," counterposed to the sounds made by those in lifeboats, by the crash of the ship as it sinks (the percussion instruments help), and by the rest of the cast, who echo key words. Meanwhile, Miranda and Prospero converse about her past: she intones the Shakespeare lines—using no end stops. As she speaks, she jumps, runs, skips, climbs the scaffolds, and once appears on the runway on top of the tent about sixty feet up. The Shakespearian lines are delivered ametrically, the object being to imagize or abstract the driving force *beyond* the symbolic word, for gesture and sound are central.

The crew lands on the island half-dead and half-blind. Miranda and Ferdinand meet and fall in love. As innocents, they touch, look (part of the "mirror" exercise), and make love in the rocking position. This is homosexually mimicked and mocked by Caliban and Ariel, while other members of the cast in turn mirror Ariel and Caliban. The possibility that Ferdinand and Miranda themselves embody monster characteristics appears to be the implication here. (The use of the "mirror" exercises becomes indispensable to the performance: every image used in the production is either contradicted, counterposed or mocked by the "mirror," perhaps a technique related to Grotowski's apotheosis-derision concept.

The awakening of the near-dead crew is a fascinating sequence. As if in The Garden of Delights, they touch, smell, look, feel, and copulate—all to the echoes and repetitions of "brave new world" and "how beauteous is man." But soon the forces of darkness are unleashed upon the "good." Caliban's mother Sycorax represents those evil and violent strains that rise from man regardless of his environment. The monster-mother is portrayed by Ronnie Gilbert, who is able to expand her face and body to enormous proportions—a fantastic emblem of the grotesque. Running to the top of the platform, she stands there, like a female King Kong, her legs spread. Suddenly, she gives a horrendous yell, and Caliban, with black sweater over his head, emerges from between her legs: Evil is born.

Prospero tries to contain Caliban (Barry Stanton) by teaching him the meaning of "I," "you," "food," "love," "master," "slave." The last two words unleash Caliban's apparent rebelliousness and brutality. Helped by the percussion instruments and the "flying" scaffoldings, he escapes from Prospero, climbs the scaffolds, jumps to the platforms, rapes Miranda, and tyranizes the islanders, then is captured and imprisoned in the "caves" (openings between the platforms). The percussion, accompanied by atonal music, begins again. Ariel moans, "Ah, ah, brave new world"; the chorus moans (or mocks) "how beauteous is man." Caliban escapes; the takeover of the island begins.

The slave Caliban is now monster-master; he and his mother dominate the scene, enacting a wild orgy, mirrored by the company's quick sexual configurations. Caliban, large and fat, but somehow acrobatic, stands on his head, legs spread; Sycorax stands behind him, her mouth on his genitals. Then they reverse positions. The others follow suit: exaggerated simulations of fellatio, cunnilingus, and other variations of oral and anal intercourse convey a monster-sexuality, a Dantesque phantasmagoria: the Garden of Delights has been transformed into the Garden of Hell. The entire cast forms a giant pyramid on the scaffoldings: Caliban on top, Sycorax on the bottom, holding Ariel prisoner. "This thing of darkness I do acknowledge mine" is the motif echoed by the group as they prepare to kill Prospero.

Prospero is pursued and captured. He is wheeled in on an operating table and then thrown to the floor. Now the group seems a pyramid of dogs: they are on top of him, they bite him, suck on him, and chew him. The leading image, as Caliban and Prospero are locked in another's arms, is homosexual rape. All at once, there are loud obscene sounds—gulping, swallowing, choking, defecating, and farting. For a moment, everything is post-coitally still: the "dogs" lie spent at Prospero's stomach and genitals, reminiscent of the moment in Milton's *Paradise Lost* when, at the gates of hell, Satan's daughter is surrounded by the dogs which are, in fact, part of her lower extremities.

The tension is broken by Ariel's arrival; he brings ribbons, costumes, bright clothing—material things—to bribe the dog pack. The group breaks into game improvisations, and the scene dissolves into Miranda's and Ferdinand's marriage ceremony, performed in a combination of Hebrew-hippie-Japanese style. The wedding over, Prospero says, "I forgot the plot." The double entendre refers to the actual play and to Caliban's plot, which threatens Prospero's position. Each actor stops where he is, thinks a moment, and then someone begins the lines from *The Tempest* epilogue: "And my ending is despair"; another picks up, "Unless I be relieved by prayer"; a third, "Which pierces so that it assaults / Mercy itself and frees all faults." The verse, spoken in various rhythms, inflections, intonations, and phrasings, mixes the sounds until everyone fades out, leaving the audience in stillness. Only the echoes of ". . . ending . . . despair . . . relieved . . . by prayer . . ." are heard in the distance. The lights stay on, there is no curtain, the empty space remains quite empty.

Peter Brook's work with *The Tempest* led to a new and radical project—the founding of an International Centre of Theatre Research in Paris, where he was to experiment with new forms and new ideas. Away from the institutionalized and commercial theatre that forces a director to produce, Brook finally was to settle down in Paris for at least two years with a select group of actors who would be committed to the work. But before starting this project, Brook directed for the Royal Shakespeare Company in 1970 a stunning and unorthodox production of *A Midsummer Night's Dream* that not only added to his personal glory, but was directly related to yet another new phase in his career.

The *Midsummer Night's Dream* prompted several critics to view Brook as the single most important theatre figure in the English-speaking world. The production received almost unanimous raves in London and New York, and the critics and audiences responded to Brook's radical approach in a surprisingly alive manner; indeed, it was hard to imagine how Brook might top this coup. Departing from his dark *Lear* and his violent *Marat/Sade*, the *Dream* was a joyous celebration that created pride in performance and a new-found delight in theatre itself. Although it was staged in a proscenium theatre and Brook used traditionally trained actors from the Royal Shakespeare Company, he turned the play into a brilliant avant-garde production.

For generations of theatregoers, *A Midsummer Night's Dream* has always meant dancing fairies, wooded greens, and gossamer wings—Oberon, Titania, and Puck flitting about, casting their magic spells with sweet sentimentality. From Garrick to Max Reinhardt, directors have leaned heavily upon this tradition of cloying romanticism, and few have had the temerity to break with it. Peter Brook did. His new production was a deliberate departure from convention—contemporary in design, Freudian in tone, and at the same time, faithful to the Shakespearian text. Here are no winged fairies, fake moons, or silver sequins, but a pristine and sensuous vision.

When Brook and Sally Jacobs, the set and costume designer, started work on the *Dream*, they resolved to create a theatrical space in which "theatricality would be celebrated" but would not impose an actual shape on the story. "Everything would be purely functional. The place must enable every difficult theatrical action to be seen out in the open, as in a gymnasium. At first we thought of starting with the actors in their work clothes on a bare stage, but it would have been too stark, too negative a statement for a celebration," Brook said. "Once having made the basic decision that this production would celebrate theatricality (as well as depict the actual wedding celebration in the text), we had to imagine the appropriate facilities—props, costumes, colors, instruments—that would convey all the elements of pure theatre."[14]

It was this concept that led Brook to stage the *Dream* on a white brightly-lit open stage with galleries reminiscent of Shakespeare's Globe running around the top and to install on the side of the walls firemen's ladders on which actors run, jump, and play; to imagine Oberon and Puck not earth-bound but flying through the air on trapezes—like sudden flashes of yellow and purple lightning, the colors of their costumes—dispensing their love juice from a silver plate spinning on a juggler's stick; to design for Titania a scarlet ostrich featherbed levitating in space, like a swing, on which the burly Ass with a Bert Lahr clown's nose, string undershirt, and worker's clogs would bed down the glamorous Queen like a fighter going into the ring; and to conceive, at this climactic point, phallic jokes and ironic stage business to signify the "wedding" of this bizarre pair.

Here, the forest was not a place where "the wild thyme grows," but trees with white metal coils cast down from the galleries like fishing nets by capricious, beefy male fairies, to entangle the two pairs of Athenian lovers, dressed in similar tie-dyed pink and blue mod outfits. Without makeup under the white lights, wearing white satin cloaks, the entire company of players—dashing, energetic, proud— start the play to the sound of drums. As in a processional, each makes his entrance, bowing to the audience to signify the beginning of the ceremony. Those not acting sit or lounge on the galleries, recalling the seating plan at the Globe Theatre, watching the unraveling of the *Dream* below like ordinary spectators.

Under the bright lights, the "magic" is made visible. On the galleries, the fairies, in nondescript gray satin slacks and shirts, play Richard Peaslee's atonal music on bongo drums, tubular bells, and Elizabethan guitars and, as in the Chinese theatre, create sound effects on washboards and metal sheets. Sometimes these fairies function as the stagehands; at other times they silently comment on the action, even participate in it. At one point, they swing on trapezes, singing erotic Arabic-Indian tunes. The ultimate magic-makers, Oberon and Puck, swinging sweepingly but nonchalantly through the air, throw their magic "western flower" (the disk) to one another from a height of about thirty feet. At another point, Puck walks on stilts, and Oberon, like a modern Tarzan, swings on a long rope suspended from the ceiling, his purple satin gown billowing in the air to "celebrate" the union of his queen with the Ass, while the rest of the company—to the tune of the Mendelsohn Wedding March—pelts the entire "wedding" party with confetti and paper plates, leaving the mischievous Puck to sweep up the mess with broom and shovel.

In his search for a fresh approach, Brook utilized old theatrical conventions: the brightly lit open stage recalls the Brechtian theatre, the fairies manipulating the sound effects right before our eyes bring to mind the Chinese theatre; the pantalooned Harlequin Puck suggests the loose improvisational techniques of the *commedia dell'arte*; the dexterity of the actors on ladders, ropes, and trapezes reminds one of the circus; the lunacy of the Athenian couples is reminiscent of the repartee of sophisticated high comedy and low farce; and the rhythmic clarity of the actors' speech recalls the dignity and grace of classical Shakespearian acting. Brook exquisitely meshed these in the *Dream* to show us that "actors can be skilled, accomplished and proud—proud of what they are, proud of dressing up and proud of performing in front of people." In this sense, Brook considers *Dream* an ode to the actor and the performing arts.

In another sense, the production is a dream about sex and love. Brook sees the play as love dissected. "It is a story about love and illusion, love and role-playing, love and all the different aspects of making love, including the most extraordinary demonic notion of Oberon having his Queen fornicate with a physically repellent object—the Ass. And why does Oberon do it? Not out of sadism, anger or revenge—but out of genuine love. It is as though in a modern sense a husband secured the largest truckdriver for his wife to sleep with to smash her illusions about sex and to alleviate the difficulties in their marriage."

Brook feels that the other characters are equally in search of a "hidden dream." Beset with midsummer madness, they are eager to express their subliminal passions and unconscious fantasy lives. To emphasize these dualities, and as if to imply double (or secret) lives, Brook cast his actors in double roles. The actors playing Theseus and Hippolyta also play Oberon and Titania (Alan Howard and Sarah Kestelman) unifying all the lovers in a common dream, thereby merging the dream world with the real one, and suggesting that neither is very different from the other.

In Brook's interpretation, the dream serves as a catharsis for the latent irrationalities and secret desires which Theseus had perceived in his sensuous Amazon queen, and whose *unconscious* fantasies, he feared, would be a deterrent to a harmonious marriage. On the other hand, Oberon and Titania are in *conscious* discord, she warning that their argument would upset the elements if a concord were not reached. In Brook's view, both pairs of lovers are seen as opposite sides of the same coin: Theseus and Hippolyta (ostensibly in concord), the Fairy King and Queen (explicitly in discord), find their solutions through the dream. Since Oberon and Titania are extensions, doubles, stand-ins of Theseus and Hippolyta, the conjuring up of the Ass for Hippolyta/Titania is Theseus/Oberon's attempt to assuage his love of her hidden sexual animality: acting out through dreams what real life forbids insures a conjugal reconciliation. And the night of dreaming works. The lovers, having purged their demons through dreaming (or imagination), convert their conscious (unconscious) discords into concords, a feat presumably impossible without fantasizing. Indeed, after the dream each of the characters experiences such inexplicable inner transformations that Bottom believes his "dream" to be "bottomless": Hermia sees everything double; Titania has the strangest vision ever, and the rest of the lovers, reeling from the night of madness in which love and lovers were exchanged, question if they are even awake.

The pivotal point of the production is the famous and funny play-within-the-play performed at Theseus' wedding. There the dream is dispelled, and illusion and reality confront and embrace each other. Brook's staging of this section is derived from the artistic questions which Shakespeare poses in it: indeed, this new production emerged from the company's work with the last scene. All the aristocratic lovers, now in embroidered velvet purple robes, gather to watch the comic melodrama *Pyramus and Thisbe* staged by the earnest artisans of Athens. Traditionally the play-within-the-play has been staged as a patronizing burlesque of the crude efforts of the naïve and unlettered representatives of the hoi polloi. Brook, wishing to evoke instead sympathy for the amateur actors and respect for their sincerity, concentrates on Shakespeare's use of the piece to comment on acting, actors, illusion and reality, and the nature of the theatre itself.

The problems of acting are clearly stated in the early discussions between Bottom and the rest of the "mechanicals." Snout wonders if Snug playing the lion too realistically will frighten the ladies, and Bottom wonders if the audience will realize that he, Bottom, is still himself while playing Pyramus. Bottom wants an additional prologue written so that the audience will know that Snug is indeed a joiner and not a lion, and that he, Bottom, is "a man as other men are." With these considerations, the mechanicals' play at the end is a mixture of illusion, melodrama, and actuality, resulting in Hippolyta's comments that their play "is the silliest stuff I ever heard." But the noble Theseus—the embodiment of Renaissance sophistication and, presumably, the voice of Shakespeare—replies "the best in this kind are but shadows; and the worst are no worse, if imagination amend them." To which she retorts, "It must be your imagination then, and not theirs."

And so a double metaphor in Brook's production rests on these statements. The play-within-the-play, the dream within the *Dream*, is made credible only by the audience's imagination, or the willingness to accept the magic woven by the imaginations of the mechanicals', Shakespeare, Brook, and the professional actors. In fact, the audience is forced to test its beliefs in the last scene. The mechanicals have presented *Pyramus and Thisbe*, a mock tragedy of what the lovers in the dream have already experienced, and what we, the audience, had already accepted as comedy. The "amateurs" believe entirely in what they are doing, as did the lovers during *their* dream: "If we imagine no worse of them than they of themselves, they may pass for excellent men" says Theseus, implying that they are no better or worse off as actors or as men than others, so long as we, the spectators, invest them with credibility. Further, to reiterate the themes of determining what is art, magic, and imagination, on the one hand, and what is reality, illusion, and acting, on the other, the actors, after the play-within-the-play is over, drop their royal robes and stand there anonymous in plain white nondescript garments, facing the audience. They are, as Bottom says, men as other men—thus breaking the illusion of the *Dream* production itself. Puck's final speech, "Give me your hands, if we be friends," delivered straight to the audience, bridges all gaps as he and the rest of the company break the third wall, jump down the aisles, and shake hands with the audience. Then actors and spectators, amateurs and professionals, fairies and mortals, aristocrats and plebians, reality and illusion all blend in Elizabethan harmony. For the audience is on its feet applauding the cast, and the cast is applauding the audience; actors whistle, make the V-sign, and wave goodby. Some in the audience run up to the stage, others embrace the actors. Drums, shouts, whistles, fill the theatre, and this "sweet comedy" is thus concluded.

Brook's work in *Dream* was not only a blow against conventional Victorian and twentieth-century Shakespearian concepts, but also against what had become standardized in the avant-garde. People had come to believe that avant-garde meant only sounds and movement as a substitute for words, nudity as a means of sensuality, confrontations with the audience in lieu of genuine audience participation, ersatz body gyrations as an extension of Meyerhold and Grotowski, dirty costumes as an emblem of hip culture, and environmentals as the only solution to space. To be sure, these aspects did derive from authentic experimentalists; Brook's new work would have been impossible without the pioneering Living Theatre which dared to involve the audience, or without the long patience of Joe Chaikin and his search for American mythic images, or without Richard Schechner's environments and his attacks on the mimetic theatre, or Grotowski's whole canon of work—or, going back further, without Meyerhold and *commedia dell'arte.*[15] None could develop independently; the history and the development of ideas—aesthetic and otherwise—is clearly dependent upon historical predecessors. The crucial point is that not only do old ideas frequently appear in new vintages, but that *both* old and new vintages synthesize and leave their mark on subsequent syntheses, thus perpetuating a genuine artistic dialectal spiral.

In this sense, Brook's body of work exemplifies the exploration of the old and the new, the search for a synthesis. Like his colleagues, he too had studied and made use of every available contemporary idea and technique. This incorporation of diverse elements on his part, far from making him a mere borrower as some critics have characterized him, is in his hands a form of originality. Brook, like a modern Rennaissance man, is determined to be part of the world around him, and to create a theatre emblematic of that living world. It is no accident that his model should be Shakespeare, whose work is the embodiment of opposites, and who had found the means of expressing the complexity and richness that synthesizing demands. Thus Brook's *Dream* is significant, because six years after his success with *Lear*, Brook is still using Shakespeare to wrestle with—but in a different way. With Shakespeare as a foundation, he is investigating whether space, language, and audience relationships can be revolutionized. In *Dream*, rather than creating an environmental, he utilized the traditional proscenium theatre; but his stage setting was conceived not as an adornment, but as a metaphor for the Elizabethan playhouse and as a vision of the dream as it appears to its chief actors and creators. Further, many of the theatrical elements Brook used are extensions of familiar theatrical techniques applied in a new way. For example, the ending of *Dream* is Brechtian in that the actors break the illusion and become themselves, but this moment is used for sheer splendid enjoyment rather than for intellectual didacticism. The occult magic of shamanism associated with primitive rituals, myths, and celebrations is reversed to disclose magic played out in the open—not for an artistic or intellectual elite, but for a multi-stratified popular audience who come to the theatre for entertainment. Illusion (mimetic art) mixes with non-illusion in that the actors as chorus comment directly to the audience, and when not performing lounge in the galleries, watching. This not only breaks the third wall, but it suggests a shift in concepts of role-playing. In fact, the play-within-the-play, staged slowly and deliberately, underscores some contemporary concerns with naturalism, illusion, and reality.

Brook also utilized modern functionalism to express the innate splendor also contained within the text. Except for a few pillows on the floor, there is no furniture. This atmosphere as backdrop for the elegantly gowned actors who seem to float against white walls gave the production an air or Renaissance regality blended with stark modernism. Shakespearian language was interspersed with nonsense music, pop music, English country songs, and workmen's dirges ("Six Pence a Day") to produce entirely original rhythms—another example of selective use of old traditions to produce the new.

Further, Brook used daring physicalizations. Aside from its skill at handling the flying trapezes and swinging ropes, the company showed an amazing ability to jump, run, trip, and tumble gracefully and deftly, all in ways that gave the verse fresh dimensions. Examples were Hermia's (Mary Henderson) amazing jump across the stage to land crosswise against a door, and her hilarious speech delivered while hanging like a monkey from one of the trapezes. The actors' continual rigorous and unpredictable movement on stage was a remarkably successful attempt to mesh opposites: strenuous movement meshed with poetic diction. The result was that conventional speech patterns were abandoned, false rhetoric was dislodged, and the production was freed from the traditional stress and pitch associated with Shakespearian acting. All of this, combined with Stanislavsky's naturalism, on the one hand (that is, the specific character delineations), and daring physicalizations on the other, was fused without any sacrifice to either. True, the images in the Shakespeare text afforded Brook and the actors the opportunity to invent outrageous "business" and still stay within the context of Shakespeare's "Such tricks hath strong imagination." Especially did the company concentrate on the power of "imagination." For the dream in the play depends upon the imagination of its main characters, while the *Dream* production depends upon the imagination of Brook and the actors, who stimulate the imagination of the audience, who, in turn—judging from their response—testified to the magic of the *Dream*.

Not content to rest on his laurels, Brook's main thrust after the success of *Dream* was his newly organized International Centre of Theatre Research in Paris. There, with a select group deliberately composed of actors from various backgrounds and theatrical training, he hopes to develop new possibilities. There, directors, actors, and designers of all nationalities can experiment with various aspects of the performing arts. And, there, they can focus on what Brook considers to be the most essential problem facing the contemporary theatre: how to bring about a profound and meaningful relationship between actor and audience, a relationship that will expand the quality of people's experiences. Having raised the bulk of the capital for the Centre from private foundations, he began work in 1971 with a nucleus company, in a huge space on the Left Bank (formerly the Gobelin tapestry factory) given to him by the French government. There Brook, with his small group (including a Japanese No actor, a Rumanian director, and Portuguese, French, American and English actors) experimented with a variety of exercises that he has developed over the years. The group worked on improvised fragments of sound and movement, gesture, and words, investigating *inauthentic* as well as authentic forms of the avant-garde. Brook aims to develop a flexible, non-institutional mobile company that will be able to play to 20, 200, 2,000 people of all strata and ages, that can play free theatre, ritual theatre, Shakespeare, or modern drama; a company that will be a fusion of temperaments, styles, techniques, and backgrounds. Brook's hope is that a company will develop that may one day be reminiscent of the tone, flavor, and ambiance of the Elizabethan theatre. There are no set rules except one—that the actor must be ready to go beyond himself.

Though committed to expanding the role of non-verbal communication because "words have either become debased or actors have become imprisoned by them," Brook does not intend to abandon words. "The non-verbal theatre has opened up a great many possibilities for us," he said. "It really makes everyone go back to the start, and ask what, in fact, is one word, or two, or three words. But of course, it isn't as though the word has got to be abolished, only re-examined."

The word "re-examined" has been for Brook a life-long obsession. In love with the language and the Elizabethans' use of it, Brook has always been fascinated by the artistry (and the questions that artistry raised) that supported the longevity of Shakespeare's work:

> It isn't only that no one writes as well as Shakespeare: The issue is that the force and the staying power of the Shakespearean theatre lie in the fantastic quantity of contradictory experiences crammed into any unit of his writing. If you want the common lusty popular theatre, if you hate the highbrow and want the earthy, it is all there at your elbow; but if your interest is introspective, private, metaphysical, mystical, this need is also met, often at the very same time.[16]

He feels that Shakespeare's richness lies in his language, but that it is not a language that functions today as it did then. Thus, ever since his experiments with "cruelty," Brook has been searching for a modern writer's poetic language or an actor's theatrical language that would equal that of Shakespeare. All his experiments, past and present, have been conducted with this in mind.

In the summer of 1971, Brook decided to continue his artistic quest, this time in Iran, since the Centre was partially financed with Iranian government funds. And there, in the ruins of Persepolis, in close and constant collaboration with the noted British poet Ted Hughes and a group of twenty actors, directors, and designers (from twelve different countries: Armenia, Britain, Cameroon, France, Iran, Japan, Mali, Portugal, Rumania, Spain, Switzerland and the United States), he worked on a new and daring production, the fruit of the Centre's first year's work.

This was *Orghast*, an experimental theatre piece written in a completely new language devised by Ted Hughes—a language that is itself called Orghast. This time the setting was not the bare white walls and trapezes that symbolized Shakespeare's forest on a

London or New York stage, but the culture, climate, history, and topography of a country viewed by Brook as the meeting place of the Occident and the Orient. In a series of performances as part of the annual Festival of Arts in Shiraz-Persepolis, Brook, Hughes, and the company sought to create a unique fusion between the drama and the environment that could not and was not intended to be achieved anywhere else.

To experience Brook's experiment, one had to cope with the environment first; one rode in buses or cars for an hour from the small provincial city of Shiraz to Persepolis. The road was bumpy, and the ride hot and dusty; donkeys, flocks of sheep, and peasants carrying provisions on their backs plodded along the way. Black-eyed children squatted in the ditches, young women peeped out from under their veils, and soldiers stood with fixed bayonets, suspiciously checking the vehicles on the road. The nearby village was depressing, typically poor, dirty, and primitive. Then, suddenly there appeared the mighty ruins of one of the most sophisticated wonders of the world—Persepolis. Once the Imperial capital of Persia, conceived by Darius, completed by Xerxes, and destroyed by Alexander, the remains of the city of Persepolis stand in all their symmetry and grace to reveal the splendor of ancient Persia. Its exquisitely sculptured staircases depict the glories of a Persia now dead, and dozens of bruised but elegant fluted columns, statues of winged bulls on fifteen-foot pedestals, enormous lion bas-reliefs, tablets, mounds, friezes, cuneiform inscriptions are all silent witness to what was once the most powerful empire in the world.

The performance of *Orghast* was not staged in the ruins, but at the top of the mountain overlooking them—the Mountain of Mercy. Getting there requires a twenty-minute climb on foot up a winding, steep road full of rock, gravel, dust, debris, and sand. The dusk had fallen, and the only illumination came from dozens of fire lamps along the road. The colors of the terrain—slate blue, muted beige, shadowy gray—made the rock enigmatic, menacing. Now one paused to catch one's breath, to look down upon those broken columns, to watch the other climbers who form a design against an undulating path of fire, to gaze in wonder upon the *mise-en-scène* that no theatrical designer in the world could ever match.

At the top of the peak was Brook's "theatre"—an open space in front of the huge tomb of King Artaxerxes III. Built into the mountain of massive rock, the tomb is surrounded by four columns; the columns support an intricate carving of the King facing the three emblems of divinity: the sun, the fire, and the Zoroastrian God of Wisdom. The front edge of the open space looks down upon the ruins of Persepolis and, in the far distance, the lights of the nearby city. Two faint spotlights shine down from the cliffs that rise still higher above the tomb; later they were to be replaced by fire and moonlight. The audience, which ranged from about one hundred to two hundred at each performance, was composed of Festival guests, international journalists, university professors, scholars, and students, middle-class professional Iranians, and the aristocracy from the Queen's court. They sit on two sides, on pillows and low benches, while the action is played out in the center. Before the tomb sit the actors in yoga position, dressed in American jeans, Persian robes, African dashikis.

Suddenly one's attention is drawn to the highest point of the cliff. There, seventy feet above the open space where the audience sits, an actor stands illuminated by the faint spotlight. Bare-chested, arms outstretched, he is chained to the rocks. There he will remain for the rest of the evening—crucified, as it were. One assumes the figure to be Prometheus, the hero of Greek mythology who, having stolen Zeus's precious fire to give to mankind, is punished for eternity. On another high cliff stands an actress, Natasha Parry.

Her long robe billows in the breeze, and her delicate, classical features and slender body are silhouetted against the sky, the curve of the mountain, and a faintly rising moon. Slowly one spies other actors stationed on various ledges of the cliffs as if to watch over the sacred mountain where Prometheus is being sacrificed. Now there is soft drumming, followed by a silence. Natasha Parry wails out a strange sound (later interpreted as the word for cow, or soul of man), followed by some words in Ted Hughes's Orghast language; the actors sitting on the level ground and the men on the mountaintops echo her cries. A fantastic theatrical moment follows—an enormous ball of fire attached to a chain is lowered from the peak near Prometheus. It is caught in a caldron and carried to the edge of the open space. There, an actor—presumably Man—lights a torch from the stolen fire; the caldron is quickly covered and the original flame snuffed out. Throughout, Prometheus looks down in agony. The stolen fire ritual over (a link also to the worship of fire by the ancient Persian Zoroastrian religion), Hughes and Brook's *Orghast*, an experiment in pure communication unfolds.

Orghast has no linear plot and few discernable characters. It is an evocative dramatic poem written entirely with a poet's tools: metaphor, image, and symbol. Hughes has drawn on ancient sources: abstractions from literary themes, allusions to Greek and Roman myths, Zoroastrian rituals, and Oriental legends. These he has meshed together to form a unified but non-literal play. Using a language with no recognizable words, Hughes and Brook force the spectator to listen to the work as they would listen to music, and to watch the action as if it were a religious experience. The sound of the language—its rhythms, tone, and texture as it reverberates and echoes all over the mountains—is virile and austere, yet touched with pity and human suffering. The actors, speaking with totally new vocal techniques, produce a symphony of sound and word which underscores their international composition, and evokes the lost memory of the comingling of tongues. Hard "or," "gr," "tr," soft "sh" sounds, and the five vowels, sliding from one to the other to blend into one word, transport the listener to Oriental-African-Semitic-Greek-Persian worlds, or perhaps to a time when language was magic and primordial. Actors speak in unpredictable inflections; they also chant, incant, wail, cry, and moan; they make the most extraordinary sounds, but always in combination with Orghast words.

Deliberately ambiguous, the play the actors are performing

summons up for each viewer personal meanings and responses. Because the drama is perceived as though in a dream, it defies total recall and literal analysis. For some, the work may be indecipherable, the language gibberish; it depends upon one's capacity to receive it on an emotional level.

The action in *Orghast*, as in a film, shifts from one spot to another; sometimes the focus is on the mountaintops, sometimes, on the level ground. The effect is a mélange of images and symbols that fade, dissolve, or meld into each other. The central theme of the play is the Prometheus myth, which links all the other sequences together. Having been chained to the rock, and already tortured by Zeus, Prometheus is further tormented by a woman vulture who, as she speaks to him in the language of the ancient Persian eagle, appears to challenge the worthiness of his having brought fire to man. Resisting the bird, Prometheus appears unmoved; but as he gazes down from his prison on the mountaintop, he discovers to his dismay that the mortals mirror the Gods.

On the level ground, an analogy based on the play *Life Is A Dream* by Calderón, the seventeenth-century Spanish playwright, and segments of Japanese legends and Seneca's *Hercules Furens*, are enacted. A tyrant-king, considering his son a threat to his throne, has incarcerated the prince in a tomb since childhood. Now released, but still dragging an enormous chain around his neck that is attached to the inside of the tomb—his umbilical cord, perhaps—the prince is so unaccustomed to freedom that he reverts back to his so-called savage nature. He, too, is tormented by women: they act as accomplices, provocateurs, avengers. One, a mother-earth figure who helped to gain the boy's release from prison, never dares to challenge the basic cruelty of the tyrant-king; another toys with a knife, as if to castrate the prince, while a third, Prometheus' castigating eagle, now uses her wicked tongue to taunt the chained prince.

The focus quickly shifts, and Katsuhiro Oida, the Japanese actor playing the tyrant-king, now resembles the tyrant-samurui who (in the Japanese legend) has been shut up in a ghost-ridden castle and awakens to find that he has murdered his family. In the most compelling part of the production, Oida, with his powerful No training at his command, reenacts the ritual killing of father, wife, and baby. During the slaughter, two versions of the wife appear, one as a helpless victim watching the murder of her child; the other, a fantastically large and powerful-looking woman with a magnificent husky voice, who challenges the bloody deed, only to be killed in the process. When the tyrant realizes the magnitude of his crime, he seeks absolution, only to be blinded by fire. Holding a huge flaming torch in one hand and a knife in the other, he is confronted in battle by an African who, carrying only a faintly lit lamp, seems to represent Wisdom. During this stylized battle of fire, the Japanese and the African capture the essence of Brook's work and the irony of Hughes's play. From two different continents, and with nothing but three props, these two transcend the cultural boundaries. In an instant, without understanding the words, the audience has been shocked by a powerful theatrical image. The fire that Prometheus stole for mankind illuminates the Japanese's tortured, guilt-ridden face to reveal the complexity of his nature—his good and evil soul. The fire enables the King to fight, and to attain spiritual revelation, even wisdom, but, paradoxically it blinds him as well. Before our eyes, the Japanese crouches on his knees, his body bent backward. His face, almost consumed by the fire, is like an exquisite Japanese mask which discloses an unfathomable and terrible beauty.

Murder, violence, and self-destruction, the slaughter of the innocent, the revenge of the women, the archetypal conflict of father and son for possession of power, the tragedy of Prometheus' sacrifice—man's receiving light only to remain among the dark forces—are themes of *Orghast*, but these are counterpointed by lyrical and touching moments: the African climbing a tall rope-ladder, holding his lamp close to his face, and singing a neo-blues hymn; the company chanting to Richard Peaslee's primitive-sounding music; and the stunning contrasts of moonlight, fire, and darkness to evoke ancient ritual. Then there are the actors (including the noted English actress Irene Worth and several young people recruited from the La Mama Troupe), unafraid to be heroic and bold, their Persian, English, American, African, Japanese, and French faces add a distinctive and individual beauty.

Hughes has, in his way, attempted a passion play. Brook directed it as if it were sacred art, and part of the audience received it as if it were an epiphany. But many were reserved. Critics challenged the value of an incomprehensible language, and claimed it was pretentious and extolled irrationality. They longed for narrative explanations, for more clearly defined relationships, for the literal, familiar word. Brook maintained that the language was created to reach the secret, hidden emotional life of human consciousness. He wanted to find a theatrical language "that transcends nationality, and the cultural and social forms that already exist. We wanted to put on stage language that is identical with the feeling *behind* the language which, when spoken properly, would evoke the intended emotional effect. A language that could hit the spectator directly and emotionally."[17]

With this goal in mind, Hughes created *Orghast* from a poet's dream world, perhaps from that state of semi-consciousness before the actual word is completed (was his model *Finnegans Wake?*). He used certain combinations and root words—including Sanskrit and Persian roots—such as "gr" for eat, "ull" for swallow, "kr" for devour, "urg" for death, "uss" for light, "gra" for fire. The title itself, *Orghast*, was understood to mean sun, light, or life.[18] (Free associations to Orghast produce organ, organism, orgasm, gasp). Hughes kept the consonants fixed, the vowels variable. He interspersed ancient Greek, Latin, and Avestan, the dead language of the Zoroastrian religion, which he claims to have used as a mantra. Like the French Symbolists, Hughes was working toward "*l'image juste*": he wanted "a precise language," he said, "one that would be an invitation to a lost world . . . a language that would be mysterious yet open, and which, like music, doesn't cut one off from the hidden world, but which is nevertheless closed to rational analysis. What we are looking for is a language . . . that will reveal man's complexity and which can be understood by all people on a biological level."

Hughes gave the actors the barest meaning of the words, although they knew the general outline of the play. Developing the drama became a dialectical process: the actors who, with Brook, had already been working on their own collective system of sound, created the emotion that the words suggested, while Hughes came up with the language that matched their emotions.

Orghast was the first part of the experiment. A few days later, four miles north of Persepolis, at Nasque Rostam where the great kings of Persia, Darius I, Darius II, Xerxes, and Artaxerxes I had built a mighty burial ground, *Orghast Part II* was played to test the effect of the language when spoken from cliffs and tombs that are over one hundred feet high. There were no seats; the audience walked about the great plain, following the action. Some people sat in the sand under the stars and just listened; the performance was given at midnight, and again at four o'clock in the morning. At midnight fires on the mountaintops created a sense of mystery, and the sight of half the cast climbing the hazardous cliffs with fires and moonlight for their guides, made the scene spectacular. Part of the action was also played on the rolling plains. One scene was acted in a scaffolded pit that resembled the environmental of *The Tempest*, but which was actually the ruins of a fire temple. Another scene took place on smaller slopes, where a group of men, carrying torches, were enactinng a battle. The story was taken from Aeschylus' *The Persians*, which Hughes combined with the mythic figures of the first part of *Orghast.* Having been conceived in a short period of time, this piece was not as well structured as the first, though the setting was spellbinding. The strength of the work was Brook's imaginative use of the gigantic space and the astonishing sound of the language as it hit the open parts of the vast terrain; indeed, it was a majestic spectacle as the roving audience, the mountains, and even the moon, became integral parts of the action.

In contrast to the first part, Part II was staged as if it were an epic. One group of actors, wearing long, flowing robes, walk in processions across the site, chanting and singing what seems to be either Greek, Orghast, or both. Another group charges across the plains, enacting the battles between the Persians and the Greeks. A third, climbing up a ladder attached to Darius' tomb, actually appeared like visions a hundred feet above the crowds; standing on ledges, their voices boom out beautiful but incomprehensible sounds. The epic quality was intended to show the relationship between history and man's actions, and the irony of man's inability to devise benevolent social order despite his knowledge. Prometheus' fire (that is, tools, as well as wisdom and light) leads men to compete, as did the Persians and the Greeks, in a war to the death. But as the sun rises, the battle is over, and Man of Part I reappears. He is leading a cow across the plain. Cow—life—alluded to at the very first the moments of the play, is the final—and wordless—image.

It was quite clear from the productions that Iran and its culture had deeply affected Brook and the tone of his work, so much that his experiment could not be separated from the place in which it was shown. Why did he chose Iran for this project? The financing by the Iranian government and the extolled physical beauty of the country were undoubtedly factors, but Brook said:

> We live in a time of emotional poverty. Emotion has reached a murky low point in the West; in fact, a Wagnerian point, so much so that Brecht had to react against it by using cool lucidity and hard thinking. Now the pendulum has swung to a search for a vehicle for more vivid, higher perceptions. There is a point in *King Lear*, for example when blind Gloucester says "I see it feelingly." To "see it feelingly" is for us to go to certain hidden sources. Persia has been this source. Our work would not have taken the same form had we stayed in London or Paris. Doing this here in Persepolis with its relationship to the sounds that belong to this place has made us look into something that we couldn't have looked into anywhere else.

What does all this mean? Some critics believe that seeking the intellectual significance in *Orghast* is beside the point, since the language was by and large incomprehensible. Many believed that creating this language was something of a hoax rather than a serious endeavor, since the relationship of syllable, sound, and sense is still a mystery, and cannot be solved with a stroke of a poet's pen. But the problems of epistemology evidently did not concern Hughes and Brook. Nor did linguistics or simple intellectual or literal comprehension. They were intent on uncovering—through a study of the sound of old languages—common primordial emotions. Apparently Avestan has confirmed their beliefs:

> When we first encountered Avesta through a remarkable Persian scholar, Mahin Tojaddad, who has done considerable research into the nature of its sound, we realised that we had come close to the source of our study [said Brook]. Avesta came into being some two thousand years ago uniquely as a ceremonial language. It was a language to be declaimed in a certain manner in rituals whose sense was sacred. The letters of Avesta carry within them concealed indications of how the particular sounds are to be produced. When these indications are followed, the deep sense begins to appear. In Avesta, there is never any distance at all between sound and content. In listening to Avesta, it never happens that one wants to know "what it means," for it is meaningful directly in relation to the quality made living by the act of speaking. Avesta proved that what we were looking for could be found, but it has to be approached with great care; it cannot be copied, it cannot be re-invented. It can only be explored and the exploration threw light on the questions with which we had lived all year."[19]

Since Brook and Hughes are searching for a language that is in itself expressive of universal emotions, their first step was to work with sound and syllable that has no fixed meaning, but which later could be developed and controlled. Accordingly, Hughes rejected working with English, claiming his mother tongue would evoke a priori meanings, literary associations, and patterned cultural and social responses. He chose instead Avestan, as well as Greek and Latin, none of which languages the actors in the company knew.

Understandably, Hughes and Brook wanted to start fresh, for in hoping to uncover root feelings expressed through sound, they hoped also to uncover the root of drama, particularly the significance of a word and its sound as a theatrical entity. But looking for a vocabulary of sound and words free from existing cultural references has obvious limitations. Something must start from somewhere, and even stripping down Western cultural forms to basic primitive ritual, or finding dead languages as models, one discovers yet another set of cultural forms indigenous to yet another tribe, community, or people, and, when applied and utilized, threaten also to become a convention. Viewing *Orghast* more than once gave one the opportunity to perceive that the language, at first startling and moving, grew familiar and even ordinary, for the ear adjusts quickly, and so Orghast, like any language, began to lose its startling effect or originality.

Another problem: Hughes was apparently aware that the Orghast language could not really stand entirely without some signs and cultural references, no matter what he theorized, and so he structured the work on Western and Oriental myths, and included some hints in the program notes. In fact, he buttressed the piece with a strong intellectual foundation—not for the sake of the audience but for the actors—in order to reach into their deepest emotional life: the more complicated the content, the more complicated the emotional reaction. Does this mean then that *Orghast* would be totally incomprehensible if there were no mythic foundation or program notes as clues? Could the ordinary public understand the piece, or is *Orghast* only for an elite few?

Further, can an unintelligible language of sounds based on an individual writer's choice be theatrically and intellectually valid? Avestan is associated with, rooted in, and developed through the Zoroastrian religion. What is the source of the Orghast vocabulary? Obviously, it is Hughes' own sensibility. Hughes makes the analogy to music, and implies that his role is equivalent to that of a composer. Here is a literal example of some of the words "scored" by Hughes (and the translation he has given):

ALTOR DATTATURGITH UDDADAKHER
all children given to death under age of speech

DRODOM
throughout the kingdom

ALTOR UDDADAKHER SLID ORGHAST
all children under age of speech this sun

DATTATURGITH
given to death

SHOORS UMBLAGRABA-OO KRISTEEAR DABITH
hear the new command of fire let the slaughter begin

DAKHERGRA
the fire has spoken

Musical sounds need no explanation and no dictionary, he claims, and he feels that verbal language could be similarly structured. But the vocabulary of music already exists; the vocabulary and syntax of the Orghast sounds do not. Even though the new Orghast words convey powerful *feelings*, they cannot convey abstract ideas. And listening to the *Orghast* "score" apart from its contextual references proves less comprehensible than listening to the language in conjunction with the actors' movements and gestures. Unlike music, Orghast words and sounds *cannot* be divorced from their environment, or from the actor's participation. Hughes' arbitrarily fixing the meaning of the word is one thing; but the meaning behind the words is inexorably linked to the place, space, and acoustics, as well as to specific actors, who must invest the sound with meaning beyond the literal one—and this is quite another thing. Since no established phonetic alphabet or "score" accompanies the *Orghast* language, the writer, director, and the actors' sensibilities (which are always subject to change) must create and agree on a phonetic system; otherwise, syllables composed of arbitrarily employed roots, even Latin and Greek ones, might prove senseless.

Where does all this leave Brook? Is finding a new theatrical language a solution to a new art? Can such a language bear the scrutiny of time and repetition? Is a theatrical language only possible as a result of a social and cultural process, and artificial when arbitrarily devised? Is there an inevitable limitation in this kind of vocabulary that must result when there is no strong linguistic foundation? Perhaps Brook's talent is not in finding definitive answers, but in finding processes and, in doing so, discovering style—a style that always has roots in tradition, but at the same time it is an outgrowth of a particular contemporary problem. In short, Brook is guided by the material at hand, rather than by a priori concepts. And in this sense, he is a pragmatist.

On the other hand, Brook's work at the Centre in Paris suggests that he may be transcending pragmatism, using it only as a means of investigation and not as an end, hoping in the process to develop a more stylistic cohesiveness despite the international character of his group. It may seem surprising, then (considering the multi-linguistics of the company), that Brook should want to experiment with language. But language has been his lifetime interest, and English drama has leaned heavily on an abundance of words—a tradition that stretches back to Elizabethan times, to the Restoration comedy of manners, to Shaw's political tracts, to Noel Coward's drawing-room comedies. Even today, some British dramatists are reluctant to relinquish their claim to verbal pyrotechnics, and as in Restoration times still strive for bon mots, antithetical phrasing, perfect parallelisms, witticisms, ironies, puns, retorts, banter, and repartee. Yet these stylistic devices express an artificial world; they tend also to be an end in themselves in that they call attention to their own cleverness.

What Brook has attempted is a breakdown of all conventional patterns of speech and language. We have noted that to give life to words, to fuse words with sound and gesture, is one of his aims. In this, Brook is still upholding tradition as well as breaking with it, because ultimately he is strengthening, expanding, and elucidating the meaning—indeed, the sound—of words. In fact, Brook's entire artistic drive has developed in this direction. To give fresh meaning to Shakespearian language, he staged groundbreaking productions (*King Lear* and *A Midsummer Night's Dream*), or combined words with sound and movement (*Oedipus*, *The Tempest*, *Marat/Sade*), or combined all of the above (*Orghast*).

In *Orghast*, he and Ted Huges have emulated the concepts of the language of the Romantic and of the Symbolist poets. William Wimsatt and Cleanth Brooks believe that the Symbolist movement actually did aim "to bring poetry to the condition of music," and that "Mallarmé's poetry is clearly musical in this sense, words being organized and orchestrated almost as if they were musical notes."[20] George Steiner claims that when poetry is divorced from conventional syntax and grammar and depends upon "sonorities" for communication, it will come closer to music. "The thought of giving to words and prosody only values equivalent to music is an ancient one."[21] Even Coleridge was looking for the "reality of the word itself," and was fascinated by the "doctrine that words can create knowledge." He wrote to Godwin: ". . . is *thinking* impossible without arbitrary signs? And how far is the word "arbitrary" a misnomer? . . . I would endeavor to destroy the old antithesis of words and Things; elevating, as it were, Words into things and living things too."[22]

The theory of words as things, words as incantation, words as music, words as having weight, body, and density, and as such, words as real objects, has been under consideration by poets, philosophers, and linguists for several centuries. The Romantics—as well as contemporary avant-gardists—were equally interested in incantation and in the origins of sounds and words; especially in the possibility of finding definitive answers by studying primitive cultures.[23] Long before the emergence of anthropology, Shelley alludes to this in his *Defence of Poetry*, while Mallarmé and some of the German Idealists believed that primitive sounds and primordial language already existed in the soul of man, but were lost to him once he became civilized. Steiner writes, in *Language and Silence*, that Mallarmé and Rimbaud "hoped to give back to the word the power of incantation . . . which it [language] possesses when it is still a form of magic." Mallarmé "made of words acts not primarily of *communication* but of *initiation* into a private mystery. . . ."[24]

Artaud also envisioned a new language to take the place of conventional syntax and grammar. He even lived among the primitive tribes in Mexico, hoping to learn their magical language, which, he presumed, was based on sounds and words that paralleled man's metaphysical being. As already stated, Artaud wanted the sound of words to have their own impact, aside from any literal meaning; he perceived words as "movements." But he admited that the "grammar" of this new language was still to be discovered. Nonetheless, he tried. Eric Sellin points out that "objectivization of words and sounds" led Artaud to interpolate into his otherwise conventional text of *Le Jet de sang* the annotations of his own invented language, which bears a remarkable resemblance to Ted Hughes's efforts:

lo kundum
a papa
da mama
la mamama
a papa
dama

lokin
a kata
repara
o leptura
o ema
lema

o ersti
o popo
erstura

or erstura
o popo
dima[25]

For Brook and Hughes, too, their interest in rituals and fragments of language is a means of discovering the "magic" and music in words through the "soul" of primitive or ancient man. The philosophical concept in *Orghast* is derived from Manicheanism—a combination of Buddhism, agnostic Christianity, and Zoroastrian religion that posits the duality of good and evil, darkness and light, and man's satanic nature until he is redeemed. In view of contemporary social problems, one questions the relevance and direction of Brook's current quest, and its relationship to ordinary audiences and their everyday lives. Brook may argue that, inasmuch as the subject of his art is universal, he is reflecting ordinary life. But the impact of *Orghast* is far from universal. Its allusions, metaphors, and symbolic paradoxes depend upon a sophisticated audience and are simply beyond the realm of the ordinary person's interest.

To be sure, Brook has been accused of being elitist, but his greatest desire is to attract all classes and all sensibilities. Perhaps in dealing with various philosophies, and in experimenting with all kinds of forms, he may be reconciling all possibilities. Since he never has been committed to any one form of theatre, all forms are open for him, for all forms may lead to what he is searching for—what he describes as "The Flower," a romantic vision that originated with a twelfth-century No actor:

> The Flower is the moment when what the actor is doing and what the audience is doing meshes—when there is a real flow of life—like an act of creation, when out of nothing something really is created and completed, and therefore you cannot say that the experience was more satisfactory for the actor than the spectator or vice versa; all of that vanishes. . . . Take a rehearsal. You've got a group of, say, twenty people, and five of them are doing an improvisation. What are the others doing? Are they watching? At that moment, are they actors or are they audience? . . . The person who is performing is the performer, the person who is watching is the watcher, so that in a studio you have performers and spectators within one group. The challenge to all of us is to look *hard and clear at this*. Whatever work we do, any of us who work with groups knows perfectly well that in miniature, an ideal

> situation can exist in which actor and performer are completely involved and related. Is it our deepest wish and aim of work to make that happen in the wider circle?
>
> . . . . .
>
> If you want to ask me what I want to do over the next ten years, what problem I want to investigate, what I want to choose, where I want to get, I would say that I want to discover how to bring about that close relationship between actor and spectator, because I don't see it happening. And I don't see it being clearly felt as the vital step. I see two separate things—there's the group working beautifully by itself and there's the outer world, and the two are not in focus. The group is a model of what could be an ideal relationship. We create that within the group. We love it, we respect it. So we say that if this can exist in our little group, then it is our responsibility to find the means to make what can happen to twenty people happen to four hundred. . . . So what I am searching for in the theatre is an act without a name—perhaps we can call it an act of communion—an experience of intense recognizable quality. . . . I've seen it in certain moments in Chekhov. I've seen it in moments in Shakespeare. But only in moments—a moment that one calls magic—"The Flower"—because it is so difficult to reach. We are so far from it, the idea of a theatre of the future in which an actor comes forward, turns his head, makes one sound, says one word, and a great breath goes through the audience, must remain a dream. We are no way near that sort of form. . . . But what we are looking for is passages—passages that lead in that direction.[26]

Brook, Hughes, and the international company are well on their way to still another passage, a continuation of the work they began in Iran. Now rather firmly imbued with mysticism, Brook and Hughes are adapting a twelfth-century Persian fable to be premiered in, of all places, the villages and schools of Africa. Judging from his past works, the chances of Brook's coming up with something new are optimal. At the very least, his work at the Centre is fascinating in itself.[27]

The Centre, in the old former Gobelin tapestry factory on the Left Bank, is the scene of intense activity. Brook, dressed in yellow cotton shirt and brown corduroys; the actors, in Japanese kimonos, karate suits, dashikis, caftans, and American tie-dyes, begin work everyday at 10 A.M.. The building is cold; the space they work in is over one hundred feet long, its ceilings one hundred feet high; there are no windows—light comes from fluorescents and baby spots—and the walls and floors are solid stone. Except for some blank tapestry cloth hanging from the ceilings to serve as separators, scaffolds of various dimensions, and pillows used for seats, the huge room is bare.

The atmosphere is casual and relaxed, though everyone is prepared for a long day. Brook sets the tone: his no-nonsense professionalism discourages emotional indulgences and theatrical exhibitionism. Never raising his voice, he displays neither the vanity nor the arrogance that afflict many famous people, and unlike some directors who relish scourging actors, he treats his group with unpatricarchal equality. But he is a shrewd and demanding observer, recognizing an actor's weaknesses instantly and handling them with British tact. In spite of the important visitors who are frequently observers, Brook shows no inclination to impress.

Nonetheless, he does. His and the company's stamina is awesome. They work until seven in the evening, sometimes through the night. A back room with refrigerator and sink serves as dining room, where they picnic on quick lunches of sausages, chicken, ham, fruit, and vegetables, and big French breads and cheeses, washed down with plenty of Beaujolais. Brook himself eats yogurt, drinks milk, and, careful not to waste a moment, confers with secretary, stage manager, and actors. Everyone returns to the mats again, stopping later only for tea. Obsessed with the idea of making theatre, they work doggedly in the windowless old factory.

One of the things that perplexes theatre people is Brook's desire to work in remote places in the world, first in Iran, and, in 1973, Nigeria, Dahomey, Togo, and Niger in Africa. Some people consider this theatrical colonialism, but Brook's involvement with foreign cultures is genuine.

> There are two worlds [says Brook], the world of every day and the world of the imagination. When children play they pass quite

naturally through the two worlds all the time, so that at one moment, a child can hold a stick and pretend its a sword. At one moment, you can tell him to drop that stick, and he responds to that. At the same time, you can tell him to drop that sword, and he responds to that. The two worlds co-exist. In most societies, particularly in Africa, the imaginary world and the everyday world intermingle from birth to death. What Western analytical minds call the superstitious attitude of the Africans is nothing but a natural, free passage of one sort of reality to another. Now, the theatre, in all its forms, contains this double element; it is the meeting place between these two worlds. But the theatre of illusion, the theatre of curtains and scenery and seats—which is rightly out of fashion and rightly despicable—is saying that the theatre speaks of a poetic world that is different from the everyday world. In the theatre of illusion, the curtain goes up and supposedly there is the world of imagination, and then the curtain goes down and we are all back in the everyday world, as though the everyday world has no imagination and the imaginary world has no every day. This is both untrue and unhealthy, and must be rejected. The healthy relationship is the co-existing one. And the co-existing one in artistic form makes it possible for an adult to find his way back to what every child knows, unaided. Which brings me a simple example: if you put a cardboard box in front of the audience and the audience can see it simultaneously as a cardboard box and a poetic object, they are seeing this in a double light. They are seeing it on an imaginary plane and on a real plane, and they respond to both simultaneously, letting whatever responses they have be perfectly natural. In Africa, we hope to find such audiences—audiences who are unconcerned with "correct" responses; in fact, in Africa, some people have no conception of theatre at all, and in some cases don't even speak the same language, but they are very close to the everyday movement of life and the imaginary world as well. . . . A sophisticated audience in London and New York can be very easily bluffed (and that's one of the reasons we're doing experimental work elsewhere). What we want is the lively response of an audience who, if he's not satisfied with what he sees, gets up seconds later and leaves. And that is what we are going to Africa to meet. We are looking for what is really human, what is the real substance of life.[28]

In this search, Brook continued to work with Ted Hughes, whose methods and interests in language are compatible with his. Both were interested in Sufism (the ideas of the mystic Muslim sect that believes in self-perfection through intuition and self-knowledge, and in the union of the mind with the Divine). It is no surprise, then, that Brook and Hughes—especially after their experience in Iran—wanted to use as a basis for their next project *The Conference of the Birds* by the twelfth-century Persian Sufi poet, Farid ud-Din Attar, whose religious and philosophical fable is dense with images, allusions, and metaphors. That the work is virtually unknown in the West (although it is reminiscent of the Holy Grail legends) offered Brook unlimited possibilities for imaginative interpretation and may, in fact, have been one of the reasons for his choice.

Attar's allegory is simple: a group of birds gathers for a conference in which they plan to undertake the search for God. In the course of the meeting, the birds become apprehensive, and lose heart. The Hoopoe (the leader and teacher) tries to convince the birds to remain firm; he tells parabolic stories corresponding to their weaknesses, and instills them with a new morality. Ashamed of their foibles, the birds finally take off. In the end, thirty survive the journey, only to discover that they themselves—their minds—are the embodiment of the Divine. Basically didactic, the story asks the reader to renounce vanity and egotism and to "enter into oneself" to find immortality.

In working with the fable, Hughes disregards the narrative, utilizing only its stories-within-stories as points of departure. Hughes's tales are plotless and cryptic, without set dialogue, and deliberately ambiguous, so that the actors can fill in their own psychological logic. The stories are also sensual and fierce, passionate and lyrical and, typical of Hughes's work, agonized. There are shootings, stabbings, and arguments—between fathers and sons, wives and husbands, kings and subjects, tyrants and slaves, victims and aggressors.

Brook has worked with Hughes's pieces the same way he worked with *Orghast*. He and the company have tried to develop a system of signs, syllables, and silence, and this time, also bird sounds. They studied Greek, not to learn the language literally, but to absorb its sonic essences, the hard sounds and the sliding vowels. These they adapted and combined with their own improvised sounds, along with elements of Japanese and African songs which require using the voice in particular ways. Hughes's stories serve as a basic structure, so that the sounds are not merely gibberish. The point is that Brook is striving for the meaning of *sound* rather than the meaning of *words*, and for a theatrical language that is more physically expressive than English and more universal, able to be grasped anywhere in the world. The greater the physicality of the language, he contends—even to the exent that one moves one's lips and chin the greater the emotionality. Thus the hard, muscular sounds of Greek offer a challenge to the contemporary English theatre's flat, colorless language that, to Brook, has become debased and meaningless.

When asked if sounds and signs could ever surpass language in the theatre, Brook said:

> I'd put the question the other way around. Do you think the so-called language theatre is satisfying? It's like the games people play. If you play the game, "Isn't the theatre terrible? I haven't been to the theatre in ages. It's perfectly dreadful, there's nothing to see," that game can go on all night. Second game: "Look what they're doing to the theatre. They're taking language away from it. They're taking away the only thing that's a real expression of civilized man." And one is up all night on that. Nobody is disputing that language is a logical development of man. But that great principle doesn't alter the fact that language in the theatre has precious little to do with language as an expression of man's highest peak of evolution, so that one would be better off playing a different game. Let's play the game that there are words and words and plays and plays and authors and authors. And there is the word that means something and the word that means nothing and then you discover that language is

> simply taken for granted. . . . When we used Avestan, Greek, and Latin, and combined it into a language that Ted Hughes called Orghast, it was not with the intention of creating a theatrical esperanto; it was simply an experiment to see how far we could go with that kind of thing and where the results would take us. We are experimenting with language now not as a basis for achievement, but as researchers. And that is quite another matter.

Some of Brook's critics have viewed his research and this particular trip to Africa as a throwback to a nineteenth-century romanticism that glorified the occult, the exotic, and the so-called primitive. On the other hand, his intended exploration of Afro-Asian culture, especially its sounds, language, and rituals, concurs with his long-standing practice of theatrical synthesis. Always eclectic, Brook wants to combine Third World sensibilities with those of the West, hoping in the process to revitalize a moribund theatre. In this sense, his work could be considered radical, although elitist—an inevitable consequence of avant-garde experimentation.

Whatever the outcome, Brook is working out the problems in his studio with serious artists from all over the world. Some mornings at the Centre, one may see the Israeli Moshe Feldenkrais putting the group (including Brook) through its paces: the gifted Japanese actor Katsuhiro Oida leading the voice exercises; the American Joe Chaikin working on Japanese and African songs; and other experts teaching Tái Chi or Greek. Most interesting among the visitors was the American Theatre of the Deaf, invited to work with Brook's group for three weeks to see what sign language could contribute to theatrical communication. (The Deaf have produced plays by Chekhov, Buchner, and Dylan Thomas—all in sign language). Some of the exercises with the Deaf indicated what Brook was looking for. On the first day of their visit, the Deaf, eager to become involved, quickly joined Brook's group in a large circle. Holding some long, thin, bamboo sticks (used in the Japanese theatre to achieve Zen calm), the two groups tapped out rhythms, formed bizarre mazes, stood on their heads, lay on their backs.

With the sticks, they challenged, cajoled, and confronted each other. Sticks became extensions of the body, the voice, the psyche; they were used to contact other actors, to measure one's relationship to space, to elicit non-verbal responses. Finally, sticks became the central object in improvisations, the actors using them metaphorically and literally. Brook (the least graceful of the company) participated in all the exercises, and all the work was silent, not simply because the Deaf use sign language and have an interpreter, but because the direction of the work is non-verbal.

Another set of exercises that became central during the Deaf's visit was the work with boxes. Apparently, boxes had occupied Brook and the company all year, so much so that they created various playlets with boxes as their themes, and performed them for deaf children in Paris. Then, when Jean-Louis Barrault invited the company to the 1972 Théâtre des Nations week of experiments, Brook's company did an improvisational piece, again using boxes. Why?

> A box is an ordinary unpoetic object of the everyday world [Brook said.] But a box is also an object that has a million identities. . . . The box is like everything that is afraid of space and has to contain it. It is like everything that is afraid of freedom and has to contain it. It is like everything that shrinks from breath. But a box can have positive meanings too. It can be what you cherish, what you guard, what you protect, what you preserve something in, what you hide in, what protects you. In other words, it can be seen in many lights. It is a good test for the actors' as well as the audience's imagination. For example, when we gave a demonstration of our work, here's what happened: a small cardboard box slowly moved from the side to the middle of the area as though by itself; in fact, you couldn't tell if there was a motor inside or what; it was all boxed up. Everyone's attention was caught. When the box stopped in the middle of the space, there was a moment's pause and then the box started breathing. Now when 500 people are looking at a cardboard box that is breathing, the very thing that I'm talking about is taking place. The audience is seeing it on another level; and they are not told anything specific, nor are they told how to respond. They can sense a

> strangely poetic thing—a breathing motion of the box—and yet they may find it funny or sad. In this case, they were surprised and yet full of laughter.

Brook is one of those people who intellectualizes his artistic concepts, but at the same time, as he proceeds from a preconceived goal and strategy, he is ready to follow new roads depending on where the actors lead him. He tries, tests, and repeats again. He looks for all kinds of variations and possibilities, for contradictory, yet logical progressions. Sometimes, as in a scientific laboratory, this process might prove boring for the viewer, at the same time that it is fascinating for the doer. For the Deaf Company, it was particularly fruitful. David Hays, their manager, said: "With Brook there is always a balance between objective evalutation and subjective involvement. He has the ability to articulate his perceptions, and he sees the world in a larger vision where others see it only personally. . . . As for the differences between us, well, the Deaf actors are more in tune with performing, they are facile and funny. Brook's actors are slow and introspective. Brook's actors lean toward the tragic; the Deaf, toward the comic. Our work with Brook certainly opened up new avenues for us. For example, we are working toward extending communications without using sign language. The Deaf are trying to use their voices on a purely emotional level since they have no way of monitoring sound."[29]

While the Deaf's work with Brook was nourishing, others had different responses. One actor, who had worked a short time at the Centre, felt that Brook was trying to impose his own personality on everyone, and that the actors were trying to please him. Another was exhausted from the demands of the daily routine, and felt that it was no longer possible to endure the long hours and the strenuous physical work. But Joe Chaikin, who was a visiting artist in 1972, came away refreshed. "You can always learn from Brook, no matter what differences you may have with him," he said. "It was wonderful as an actor to study voice and to be criticized, steered, and directed by someone who is as developed as Brook.

Of course I don't share his interest in Greek; I believe it's possible to deal with the same problems of sound and speech using English. As for Brook's actors, they are beautifully trained."[30]

Brook's company is guarded about the work, in fact, uncommunicative. One exception, the British actor, Bruce Myers, formerly with the Royal Shakespeare Company and now in his second year at the Centre, said: "One must feel free to work with Brook and not crave stardom. One must be ready to develop one's psyche as well. For English actors, this is difficult. They have developed a façade of calm and cool, and they play this off well, but underneath, many are intersted in something more than that. . . . On the other hand, many fine actors who have hidden behind this cool and have sought it as a refuge against real feelings could never work with Brook; it means too much exposure. And one must be ready for that."

In Parisian theatrical circles, where jealousy and carping run second to that of no other place, one producer felt that Brook was wasting his enormous funds on techniques that would lead him nowhere; another believed that Brook was a sacred cow in the West, and that his name and position could never be attacked. A third claimed, "Brook has been brought up on rationalism, and regardless of his bent toward Asian-African occultism, he will remain an English rationalist."

Brook is accustomed to being the center of controversy. At twenty, he was considered *l'enfant terrible* of the West End; at twenty-six, as director of Covent Garden Opera, he fought all the divas; today, at almost fifty, he has enemies, but also powerful friends in many circles, who back him unequivocally with money.

Nevertheless, there are people in the conventional theatre in Paris, London, and New York unaccustomed to artistic and intellectual depth in successful directors, who find it hard to understand Peter Brook. Why does he have to go on painfully experimenting when he could mount any production he wanted and in any way he wanted? And Brook agrees: Yes, doing productions *is* more fun—if fun is one's main purpose in life. But not for him.

> My main purpose is neither fun, nor prestige, nor success, nor any of these things. Of course I am delighted if a play I do is a hit. I like playing the game of the commercial theatre, of going into the box office and seeing what the advance sales is and so forth—but that's all fringe. They're totally unimportant and in no way connected with my real work. Fundamentally, all the work I've done has been like an airplane circling to land. It has been spiralling around dealing with one question only—what is the nature of the theatre? What am I doing it for? What is it all about? I've worked in every form—West End farces, comedies, TV, movies—I've worked just to explore the field. But exploring the field doesn't mean going on in the same way, for that would mean being locked into an eternal adolescence. Circling the field eventually narrows, and now I have come closer to the point of landing, and discovering what I want to discover. I'm in Paris, I was in Iran, and now I'm going to Africa. Africa is not going out of my way at all. Staying in Paris would be, staying in New York would be. Africa is directly in the line of what needs to be explored—the place of the theatre in the world today, now. After all, I'm living all my life in the theatre. I have made my cash there, and have proved my ability to live in the competitive world through a form, the theatre. Now I want to know what that theatre is—and to know what it is, is to know what it could be.

If no ultimate answer is forthcoming, Brook has in many ways gone beyond other experimentalists in that, not content with finding a single doctrinaire way, he constantly seeks to forge traditional elements with the new, and lets the search itself provide alternatives that thus far have continued to entrance audiences, while he himself remains unpredictable.

Epilogue

By 1973 the non-literary experimental theatre appeared to be on the decline. The Living Theatre and the Open Theatre were disbanded, the Performance Group was reorganized (but its new productions were not successful), and Grotowski's Polish Laboratory Theatre seemed to be promoting anti-theatre. Indeed, when Grotowski returned to lecture in New York, he advised young people not to learn to act but to learn to live. Only Peter Brook seemed to retain his zest, experimenting with form and language in exotic environments, an involvement viewed by some with skepticism. In theatre circles the opponents of experimentation were proclaiming its death, as were many of its erstwhile supporters. The editor of a promising new theatrical journal *Performance*, dismissed the 1960's in four paragraphs: in a *New York Times* article, a leading experimentalist of that decade (Richard Schechner) disclaimed his former theories. Some people were clearly embarrassed by the past; others looked back with nostalgia.

At the same time the Broadway theatre, despite infusions of money and musicals, showed little evidence of revitalization. But, interestingly enough, some of its most massive failures, as well as a few moderate successes, demonstrated that the ideas of the avant-gardists had penetrated the established theatre. New "hip" versions of Shakespeare's comedies were clearly influenced by Brook's *Dream*, and other productions used scaffoldings, trapezes, trampolines, rock music, psychedelic effects, audience participation. Nudity and obscene language, so shocking when the Becks first used them, have become a commonplace on stage and in film.

As happened in the country as a whole, the styles of the radicals became more acceptable but not their principles—as stunningly expressed by the McGovern debacle and the Nixon landslide in November 1972. The radicals themselves seemed spent and gloomy or at least were rethinking their positions in a new situation in which the victory of the "silent majority" was counterpoised by the sensational disclosures of Watergate. While the ceasefire in Vietnam may have signaled the beginning of the end of American hegemony, and Watergate might rock the nation, the socio-economic power structure in the United States remained intact, and the basic social problems persisted. The rebellion of the sixties had effected little fundamental change, and it did not look as if the demoralized, disunited Left could mobilize for change in the seventies. On the cultural front, in the endless search for newness and appeals to the youth, the media had succeeded in coopting the trappings of radical life styles so well that the word "counterculture" had little meaning any more, and authentic artistic and social alternatives appeared impossible except in isolated instances. The Establishment had used its not so-secret weapon: it tolerated new ideas and new life styles and then quickly merchandised them out of existence. Everyone had long hair, wore jeans and beads, smoked pot and played the guitar. The exciting ferment of the sixties had turned sour.

And so went the experimental theatre. Not so surprising, really. In the United States especially, popular ambivalence about art and intellect has traditionally created an inhospitable environment for serious, searching artists. This is more true for the performing artists so dependent upon financial backing. Theatre in particular is a social enterprise: actors, directors, playwrights, designers must be able to work together. Opposition to the established commercial stage has always been difficult in the theatre, and perhaps most difficult of all in the mad, variegated American cultural scene of the late sixties and the early seventies when other media (such as film) seemed to be captivating creative artists.

Those who chose to work within the system found their idealism was in danger of being compromised by the demands of the system. As ever, how to function effectively and retain one's integrity was a problem. For those who remained outside, their politics and social philosophies were continually diluted by practical realties of everyday life. At the same time, radical political commitments were not always compatible with the artists experimentation and concentration. The avant-garde was caught by American romantic innocence, New Left anarchism and self-seeking opportunism.

As in the case of movements composed of all kinds of personalities, and especially where personality was itself supposed to be an artistic vehicle, some individuals lost sight of their original aim of building an authentic new theatre and got caught up in all sorts of fads and ego trips. Others, remaining true to their muse, took the same paths in a sincere search for new forms, new young audiences, and new ways of coping with life. So untried techniques were grafted onto undigested philosophies, and gestalt therapy theories mixed with R. D. Laing, confrontation politics with Artaud, consciousness expansion with Yoga, spontaneity with disciplined exercise, guruism with collective living, freakism with simplicity.

A serious problem, and one that affected radical political movements as well, was the experimentalists reliance on self-expression as a predominant aesthetic—the old romantic tenet. Self-expression became the answer to all arguments and served to hide a dearth of shallow ideas and unworkable theatrics. To be anti-rational and surrender intellect to extreme emotion was to be hip; it was to be in tune with the "here and the now," no matter what the consequences. True, self-expression contributed to several major artistic breakthroughs, but it also encouraged all sorts of extremes that became absurdities; it cultivated an intense and limited subjectivism and bred, in the name of an ill-defined individualism, a new anti-intellectualism. Finally, self-expression encouraged the cult of guruism among the artists, with some beginning to believe in their own invincibility. The austere Grotowski, profoundly influenced by the "counterculture" ambiance of the West, exchanged his black business suit for dungarees, let his hair and beard grow long and came to pontificate before college audiences in the United States.

Linked to this problem was the old quandry faced by innovators who want to reach a popular audience but whose experimentation by its nature appeals to a relatively few cognoscenti open to new forms and ideas. And in theatre groups that tended to tie their art to political ideology, this situation, along with focus on self-expression, presented an acute dilemma that experimentalists were not able to resolve. And there were some who were consciously elitist at the onset, like Grotowski, who played to limited numbers and did not care about reaching larger audiences. Thus he was cut off from those who might have been enriched by his efforts, a problem that he never worked through. Peter Brook, though he has not solved the problem of the relationship between audience and performance, is aware of it and groping for answers. His work in Africa was an attempt, among other things, to test group living under difficult conditions and to try to play to unsophisticated audiences. Only Peter Schumann had a simple view—he continued to take his puppets everywhere and anywhere. His art is conducive to street and informal settings.

That the avant-garde would have touched a wide public even if they could reach them is another question. There is no strong theatrical tradition in the United States, and avant-garde theatrical artists have never been embraced by the populace, though their ideas eventually may become acceptable, conventional, and often debased. To the extent that the contemporary experimentalists aimed to alter public sensibilities, however, they were in a good measure successful and with all their weaknesses, which were not unique to them, expressed the problem of the sixties counterculture as a whole. The experimentalists brought excitement, vision and refreshing new possibilities to a stale theatre. Some of their work may have been flawed and most of the groups did not survive, but any serious theatrical artist has to reckon with their innovations and their attempt to find ways to renew the theatre. And in the process experimentalists were able to create beautiful, thrilling moments.

Certainly they did not work out all the answers—who could—but they asked the right questions. The experimentalists questioned the validity of relying on the spoken word in an age of the visual, in an age where television and film techniques could rivet the attention of the population by one image on a screen. The experimentalists challenged conventions of language, space, and seating arrangements, and proved that it was possible to play without mechanized stage trappings and standard theatrics. They urged writers and directors to utilize filmic techniques and poetic devices—images, metaphors, myths—to depict contemporary sensibilities. Above all, they called upon artists to redefine the function of the theatre and its ultimate social value. Thus while the experimentalists of the 1960's were no longer working in the same way, if they were working at all, they did call attention to the limited life expectancy of the traditional theatre. And some of them, sensing that a new decade would precipitate new problems, attempted to formulate still other solutions.

Grotowski in 1973 repudiated his concept of the "holy theatre" and predicted that the term "theatre" would eventually vanish. Living and working together with his company in a kind of semi-commune, he chose a new vocabulary designed to redefine the theatre. A piece he now calls a "meeting"; a spectator, a "visitor"; and a theatre, "holiday"—a time for a fresh look at the essentials in life. Peter Brook, after returning from Africa where he and his company camped in tents, slept under the stars, and performed for natives in their own villages, is still searching for new forms. How all this will work out in concrete theatrical terms is still unclear. But for both Grotowski and Brook, this may be beside the point; perhaps their search is more fascinating than their findings. The Living Theatre and Joe Chaikin are also thinking things out quietly and may be taking still other directions. But even if none of these theatre artists ever comes up with anything further, their quest was a remarkable one. They tried against all odds to break the establishment's hold on the theatre, and like all pioneers in all fields they were targets for criticism. Especially was this true of the Living Theatre, which bore the brunt of poverty as well. *La bête noire* of the movement, it was unafraid to "signal through the flames" and leave its ashes for others to build on. Unsubsidized by foundations, with no consistent place to work, and with little peace of mind, it audaciously explored new territory here and abroad. While Grotowski and Brook refined, distilled and brought to the scene their years of professionalism and exquisite taste and tradition, the Living Theatre continued to the end to be the metaphor for American romanticism. It is the Living that represented in theatre the revolutionary spirit of the students of the 1960's and it was the Living that symbolized the exhilarating heights and the awful lows of that revolution.

Now in the 1970's we look back and realize that our lives were far from romantic or revolutionary and that no theatre experience of that decade could make our lives any different. In America the gap continues—between what we believe and how we act, between how we live and what we want, between what we think is art and what we support as art. In theatre the gap has widened even more. Now, as the theatre may be at the threshold of artistic anachronism, we wonder again. If the theatre is not a place for shouting, laughing, crying, thinking, teaching, feeling, then what's the theatre for?

Notes

In the notes that follow, *TDR* refers to *Tulane Drama Review* (now *The Drama Review*).

Chapter 1. The Symbolists and the Naturalists

1. Wallace Fowlie, *Mallarmé* (Chicago: University of Chicago, 1953), p. 64.
2. Enid Starkie, *Arthur Rimbaud* (New York: New Directions, 1961), p. 235.
3. See Enid Starkie's *Baudelaire* (1933 Reprint, New York: New Directions, 1958) for a moving and detailed depiction of the poet's life.
4. Arthur Symons, from Preface to his translation of *Les Fleurs du Mal* as quoted in Edward Engelberg, *The Symbolist Poem* (New York: Dutton, 1967), p. 309.
5. Enid Starkie, *Arthur Rimbaud*, pp. 104–111.
6. *Ibid.*, pp. 158–159.
7. *Ibid.*, p. 235.
8. *Ibid.*, p. 125.
9. *Ibid.*, p. 118–128.
10. Wallace Fowlie, *Age of Surrealism* (Bloomington: Indiana University, 1960), p. 53.
11. Fowlie, *Mallarmé*, p. 17.
12. As quoted in Haskell M. Block, *Mallarmé and the Symbolist Drama* (Detroit: Wayne State University, 1963), pp. 11–12.
13. For an excellent and invaluable discussion of Mallarmé's aesthetics, see Block.

14. *Revue Indépendante*, January 1887, p. 56 as quoted in Block, p. 85.

15. Block, Chapter 4, *passim*, and p. 93.

16. *Ibid.*, p. 88.

17. Arthur Symons, "The Decadent Movement in Literature," *Harper's New Monthly Magazine* (November 1893), as quoted in Engelberg, *The Symbolist Poem*, pp. 195–197.

18. Roger Shattuck, *The Banquet Years* (1958 Reprint. New York: Vintage-Random House, 1968), p. 206.

19. George E. Wellwarth, *The Theatre of Protest and Paradox* (New York: New York University, 1964), p.3.

20. Shattuck, pp. 213–214.

21. *Ibid.*, pp. 187–222.

22. Arthur Symons, *Studies in Seven Arts*, as quoted in Shattuck, p. 207.

23. As quoted in Shattuck, p. 209.

24. As quoted in Shattuck, p. 241.

25. *Ibid.*

26. Shattuck, p. 239.

27. *Ibid.*, p. 243.

28. Emile Zola, *Le Naturalisme au théâtre*, quoted in Martin Esslin, "Naturalism in Context," *TDR* (Winter 1968), p. 69.

29. For a good discussion of this, see Lawson A. Carter, *Zola and the Theatre* (New Haven: Yale University, 1963).

30. *Ibid.*, *passim.*

31. Edward Gordon Craig, *On the Art of the Theatre* (New York: Theatre Arts, 1956), pp. 139–140.

32. *Ibid.*, p. 144.

33. Gerald E. Weales, in *The Reader's Encyclopedia of World Drama*, eds. John Gassner and Edmund Quinn (New York: Crowell, 1969), p. 256.

34. *Ibid.*

35. Bernard S. Meyers, *The German Expressionists* (New York: 1956). p. 10.

36. Lothar-Günther Buchheim, *The Graphic Art of German Expressionism* (New York: Universe, 1960), p.21.

37. See Walter H. Sokol, *The Writer in Extremis* (Stanford: Stanford University, 1959).

38. Sokol, p. 18.
39. *Ibid.*, pp. 24–64.

Chapter 2. The Russians Take Over

1. Marc Slonim, *Russian Theatre: From the Empire to the Soviets* (New York: Collier Books, 1961), p. 116.
2. For an excellent description of the production, see Slonim, Chapter 4.
3. *Ibid.*
4. *Ibid.*, p. 159.
5. Vsevolod Meyerhold, *Meyerhold on Theatre*, Edward Braun, ed. and trans., (London: Methuen, 1969), p. 199. All quotations from Meyerhold, unless otherwise specified, are from this source.
6. *Ibid.*, p. 54.
7. *Ibid.*, p. 56.
8. Quoted in E. T. Kirby, ed., *Total Theatre* (New York: Dutton, 1969), p. 136, from Nikolai A. Gorchakov, *The Theatre in Soviet Russia*, trans. Edgar Lehram (New York: Columbia University, 1957).
9. Braun, p. 56.
10. Grotowski does a series of exercises called corporeal and plastiques—gymnastics—that are presumably adaptations of biomechanics.
11. Braun, p. 199.
12. *Ibid.*, p. 201.
13. *Ibid.*, p. 203.
14. *Ibid.*, p. 202.
15. Oliver M. Sayler, *Russian Theatre Under the Revolution* (Boston: Little, Brown, 1920), p. 210.
16. As quoted in Braun, p. 250.
17. See Braun, p. 252, in which he cites as his source for the circumstances of Meyerhold's death the *Teatralnaya entsiklopedia*, Moscow, 1964, Vol. 3, col. 768.
18. Alexander Tairov, *Notes of a Director*, William Kuhlke, trans. and ed., (Coral Gables: University of Miami, 1969). See Kuhlke's excellent Introduction.
19. *Ibid.*, p. 29.
20. Tairov, *Notes of a Director*, p. 136.

21. Kuhlke in Tairov, p. 37.

22. William Kuhlke, "Vakhtangov and the American Theatre of the 1960's," in *Total Theatre*, ed. E. T. Kirby, p. 150. Apparently this concept implied a blend of the grotesque and the real.

23. *Ibid.*, pp. 152–154.

Chapter 3. The Surrealists

1. Georges Hugnet, "L'esprit dada dans la peinture" (*Cahiers d'Art*, 1932–1934), as quoted in Maurice Nadeau, *The History of Surrealism*, trans. Richard Howard (1965 Reprint. New York: Collier Books, 1967), p. 56.

2. Quoted in Robert Motherwell, ed., *The Dada Painters and Poets: An Anthology* (New York: Wittenborn & Schultz, 1951), p. 81.

3. Georges Hugnet, *op. cit.*, quoted in Nadeau, p. 63.

4. *Ibid.*, pp. 61–62.

5. *Ibid.*, p. 62.

6. Sarane Alexandrian, *Surrealist Art*, trans. Gordon Clough (New York: Praeger, 1970), p. 45.

7. *Ibid.*, pp. 45–46.

8. Marcel Janco, as quoted in Hans Richter, *Dada Art and Anti-Art* (New York: McGraw-Hill, 1965), p. 25.

9. Richter, p. 30.

10. Nadeau, pp. 66–67.

11. André Breton, *Le Manifeste du surréalisme*, (1924) as quoted in Patrick Waldberg, *Surrealism* (New York: McGraw-Hill, 1965), p. 72.

12. Breton, *Le Manifeste du surréalisme* (1924) as quoted in Nadeau, p. 90.

13. Louis Aragon, "Une vague de rêves," in *Commerce* (Autumn 1924), quoted in Nadeau, pp. 82—83.

14. Alexandrian, pp. 66–67.

15. *Ibid.*, pp. 71–74.

16. Nadeau, pp. 83–84.

17. Breton, *Le Second Manifeste du surréalisme* (1929) as quoted in Waldberg, p. 76.

18. Breton, *Le Manifeste du surréalisme* (1924) as quoted in Waldberg, p. 70.

19. Quoted in Nadeau, p. 240.

20. *La Révolution surréaliste*, No. 4, quoted in Nadeau, p. 111.
21. *Ibid.*
22. Waldberg, pp. 34–35.
23. Quoted in Nadeau, p. 112.
24. For a detailed description, see Nadeau, pp. 112–114.

Chapter 4. Artaud's Plague

1. Albert Camus, *The Myth of Sisyphus*, trans. Justin O'Brien (New York: Knopf, 1955).

2. The Public Theater under the leadership of Joseph Papp in 1967 produced *Hair* and some new European playwrights in its first season, but the company was not a leader in experimental theatre.

3. See Chapter 10 for an extensive discussion of the *Marat/ Sade.*

4. See Bettina L. Knapp, *Antonin Artaud, Man of Vision* (New York: David Lewis, 1969) for details on Artaud's youth.

5. Dullin was probably the first French artist to use improvisation as a means of sharpening technique, and the first in France to recognize that only in the atmosphere of the studio could the actor develop.

6. A good discussion of this appears in Knapp, Chapter 2.

7. Antonin Artaud, *The Theatre and Its Double*, tr. Mary Caroline Richards (New York: Grove, 1958), p. 54.

8. Artaud, p. 27. All quotations from Artaud are from this source, unless otherwise specified.

9. *Ibid.*, pp. 30–32.

10. *Ibid.*, p. 90.

11. Quoted in Antonin Artaud, "States of Mind: 1921–1945," trans. Ruby Cohn, *TDR* (Winter 1963), p. 44.

12. Artaud, *The Theatre and Its Double*, p. 81.

13. *Ibid.*, p. 80.

14. *Ibid.*, p. 79.

15. *Ibid.*, p. 80.

16. *Ibid.*, *passim.*

17. Bosch, El Greco, and Goya were subsequently used by the Living Theatre, Peter Brook, and Grotowski as stimuli for their work, although Grotowski tended to use the Christian icons more than he used Bosch.

18. Artaud, *The Theatre and Its Double*, p. 93.
19. *Ibid.*, p. 116.
20. *Ibid.*, pp. 99–100.
21. *Ibid.*, p. 119. See later descriptions of Grotowski's work and Brook's experiments for obvious similarities.
22. *Ibid.*, Chapter 12. See also Knapp, pp. 95–97.
23. Artaud, p. 71.
24. *Ibid.*, p. 96.
25. *Ibid.*, pp. 101–102.
26. Ihab Hassan, *The Literature of Silence: Henry Miller and Samuel Beckett* (New York: Knopf, 1967), pp. 15–16.

Chapter 5. Happenings

1. Michael Kirby, *Happenings* (New York: Dutton, 1966), p. 74.
2. For an excellent description of Kaprow's happening, see Kirby, pp. 53–83. I am especially grateful for this and for the additional information in Kirby's detailed book.
3. Jim Dine, quoted in Kirby, p. 185.
4. Allan Kaprow, *Assemblage, Environments & Happenings* (New York: Abrams, n.d.).
5. Kirby, p. 31.
6. In early happenings, the audience could participate as well as observe; in later ones, there was no audience—they all had become participants.
7. Richard Schechner, "Extensions in Time and Space, An Interview with Allan Kaprow," *TDR* (Spring 1968), p. 155.
8. *Ibid.*, p. 156.
9. Quoted in Kirby, p. 202.
10. See Kirby, p. 17 and *passim.*
11. Robert Rauschenberg in an interview with Richard Kostelanetz, *The Theatre of Mixed Means* (New York: Dial, 1968), p. 86.
12. Kaprow, *Assemblage, Environments & Happenings*, pp. 188–198.
13. Taped interview with me, May 1969.
14. *Ibid.*
15. *Ibid.*
16. See Kaprow, *Assemblage, Environments & Happenings* for what appears to be the original scenario, p. 228.

17. *Ibid.*, p. 234.
18. Jean-Jacques Lebel, "On the Necessity of Violation," *TDR* (Fall 1968), p. 90.
19. "Collective Dream" was also part of the Living Theatre's *Paradise Now.*
20. Lebel, "On the Necessity of Violation." See Chapter 6 on the Living Theatre for comparisons.
21. Lebel, p. 94.
22. *Ibid.*, p. 105.

Chapter 6. The Living Theatre—The Mother of Them All

1. Julian Beck, "How to Close a Theatre," *TDR* (Spring 1964), pp. 180–190.
2. As quoted by Steven Ben Israel in *Yale/Theatre* (Spring 1969), p. 134. These are excerpts from Mary Shelley's novel, *Frankenstein.* The lines are not consecutive; the Becks apparently pieced them together.
3. See William Godwin, *Enquiry Concerning Political Justice.*
4. Quoted in Antonin Artaud, "States of Mind: 1921–1945," trans. Ruby Cohn, *TDR* (Winter 1963), p. 49.
5. Clarence L. Barnhart, ed., *The New Century Handbook of English Literature* (New York: Appleton-Century-Crofts, 1956), p. 384.
6. See Stefan Brecht's interpretation of *Mysteries* in "Revolution at the Brooklyn Academy of Music," *TDR* (Spring 1969), as well as his detailed discussion of the Living Theatre's entire repertory.
7. See Knapp, *Antonin Artaud, Man of Vision*, p. 24.
8. Quoted in *Yale/Theatre* (Spring 1969), p. 117. The entire issue is devoted to the Living Theatre, and is extremely helpful in conveying the background, atmosphere, and incidents of the company's American tour.
9. "Containment is the Enemy; Judith Malina and Julian Beck Interviewed by Richard Schechner," *TDR* (Spring 1969), pp. 24–44.
10. It is true that the preparation of *Paradise Now* had begun before the uprising, but my contention is that the experience in the Paris events contributed to the final form of the piece.
11. Quoted in *Yale/Theatre* (Spring 1969), p. 16.

12. I have seen *Paradise Now* three times, once in France and twice at the Brooklyn Academy. This description is based on the final week of the run at the Academy in March 1969.

13. Taped interview with me, Avignon, August 1968.

14. "Inside Paradise," (conversations recorded during a performance of *Paradise Now*, September 27, 1968), *Yale/Theatre*, pp. 34–39.

15. Michael Thomas, "Expecting to Fly: Advertisements for the Living Theatre," in *US* (New York: Bantam, 1969), p. 61.

16. *Yale/Theatre* (Spring 1969), pp. 52–84.

17. *Ibid.*

18. *Ibid.*

19. Any takeover of a theatre or a meeting defies institutional forms; it is a step closer to the anarchist revolution. Therefore the Becks looked kindly upon their company's disruption of a meeting at the Fillmore theatre in New York one night, and similarly at the company's takeover and disruption of a forum at the Theatre for Ideas, where, ironically, Julian Beck and Judith Malina were to be the principle speakers.

20. See Herbert Marcuse, *Eros and Civilization* (Boston: Beacon, 1955) for his comprehensive and fascinating discussion of this problem.

21. This theory is reminiscent of Earl Browder's enlightened capitalism doctrine, which maintained that the capitalist class will relinquish power in order to save itself.

22. Taped interview with me, Avignon, August 1968.

23. "Inside Paradise," *Yale/Theatre* (Spring 1969), p. 35.

24. For a highly personal account of her trip to California with the company, see Renfreu Neff, *The Living Theatre: USA* (New York: Bobbs-Merrill, 1970).

25. All these and the following quotes by Judith Malina and Julian Beck, unless otherwise specified, are from taped interviews sent to me from Paris in 1970 via the *New York Times.* Parts were used as the basis for my article, "After 'Paradise,' Where?", *New York Times*, Sunday, March 8, 1970.

26. Herbert Marcuse, *An Essay on Liberation* (Boston: Beacon, 1969), pp. 27–41.

Chapter 7. The Phenomenon of Jerzy Grotowski

1. Szymon Datner, *The Wehrmacht's 55 Days in Poland*, quoted in *Poland* (November 1969), pp. 37–38.

2. W. F. Reddaway, J. H. Penson, O. Halecki, and R. Dyboski, eds., *The Cambridge History of Poland* (Cambridge: Cambridge University, 1951), p. 324. Much of the material on Polish Romanticism that follows is based on the extensive discussion that appears here. See also Peter Brock, "Polish Nationalism," *Nationalism in Eastern Europe,* eds. Peter F. Sugar and Ivo J. Lederer (Seattle: University of Washington, 1969), pp. 310–372.

3. Jan Kott, *Theatre Notebook: 1947–1967*, trans. Boleslaw Taborski (New York: Doubleday, 1968), pp. 52–53.

4. *Cambridge History of Poland*, p. 329.

5. Kott, p. 56.

6. *Cambridge History of Poland*, p. 322.

7. Adam Tarn, "The Roots of Polish Drama," *Drama in Calgary*, 3, No. 3, p. 4 and *passim.*

8. Claude Backvis, "Genius of the Theatre," *Poland* (November 1969) p. 35. I am grateful for this long and informative article, as well as for Aniela Lempicka, "In the Sphere of European Intellectual Revolution," *Poland* (November 1969).

9. Julian Krzyzanowski, "Stanislaw Wyspianski," *Polish Review* (Autumn 1957), pp. 25–26.

10. Kazimierz Braun, "Wyspianski and the New Poetic Theatre," quoted in *The Theatre in Poland* (April 1969), p. 20.

11. Slawomir Mrozek, a leading Polish playwright, has been exiled from Poland for criticizing the Party; so has the well-known Marxist philosopher Leszek Kolakowski. The Jewish actress Ida Kaminska told me in a taped interview in 1970 that she left Poland because she refused to join in a campaign against Polish Jews "known" to be Zionists. For a description of repressive bureaucracy in Polish government, see Leszek Kolakowski, *Toward a Marxist Humanism*, trans. Jane Zielonko Peel (New York: Grove, 1968).

12. *Teatr*, No. 23 (1968), quoted in *The Theatre in Poland* (April 1969), p. 23.

13. Jerzy Grotowski, *Towards a Poor Theatre* (Holstebro, Denmark: Odin Teatrets Forlag, 1968), p. 22.

14. Ludwik Flaszen, "After the Avant-Garde," *The Theatre in Poland* (July-August 1968), p. 17.

15. Kolakowski, *Toward a Marxist Humanism, passim.*

16. *Ibid.*, pp. 34–36.

17. Kolakowski was expelled from the Communist Party in 1967. He continued to teach philosophy at the University of Warsaw but was dismissed from his post in March 1968. He has taught at Berkeley and is now Professor of Philosophy at Oxford.

18. Elizabeth Hardwick, "The Theater of Grotowski," *New York Review of Books*, February 12, 1970, pp. 3–5.

19. Gustave Thibon, in his Introduction to *Gravity and Grace*, by Simone Weil, trans. Emma Craufurd (London: Routledge & Kegan Paul, 1952). p. xi.

20. Ludwik Flaszen, "After the Avant-Garde."

21. In conversation with me, 1969.

22. As quoted in Grotowski, *Towards a Poor Theatre*, p. 109.

23. Elizabeth Drew, *T. S. Elliot: The Design of His Poetry* (New York: Scribner's 1949), p. 48.

24. This material is based on Grotowski's public lectures and on interviews with me.

25. See my discussion of the Russian avant-gardists in Chapter 2.

26. Eugenio Barba, "The Kathakali Theatre," *TDR* (Summer 1967), pp. 38–40.

27. *Ibid.,* p. 42.

28. *Ibid.,* p. 50.

29. Grotowski, *Towards a Poor Theatre, passim.*

30. *Ibid.*, p. 38.

31. *Ibid.*, p. 35.

32. *Ibid.*, p. 39.

33. For specific details about the exercises, see Grotowski, *Towards a Poor Theatre*. Actually, many of these exercises have been reworked, reevaluated, and even discarded. Grotowski believes strongly that exercises themselves can become stereotyped.

34. Anthony Abeson, "The Many Sides of Silence," *Village Voice*, October 9, 1969, p. 47.

35. Grotowski, p. 183.
36. *Ibid.*, p. 147.
37. *Ibid.*, p. 166.
38. *Ibid.*, p. 176.
39. Abeson, "The Many Sides of Silence."
40. Andre Gregory in an interview with me, 1970.
41. Interview with me, *Camera Three*, CBS-TV, New York, January 1969.
42. Bohdan Drozdowski in *Kultura* (No. 4, 1969) quoted in *The Theatre in Poland* (April 1969), p. 21.
43. Interview with me, *Camera Three.*
44. *Ibid.*

Chapter 8. The Open Theatre

1. Chaikin in a taped interview with me, September 1969.
2. All quotations by Peter Feldman are from his unpublished notes, which he kindly lent me.
3. Taped interview with me, 1968.
4. *Ibid.*
5. This description is based on the last New York performance of *The Serpent* in Spring 1970.
6. Jean-Claude van Itallie, *The Serpent* (New York: Atheneum, 1969), pp. 16–17.
7. *Ibid.*, p. 10.
8. *Ibid.*, pp. 12–14.
9. I am grateful to Roberta Sklar, co-director of *The Serpent* and *Terminal*, for her valuable talks with me about the Open Theatre.
10. I have seen the work performed several times. This description is based on the final performance at Washington Square Methodist Church in New York.
11. Taped interview with me, September 1969.

Chapter 9. The Environmentalists and Some Others

1. Richard Schechner, *Public Domain* (New York: Bobbs-Merrill, 1969), pp. 185–187.
2. From Richard Schechner's unpublished manuscript, which he kindly lent me.

3. Parviz Sayyad, writing in *Bulletin of the Fourth Festival of Arts* (Shiraz-Persepolis, Iran: September 4, 1970).

4. *Ibid.*

5. Schechner's unpublished manuscript.

6. Richard Schechner, ed. *Dionysus in 69* (New York: Farrar, Straus and Giroux, 1970), no pagination.

7. *Ibid.*

8. See Benjamin Hunningher, *The Origin of the Theatre* (1955 Reprint. New York: Hill & Wang, 1961), pp. 11–24.

9. *Dionysus in 69.*

10. *Ibid.*

11. *Ibid.*

12. Schechner, *Public Domain*, p. 228.

13. *TDR*, 12, No. 3 (1968), pp. 41–64.

14. In the summer of 1971 in Iran, Peter Brook, taking a cue from Ronconi, staged *Orghast* Part II in a huge open space with no seats.

15. Andre Gregory's remarks to John Lahr on "Why Alice", *Camera Three*, CBS-TV. December 6, 1970.

16. Stefan Brecht, "Family of the f. p.; Notes on the Theatre of the Ridiculous," *TDR* (Fall 1968), p. 117.

17. Quoted from *Les Lettres françaises*, trans. Linda Moses, June 2, 1971.

18. Robert Wilson, in conversation with me, Paris, May 1972.

19. Interview with me, Paris, May 1972.

20. Wilson in conversation with me, New York, February 1972.

21. Quoted from an interview with Vladimir Predic, *The Belgrade Literary Gazette*, September 16, 1971.

22. Peter Schumann, "The World Has to be Demonstrated Anew," *Poland* (March 1970), p. 4.

23. Peter Schumann in a taped interview with me, April 1971.

24. *Ibid.*

25. For a fuller description, and a good discussion of the group, see Stefan Brecht, "Peter Schumann's Bread & Puppet Theatre," *TDR*, 14, No. 3 (1970), pp. 44–96.

Chapter 10. The Achievement of Peter Brook: From Commercialism to the Avant-Garde

1. Peter Hall, "Shakespeare and the Modern Director," in *Royal Shakespeare Theatre Company 1960–1963* (London: Max Reinhardt, 1964), p. 47.

2. Jan Kott, *Shakespeare Our Contemporary* (1964. Reprint. New York: Anchor Books, 1966), p. 152.

3. *Ibid.*, p. 130.

4. *Ibid.*, p. 147.

5. *Ibid.*, p. 157.

6. *Ibid.*, p. 162.

7. See Charles Marowitz, "Notes on the Theatre of Cruelty," *TDR* (Winter 1966).

8. Michael Kustow, Geoffrey Reeves, and Albert Hunt, eds., *Tell Me Lies* (New York: Bobbs-Merrill, 1968), p. 12.

9. *Ibid.*, p. 191 and *passim.*

10. Martin Esslin, "Oedipus Wanted Power, Not His Mother," *New York Times*, March 31, 1968.

11. Charles Marowitz, "Peter Brook's 'Oedipus'," *Village Voice*, March 28, 1968.

12. From Brook's program notes, *The Tempest*, June 1968.

13. Taped interview with me, London, June 1968. Parts of this appear in "Peter Brook's *Tempest*," my article in *TDR* (Spring 1969).

14. Taped interview with me in Brook's Paris apartment, November 1970. All quotations from Brook that pertain to *A Midsummer Night's Dream* are based on this interview, unless otherwise specified. Parts of it formed the basis for "A Hidden 'Dream' of Sex and Love," my article about the production in the *New York Times,* Sunday, January 17, 1971.

15. See description of Meyerhold production in Slonim, *Russian Theater,* p. 268, in which Slonim describes Meyerhold's use of acrobatic techniques to "modernize" productions, and Meyerhold's arguments with the authorities on this point.

16. *New York Herald Tribune*, December 20, 1965.

17. This and all other quotations regarding *Orghast* are based on personal interviews with Peter Brook and Ted Hughes in Shiraz, Iran, August-September 1971, unless otherwise specified. Parts were used in my article, "Peter Brook Learns to Speak Orghast," *New York Times*, Sunday, October 3, 1971.

18. See Tom Stoppard, "'Orghast'," *Times Literary Supplement*, October 1, 1971.

19. Peter Brook, "Orghast: Talking Without Words," *British Vogue*, December 1971.

20. William K. Wimsatt, Jr. and Cleanth Brooks, *Literary Criticism* (New York: Knopf, 1962), p. 593.

21. George Steiner, *Language and Silence* (New York: Atheneum, 1970), pp. 27–28.

22. Quoted in Wimsatt and Brooks, p. 584.

23. A good discussion of this appears in Wimsatt and Brooks.

24. Steiner, p. 28.

25. Eric Sellin, *The Dramatic Concepts of Antonin Artaud* (Chicago: University of Chicago, 1968), p. 88.

26. Taped interview with me, New York, November 1970.

27. The following description and quotations are based on my visit to the Centre, and interviews with Brook, in May 1972; much of this material appeared in my article, "Peter Brook's 'Birds' Fly to Africa," *New York Times*, Sunday, January 21, 1973.

28. *Ibid.* All quotations are based on the May 1972 interviews, unless otherwise specified.

29. Conversations with David Hays in Paris and New York, 1972.

30. Conversations in New York, Fall 1972.

Bibliography

Abeson, Anthony. "The Many Sides of Silence." *Village Voice*, 9 October 1969.

Alexandrian, Sarane. *Surrealist Art*. Translated by Gordon Clough. New York: Praeger, 1970.

Alquié, Ferdinand. *The Philosophy of Surrealism.* Translated by Bernard Waldrop. Ann Arbor: Univ. of Michigan, 1965.

Antoine, André. *Memories of the Théâtre-Libre.* Translated by Marvin A. Carlson. Coral Gables: Univ. of Miami, 1964.

Artaud, Antonin. *Antholgy*. Edited by Jack Hirschman. San Francisco: City Lights, 1965.

———. "States of the Mind: 1921-1945." Translated by Ruby Cohn. *TDR*, Winter 1963.

———. *The Theatre and Its Double*. Translated by Mary Caroline Richards. New York: Grove, 1958.

Arnued, Paul. "The Artaud Experiment." *TDR*, Winter, 1963.

Backvis, Claude. "Genius of the Theatre." *Poland* 10 (November 1969).

Balakian, Anna. *The Literary Origins of Surrealism.* New York: New York Univ., 1947.

———. *Surrealism*. New York: Noonday, 1959.

Barba, Eugenio. "The Kathkali Theatre." *TDR*, Summer 1967.

Barnhardt, Clarence L., ed. *The New Century Handbook of English Literature.* New York: Appleton-Century-Crofts, 1956.

Baudelaire, Charles. *Art in Paris, 1845-1862*. Translated and edited by Jonathan Mayne. London: Phaidon, 1965.

———. *Artificial Paradise.* Translated by Ellen Fox. New York: Herder & Herder, 1971.

———. *The Flowers of Evil.* Translated by Florence Louie Friedman. Philadelphia: Dufour Editions, 1966.

———. *The Mirror of Art.* Translated by Jonathan Mayne. New York: Doubleday, 1956.

Beck, Julian. "How to Close a Theatre." *TDR*, Spring 1964.
Benedikt, Michael and Wellwarth, George E. *Modern French Theatre*. New York: Dutton, 1966.
Biner, Pierre. *Le Living Théâtre*. Lausanne: L'Age d'Homme, n.d.
Block, Haskell M. *Mallarmé and the Symbolist Drama*. Detroit: Wayne State Univ., 1963.
Bowers, Faubion. *Theâtre in the East*. New York: Grove, 1956.
Braun, Kazimierz, "Wyspianski and the New Poetic Theatre." *The Theatre in Poland, April 1969.*
Brecht, Bertolt. Brecht on Theatre. Translated by John Willett. New York: Hill & Wang, 1964.
Brecht, Stefan. "Family of the f.p.: Notes on the Theatre of the Ridiculous." *TDR*, Fall 1968.
———. "Peter Schumann's Bread and Puppet Theatre." *TDR* 14, no. 3 (1970).
———. "Revolution at the Brooklyn Academy of Music." *TDR*, Spring 1969.
Brinton, Crane. *The Political Ideas of the English Romanticists.* 1926. Reprint. New York: Russell & Russell, 1962.
Brock, Peter. "Polish Nationalism" in *Nationalism in Eastern Europe.* Peter F. Sugar and Ivo J. Lederer, eds. Seattle: Univ. of Washington, 1969.
Brockett, Oscar G. *The Theatre: An Introduction*. New York: Holt, 1966.
Brook, Peter. *The Empty Space.* New York: Atheneum, 1968.
———. "Orghast: Talking without Words." *British Vogue*, December 1971.
Brown, Norman O. *Life Against Death*. Middletown: Wesleyan Univ., 1959.
Brunvand, Jan Harold. *The Study of American Folklore.* New York: Norton, 1968.
Buchheim, Lothar-Günther. *The Graphic Art of German Expressionism* New York: Universe, 1960.
Cage, John. *A Year from Monday*. Middletown: Wesleyan Univ., 1969.
———. "An Interview." *TDR*, Winter 1965.
———. *Silence*. 1961. Reprint. Cambridge: MIT, 1966.
Campbell, Joseph. *The Hero with a Thousand Faces*. New York: World, 1956.
Camus, Albert. *The Myth of Sisyphus*. Translated by Justin O'Brien. New York: Knopf, 1955.
Caputi, Anthony. *Classical Greece*. Lexington, Mass.: D. C. Heath, 1968.
Carter, A. E. *The Idea of Decadence in French Literature, 1840–1900.* Toronto: Univ. of Toronto, 1958.
Carter, Lawson A. *Zola and the Theatre*. New Haven: Yale Univ., 1963.
Chaikin, Joseph. *The Presence of the Actor.* New York: Atheneum, 1972.

Checkhov, Michael. *To the Actor*. New York: Harper & Row, 1953.
Cornell, Kenneth. *The Symbolist Movement*. New Haven: Yale Univ., 1951.
Corrigan, Robert W. *The Modern Theatre*. New York: Macmillan, 1964.
Craig, Edward Gordon. *Books and Theatre*. London: Dent, 1925.
———. *On the Art of the Theatre*. New York; Theatre Arts, 1956.
———. *The Theatre—Advancing*. Boston: Little, Brown, 1919.
———. *Towards a New Theatre*. London: Dent, 1913.
Crosby, Harry H. and Bond, George R. *The McLuhan Explosion*. New York: American Book, 1968.
Croyden, Margaret. "A Hidden 'Dream' of Sex and Love." *New York Times*, 17 January, 1971.
———. "After 'Paradise,' Where?" *New York Times, 8 March, 1970.*
———. *"The Blood of Poets." Village Voice*, 8 January, 1970.
———. "Burning Bridges is Natural." *New York Times,* 29 March, 1970.
———. "Exploration of the Ugly: Brook's Work on *Oedipus*." *TDR*, Spring 1969.
———. "An Interview with Jerzy Grotowski." *Village Voice*, 23 January, 1969.
———. "The Most Avant-Garde of Them All?" *New York Times*, 5 October, 1969.
———. "Peter Brook's 'Birds' Fly to Africa." *New York Times*, 21 January, 1973.
———. "Peter Brook Learns To Speak Orghast." *New York Times*, 3 October, 1971.
———. "Peter Brook's *Tempest*." *TDR*, Spring 1969.
———. "Shakespeare—Cruel and True." *Antioch Review* XXVII, 3 (Fall 1967).
Datner, Szymon. *The Wehrmacht's 55 Days in Poland*, quoted in *Poland* 10, (November 1969).
Drew, Elizabeth. *T. S. Eliot: The Design of His Poetry*. New York: Scribners, 1949.
Drozdowski, Bohdan. *Kultura* (1969), quoted in *The Theatre in Poland*, April 1969.
Durant, Will and Ariel. *Rousseau and Revolution*. New York: Simon & Schuster, 1967.
Duchartre, Pierre Louis. *The Italian Comedy*. Translated by Randolph T. Weaver. 1939. Reprint. New York: Dover, 1966.
Engelberg, Edward. *The Symbolist Poem*. New York: Dutton, 1967.
Esslin, Martin. *Brecht*. New York: Doubleday, 1960.
———. "Naturalism in Context." *TDR*, Winter 1968.
———. "Oedipus Wanted Power, Not His Mother." *New York Times*, 31 March, 1968.

———. *The Theatre of the Absurd*. New York: Doubleday, 1967.

Ewen, Frederic. *Bertolt Brecht*. New York: Citadel, 1969.

Feldenkrais, Moshe. *Awareness Through Movement*. New York: Harper & Row, 1972.

Flaszen, Ludwik. "After the Avant-Garde." *The Theatre in Poland*, July-August 1968.

Fowlie, Wallace. *Age of Surrealism*. Bloomington: Indiana Univ., 1960.

———. *Mallarmé*. Chicago: Univ. of Chicago, 1953.

Frazer, James George. *The Golden Bough*. New York: Macmillan, 1963.

Gassner, John and Quinn, Edmund, eds. *The Reader's Encyclopedia of World Drama*. New York: Crowell, 1969.

Gorchakov, Nikolai M. *Stanislavsky Directs*. Translated by Miriam Goldina. New York: Minerva, 1968.

———. *The Theatre in Soviet Russia*. Translated by Edgar Lehram. New York: Columbia Univ., 1957.

Green, Naomi. *Antonin Artuad: Poet Without Words*. New York: Simon & Schuster, 1970.

Grossman, Manuel L. *Dada*. New York: Bobbs-Merrill, 1971.

Grotowski, Jerzy. *Towards a Poor Theatre*. Holstebro, Denmark: Odin Theatrets Forlag, 1968.

Hall, James B. and Ulanov, Barry. *Modern Culture and the Arts*. New York: McGraw-Hill, 1967.

Hall, Peter. "Shakespeare and the Modern Director" in *Royal Shakespeare Theater Company, 1960-1963*. London: Max Reinhardt, 1964.

Hardwick, Elizabeth. "The Theatre of Grotowski." *New York Review of Books*, 12 February, 1970.

Hassan, Ihab, *The Literature of Silence: Henry Miller and Samuel Beckett*. New York: Knopf, 1967.

Hewitt, Barnard. *History of the Theatre from 1800 to the Present*. New York: Random House, 1970.

———, ed. *The Renaissance Stage*. Translated by Allardyce Nicoll, John H. McDowell and George R. Kernodle. Coral Gables: Univ. of Miami, 1958.

Hoffman, Frederick J. *Samuel Beckett*. 1962. Reprint. New York: Dutton, 1964.

Hunningher, Benjamin. *The Origin of the Theatre*. 1955. Reprint. New York: Hill & Wang, 1961.

Hyslop, Lois Boe and Francis E., Jr., eds. and trans. *Baudelaire as a Literary Critic*. University Park, PA: Pennsylvania State Univ., 1964.

Jacobsen, Josephine and Mueller, William R. *The Testament of Samuel Beckett*, New York: Hill & Wang, 1964.

Jotterand, Franck. *Le nouveau théatre américain*. Paris: Editions du Seuil, 1970.

Jung, C. G. *Symbols of Transformation.* Vol. I. Translated by R. F. C. Hull. 1956. Reprint. New York: Harper & Row, 1962.

Kaprow, Allan. *Assemblage, Environment & Happenings.* New York: Abrams, n.d.

Kirby, E. T., ed. *Total Theatre.* New York: Dutton, 1969.

Kirby, Michael. *Art of Time.* New York: Dutton, 1969.

———. *Happenings.* New York:Dutton, 1966.

Knapp, Bettina L. *Antonin Artuad, Man of Vision.* New York: David Lewis, 1969.

Knight, G. Wilson. *The Golden Labyrinth.* New York: Norton, 1962.

Kolakowski, Leszek. *Toward a Marxist Humanism.* Translated by Jane Zielenko Peel. New York: Grove, 1968.

Kostelanetz, Richard. *The Theatre of Mixed Means.* New York: Dial, 1968.

Kott, Jan. *Shakespeare Our Contemporary.* 1964. Reprint. New York: Anchor, 1966.

———. *Theatre Notebook: 1947-1967.* Translated by Boleslaw Taborski. New York; Doubleday, 1968.

Kristiansen, Donna M. "What is Dada?" *Eduational Theatre Journal,* October 1968.

Krzyzanowski, Julian. "Stanislaw Wyspianski." *Polish Review,* Autumn 1957.

Kustow, Michael; Reeves, Geoffrey, and Hunt, Albert, eds. *Tell Me Lies.* New York: Bobbs-Merrill, 1968.

Laing, R. D. *The Divided Self.* 1960. Reprint. Baltimore: Pelican, 1965.

———. *The Politics of Experience.* New York: Random House, 1967.

Langer, Susanne K. *Feeling and Form.* New York: Scribner, 1953.

Lebel, Jean-Jacques. *Entretiens avec le living théâtre.* Paris: Pierre Belfond, 1969.

———. "On the Necessity of Violation." *TDR,* Fall 1968.

———. "Notes on Paris Street Theatre." *TDR,* Summer 1969.

Lempicka, Aniela. "In the Sphere of European Intellectual Revolution." *Poland,* November 1969.

MacGowen, Kenneth and Melnitz, William. *Golden Ages of the Theatre.* Englewood Cliffs, N. J.: Prentice-Hall, 1959.

Magarshack, David, *Chekhov the Dramatist.* New York: Hill & Wang, 1960.

Malina, Judith and Beck, Julian. *Paradise Now.* New York: Vintage, 1971.

Marcuse, Herbert. *An Essay on Liberation.* Boston: Beacon, 1969.

———. *Eros and Civilization.* Boston: Beacon, 1955.

———. *One-Dimensional Man.* Boston: Beacon, 1964.

Marowitz, Charles. "Notes on the Theatre of Cruelty." *TDR,* Winter 1966.

———. "Peter Brook's 'Oedipus'" *Village Voice,* 28 March, 1968.

Meyerhold, Vsevolod. *Meyerhold on Theatre.* Translated and edited by

Edward Braun. London: Methuen and New York: Farrar, Straus, and Giroux, 1969.

Meyers, Bernard S. *The German Expressionists.* New York: 1956.

Millett, Fred B. and Bentley, Gerald Eades, *The Art of the Drama.* New York: Appleton-Century-Crofts, 1935.

Motherwell, Robert, ed. *The Dada Painters and Poets: An Anthology.* New York: Wittenborn & Schultz, 1951.

Murray, Henry A., ed. *Myth and Mythmaking.* 1960. Reprint. Boston: Beacon, 1968.

Nadeau, Maurice. *The History of Surrealism.* Translated by Richard Howard. 1965. Reprint. New York: Collier, 1967.

Nagler, A. M. *A Source Book in Theatrical History.* New York: Dover, 1959.

Neff, Renfreu. *The Living Theatre: USA.* New York: Bobbs-Merrill, 1970.

Noyes, Russell. *English Romantic Poetry and Prose.* New York: Oxford Univ, 1956.

Oreglia, Giacomo. *The Commedia dell'Arte.* Translated by Lovett F. Edwards, New York: Hill & Wang, 1968.

Pasolli, Robert. *A Book on the Open Theatre.* New York: Bobbs-Merrill, 1970.

Performance I: Growing Out of the Sixties. I, no. I (December 1971).

Perls, Frederick; Hefferline, Ralph F.; and Goodman, Paul. *Gestalt Therapy.* New York: Dell, 1951.

Poggioli, Renato. *The Theory of the Avant-Garde.* Translated by Gerald Fitzgerald. Cambridge: Harvard Univ., 1968.

Pronko, Leonard Cabell. *Avant-Garde: The Experimental Theatre in France.* Berkeley: Univ. of California, 1962.

———. *Theatre East and West.* Berkeley: Univ. of California, 1967.

Quadri, Franco. "Orlando Furioso." *TDR* 14, no. 3 (1970).

Raymond, Marcel. *From Baudelaire to Surrealism.* New York: Wittenborn, 1950.

Reddaway, W. F.; Penson, J. H.; Halecki, O.' and Dyboski, R., eds. *The Cambridge History of Poland.* Cambridge, England: Cambridge University, 1951.

Reik, Theodor. *Ritual.* Translated by Douglas Bryan. New York: Grove, 1962.

Richter, Hans. *Dada Art and Anti-Art.* New York: McGraw-Hill, 1965.

Rimbaud, Arthur. *A Season in Hell and The Drunken Boat.* Translated by Louise Varèse. New York: New Directions, 1961.

———. *Illuminations.* Translated by Louise Varèse. New York: New Directions, 1957.

Roose-Evans, James. *Experimental Theatre.* New York: Grove, 1971.

Rostagno, Aldo with Julian Beck and Judith Malina. *We, The Living Theatre.* New York: Ballantine, 1970.

Ruff, M. A. *Baudelaire*. Translated by Agnes Kertesz. New York: New York Univ., 1966.

Skidmore College. "R. D. Laing and Anti-Psychiatry." *Salmagundi* 16 (Spring 1971).

Sartre, Jean-Paul. *Baudelaire*. Translated by Martin Turnell. 1950. Reprint. New York: New Directions, 1967.

Sayler, Oliver M. *Russian Theatre Under the Revolution*. Boston: Little, Brown, 1920.

Schechner, Richard. "Containment is the Enemy: Judith Malina and Julian Beck Interviewed." *TDR*, Spring 1969.

———, ed. *Dionysus in 69*. New York: Farrar, Straus & Giroux, 1970.

———. "Extensions in Time and Space, an Interview with Allan Kaprow." *TDR*, Spring 1968.

———. *Public Domain*. New York: Bobbs-Merrill, 1969.

Schlemmer, Oskar; Moholy-Nagy, Laszlo; and Molnar, Farkes. *The Theatre of the Bauhaus*. Edited and with an intro. by Walter Gropius. Translated by Arthur S. Wensinger. Middletown: Wesleyan Univ., 1961.

Schumann, Peter. "The World has to be Demonstrated Anew." *Poland*, March 1970.

Scott, A. C. *The Kabuki Theatre of Japan*. 1955. Reprint. New York: Collier, 1966.

Sellin, Eric. *The Dramatic Concepts of Antonin Artaud*. Chicago: Univ. of Chicago, 1968.

Shah, Idries. *The Sufis*. 1964. Reprint. New York: Doubleday, 1971.

Shattuck, Roger. *The Banquet Years*. 1958. Reprint. New York: Vintage, 1968.

——— and Taylor, Simon Watson, eds. *Selected Words of Alfred Jarry*. New York: Grove, 1965.

Simonov, Ruben. *Vakhtangov*. Translated by Miriam Goldina. New York: DBS Publications, 1969.

Slonim, Marc. *Russian Theatre: From the Empire to the Soviets*. New York: Collier, 1961.

Smith, Michael. *Theatre Trip*. New York: Bobbs-Merrill, 1969.

Sokol, Walter H. *The Writer in Extremis*. Stanford: Stanford Univ. 1959.

Southern, Richard. *The Seven Ages of the Theatre*. New York: Hill & Wang, 1961.

Spolin, Viola. *Improvisation for the Theatre*. Evanston: Northwestern Univ., 1963.

Stanislavski, Constantin. *Creating a Role*. Translated by Elizabeth Reynolds Hapgood. New York: Theatre Arts, 1961.

———. *My Life in Art*. Translated by J. J. Robbins. 1924. Reprint. New York: World, 1956.

———. *On the Art of the Stage*. Translated by David Magarshack. New York: Hill & Wang, 1961,

Starkie, Enid. *Arthur Rimbaud*. New York: New Directions, 1961.

———. *Baudelaire*. 1933. Reprint. New York: New Directors, 1958.

Steiner, George. *Language and Silence*. New York: Atheneum, 1970.

Stokoe, F. W. *German Influence in the Romantic Period*. Cambridge, England: Cambridge Univ., 1926.

Stoppard, Tom. "Orghast." *Times Literary Supplement*, 1 October, 1971.

Symons, Arthur. Introduction to *Les Fleurs du Mal*, by Charles Baudelaire. Translated by Arthur Symons. London: Casanova Society, 1925.

———. *The Symbolist Movement in Literature*. 1919. Reprint. New York: Dutton, 1958.

Tairov, Alexander. *Notes of a Director*. Translated and edited by William Kuhlke. Coral Gables: Univ. of Miami, 1969.

Tarn, Adam. "The Roots of Polish Drama." *Drama in Calgary 3, no. 3.*

Temkine, Raymonde. *Grotowski*. Lausanne: L'Age d'Homme, n.d.

Theatr 23 (1968) quoted in *The Theatre in Poland*, April 1969.

Le Theatre. 1971-1. Paris: Christian Bourgois, 1971.

Thomas, Michael. "Expecting to Fly: Advertisements for the Living Theatre." in *US*. New York: Bantam, 1969.

van Itallie, Jean-Claude. *America Hurrah*. 1966. Reprint. New York: Pocket Books, 1968.

———. *The Serpent*. New York: Atheneum, 1969.

van Roosbroeck, G. L. *The Legend of the Decadents*. New York: Columbia Univ., 1927.

Waldberg, Patrick. *Surrealism*. New York: McGraw-Hill, 1965.

Weil, Simone. *Gravity and Grace*. Translated by Emme Crauford. London: Routledge & Kegan Paul, 1952.

Weiss, Peter. *Marat/Sade*. English version of by Geoffrey Skelton. 1965. Reprint. New York: Pocket Books, 1966.

Wellwarth, George E. *The Theatre of Protest and Paradox*. New York: New York Univ., 1964.

Weston, Jessie L. *From Ritual to Romance*. Reprint. New York: Doubleday, 1957.

Willett, John. *The Theatre of Bertolt Brecht*. New York: New Directions, 1959.

Wimsatt, William K., Jr., and Brooks, Cleanth. *Literary Criticism*. New York: Knopf, 1962.

Yale/Theatre. Spring 1969.

Yankowitz, Susan. *Terminal* in *Scripts* I, no. 1 (November 1971).

Index

INDEX

INDEX

INDEX

INDEX

INDEX

About the Author

Margaret Croyden is a well-known writer and critic of the contemporary theatre. Her work has appeared in *The New York Times*, the *Village Voice, The Drama Review,* the *Antioch Review,* the *Texas Quarterly* and the *Transatlantic Review*. Miss Croyden has conducted her own theatre programs on radio station WBAI. Television audiences have seen her exclusive interviews with Peter Brook and Jerzy Grotowski on CBS's *Camera Three* as well as her numerous appearances as an analyst and commentator on leading contemporary theatre artists.

A former actress turned scholar, Miss Croyden had studied with Lee Strasberg and Stella Adler. Then, "fed up with the struggles of an actress," she embarked on an academic career. With the assistance of a scholarship, she earned her BA from Hunter College in New York City and her MA from New York University. Miss Croyden is currently Associate Professor of English and Dramatic Literature at Jersey City State College. She resides in New York City.